ASPEN PUBLISHERS

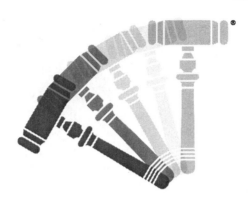

Casenote™ *Legal Briefs*

FEDERAL COURTS

Keyed to Courses Using

Hart and Wechsler's
The Federal Courts and The Federal System
Sixth Edition
by Fallon, Manning, Meltzer, and Shapiro

™ Wolters Kluwer
Law & Business

AUSTIN   BOSTON   CHICAGO   NEW YORK   THE NETHERLANDS

This publication is designed to provide accurate and authoritative information in regard to the subject matter covered. It is sold with the understanding that the publisher is not engaged in rendering legal, accounting, or other professional services. If legal advice or other expert assistance is required, the services of a competent professional person should be sought.

— From a Declaration of Principles adopted jointly by a Committee of the American Bar Association and a Committee of Publishers and Associates

To contact Customer Care, e-mail customer.care@aspenpublishers.com, call 1-800-234-1660, fax 1-800-901-9075, or mail correspondence to:

Aspen Publishers
Attn: Order Department
P.O. Box 990
Frederick, MD 21705

Printed in the United States of America.

1 2 3 4 5 6 7 8 9 0

ISBN 978-0-7355-8947-6

About Wolters Kluwer Law & Business

Wolters Kluwer Law & Business is a leading provider of research information and workflow solutions in key specialty areas. The strengths of the individual brands of Aspen Publishers, CCH, Kluwer Law International and Loislaw are aligned within Wolters Kluwer Law & Business to provide comprehensive, in-depth solutions and expert-authored content for the legal, professional and education markets.

CCH was founded in 1913 and has served more than four generations of business professionals and their clients. The CCH products in the Wolters Kluwer Law & Business group are highly regarded electronic and print resources for legal, securities, antitrust and trade regulation, government contracting, banking, pension, payroll, employment and labor, and health-care reimbursement and compliance professionals.

Aspen Publishers is a leading information provider for attorneys, business professionals and law students. Written by preeminent authorities, Aspen products offer analytical and practical information in a range of specialty practice areas from securities law and intellectual property to mergers and acquisitions and pension/benefits. Aspen's trusted legal education resources provide professors and students with high-quality, up-to-date and effective resources for successful instruction and study in all areas of the law.

Kluwer Law International supplies the global business community with comprehensive English-language international legal information. Legal practitioners, corporate counsel and business executives around the world rely on the Kluwer Law International journals, loose-leafs, books and electronic products for authoritative information in many areas of international legal practice.

Loislaw is a premier provider of digitized legal content to small law firm practitioners of various specializations. Loislaw provides attorneys with the ability to quickly and efficiently find the necessary legal information they need, when and where they need it, by facilitating access to primary law as well as state-specific law, records, forms and treatises.

Wolters Kluwer Law & Business, a unit of Wolters Kluwer, is headquartered in New York and Riverwoods, Illinois. Wolters Kluwer is a leading multinational publisher and information services company.

Format for the Casenote Legal Brief

Nature of Case: This section identifies the form of action (e.g., breach of contract, negligence, battery), the type of proceeding (e.g., demurrer, appeal from trial court's jury instructions), or the relief sought (e.g., damages, injunction, criminal sanctions).

Fact Summary: This is included to refresh your memory and can be used as a quick reminder of the facts.

Rule of Law: Summarizes the general principle of law that the case illustrates. It may be used for instant recall of the court's holding and for classroom discussion or home review.

Facts: This section contains all relevant facts of the case, including the contentions of the parties and the lower court holdings. It is written in a logical order to give the student a clear understanding of the case. The plaintiff and defendant are identified by their proper names throughout and are always labeled with a (P) or (D).

Palsgraf v. Long Island R.R. Co.

Injured bystander (P) v. Railroad company (D)

N.Y. Ct. App., 248 N.Y. 339, 162 N.E. 99 (1928).

NATURE OF CASE: Appeal from judgment affirming verdict for plaintiff seeking damages for personal injury.

FACT SUMMARY: Helen Palsgraf (P) was injured on R.R.'s (D) train platform when R.R.'s (D) guard helped a passenger aboard a moving train, causing his package to fall on the tracks. The package contained fireworks which exploded, creating a shock that tipped a scale onto Palsgraf (P).

🏛 RULE OF LAW
The risk reasonably to be perceived defines the duty to be obeyed.

FACTS: Helen Palsgraf (P) purchased a ticket to Rockaway Beach from R.R. (D) and was waiting on the train platform. As she waited, two men ran to catch a train that was pulling out from the platform. The first man jumped aboard, but the second man, who appeared as if he might fall, was helped aboard by the guard on the train who had kept the door open so they could jump aboard. A guard on the platform also helped by pushing him onto the train. The man was carrying a package wrapped in newspaper. In the process, the man dropped his package, which fell on the tracks. The package contained fireworks and exploded. The shock of the explosion was apparently of great enough strength to tip over some scales at the other end of the platform, which fell on Palsgraf (P) and injured her. A jury awarded her damages, and R.R. (D) appealed.

ISSUE: Does the risk reasonably to be perceived define the duty to be obeyed?

HOLDING AND DECISION: (Cardozo, C.J.) Yes. The risk reasonably to be perceived defines the duty to be obeyed. If there is no foreseeable hazard to the injured party as the result of a seemingly innocent act, the act does not become a tort because it happened to be a wrong as to another. If the wrong was not willful, the plaintiff must show that the act as to her had such great and apparent possibilities of danger as to entitle her to protection. Negligence in the abstract is not enough upon which to base liability. Negligence is a relative concept, evolving out of the common law doctrine of trespass on the case. To establish liability, the defendant must owe a legal duty of reasonable care to the injured party. A cause of action in tort will lie where harm, though unintended, could have been averted or avoided by observance of such a duty. The scope of the duty is limited by the range of danger that a reasonable person could foresee. In this case, there was nothing to suggest from the appearance of the parcel or otherwise that the parcel contained fireworks. The guard could not reasonably have had any warning of a threat to Palsgraf (P), and R.R. (D) therefore cannot be held liable. Judgment is reversed in favor of R.R. (D).

DISSENT: (Andrews, J.) The concept that there is no negligence unless R.R. (D) owes a legal duty to take care as to Palsgraf (P) herself is too narrow. Everyone owes to the world at large the duty of refraining from those acts that may unreasonably threaten the safety of others. If the guard's action was negligent as to those nearby, it was also negligent as to those outside what might be termed the "danger zone." For Palsgraf (P) to recover, R.R.'s (D) negligence must have been the proximate cause of her injury, a question of fact for the jury.

▶ ANALYSIS

The majority defined the limit of the defendant's liability in terms of the danger that a reasonable person in defendant's situation would have perceived. The dissent argued that the limitation should not be placed on liability, but rather on damages. Judge Andrews suggested that only injuries that would not have happened but for R.R.'s (D) negligence should be compensable. Both the majority and dissent recognized the policy-driven need to limit liability for negligent acts, seeking, in the words of Judge Andrews, to define a framework "that will be practical and in keeping with the general understanding of mankind." The Restatement (Second) of Torts has accepted Judge Cardozo's view.

Quicknotes

FORESEEABILITY A reasonable expectation that change is the probable result of certain acts or omissions.

NEGLIGENCE Conduct falling below the standard of care that a reasonable person would demonstrate under similar conditions.

PROXIMATE CAUSE The natural sequence of events without which an injury would not have been sustained.

Party ID: Quick identification of the relationship between the parties.

Concurrence/Dissent: All concurrences and dissents are briefed whenever they are included by the casebook editor.

Analysis: This last paragraph gives you a broad understanding of where the case "fits in" with other cases in the section of the book and with the entire course. It is a hornbook-style discussion indicating whether the case is a majority or minority opinion and comparing the principal case with other cases in the casebook. It may also provide analysis from restatements, uniform codes, and law review articles. The analysis will prove to be invaluable to classroom discussion.

Issue: The issue is a concise question that brings out the essence of the opinion as it relates to the section of the casebook in which the case appears. Both substantive and procedural issues are included if relevant to the decision.

Holding and Decision: This section offers a clear and in-depth discussion of the rule of the case and the court's rationale. It is written in easy-to-understand language and answers the issue presented by applying the law to the facts of the case. When relevant, it includes a thorough discussion of the exceptions to the case as listed by the court, any major cites to the other cases on point, and the names of the judges who wrote the decisions.

Quicknotes: Conveniently defines legal terms found in the case and summarizes the nature of any statutes, codes, or rules referred to in the text.

Aspen Publishers is proud to offer *Casenote Legal Briefs*—continuing thirty years of publishing America's best-selling legal briefs.

Casenote Legal Briefs are designed to help you save time when briefing assigned cases. Organized under convenient headings, they show you how to abstract the basic facts and holdings from the text of the actual opinions handed down by the courts. Used as part of a rigorous study regimen, they can help you spend more time analyzing and critiquing points of law than on copying bits and pieces of judicial opinions into your notebook or outline.

Casenote Legal Briefs should never be used as a substitute for assigned casebook readings. They work best when read as a follow-up to reviewing the underlying opinions themselves. Students who try to avoid reading and digesting the judicial opinions in their casebooks or online sources will end up shortchanging themselves in the long run. The ability to absorb, critique, and restate the dynamic and complex elements of case law decisions is crucial to your success in law school and beyond. It cannot be developed vicariously.

Casenote Legal Briefs represents but one of the many offerings in Aspen's Study Aid Timeline, which includes:

- *Casenote Legal Briefs*
- *Emanuel Law Outlines*
- *Examples & Explanations* Series
- *Introduction to Law* Series
- Emanuel *Law in a Flash* Flashcards
- Emanuel *CrunchTime* Series

Each of these series is designed to provide you with easy-to-understand explanations of complex points of law. Each volume offers guidance on the principles of legal analysis and, consulted regularly, will hone your ability to spot relevant issues. We have titles that will help you prepare for class, prepare for your exams, and enhance your general comprehension of the law along the way.

To find out more about Aspen Study Aid publications, visit us online at *http://lawschool.aspenpublishers.com* or email us at *legaledu@wolterskluwer.com*. We'll be happy to assist you.

Free access to Briefs online!

Download cases from this Casenote Legal Brief. Simply fill out this form for full access to this useful feature provided by Loislaw. Learn more about Loislaw services on the inside front cover of this book or visit *www.loislawschool.com*.

Name	Phone ( )
Address	**Apt. No.**
City	**State** **ZIP Code**
Law School	**Year** (check one) ☐ 1st ☐ 2nd ☐ 3rd

Cut out the UPC found on the lower left-hand corner of the back cover of this book. Staple the UPC inside this box. Only the original UPC from the book cover will be accepted. No photocopies or store stickers are allowed.

Attach UPC inside this box.

Email (Print legibly or you may not get access!)
Title of this book (course subject)
Used with which casebook (provide author's name)

Mail the completed form to:

Aspen Publishers, Inc.
Legal Education Division
Casenote Online Access
130 Turner Street, Building 3, 4th Floor
Waltham, MA 02453-8901

I understand that online access is granted solely to the purchaser of this book for the academic year in which it was purchased. Any other usage is not authorized and will result in immediate termination of access. Sharing of codes is strictly prohibited.

Signature _____

Upon receipt of this completed form, you will be emailed codes with which to access the briefs for this Casenote Legal Brief. Online briefs are not available for all titles. For a full list of Casenote Legal Brief titles, please visit *http://lawschool.aspenpublishers.com*.

Make a photocopy of this form and your UPC for your records.

For detailed information on the use of the information you provide on this form, please see the PRIVACY POLICY at www.aspenpublishers.com.

How to Brief a Case

A. Decide on a Format and Stick to It

Structure is essential to a good brief. It enables you to arrange systematically the related parts that are scattered throughout most cases, thus making manageable and understandable what might otherwise seem to be an endless and unfathomable sea of information. There are, of course, an unlimited number of formats that can be utilized. However, it is best to find one that suits your needs and stick to it. Consistency breeds both efficiency and the security that when called upon you will know where to look in your brief for the information you are asked to give.

Any format, as long as it presents the essential elements of a case in an organized fashion, can be used. Experience, however, has led *Casenotes* to develop and utilize the following format because of its logical flow and universal applicability.

NATURE OF CASE: This is a brief statement of the legal character and procedural status of the case (e.g., "Appeal of a burglary conviction").

There are many different alternatives open to a litigant dissatisfied with a court ruling. The key to determining which one has been used is to discover *who is asking this court for what.*

This first entry in the brief should be kept as *short as possible.* Use the court's terminology if you understand it. But since jurisdictions vary as to the titles of pleadings, the best entry is the one that addresses who wants what in this proceeding, not the one that sounds most like the court's language.

RULE OF LAW: A statement of the general principle of law that the case illustrates (e.g., "An acceptance that varies any term of the offer is considered a rejection and counteroffer").

Determining the rule of law of a case is a procedure similar to determining the issue of the case. Avoid being fooled by red herrings; there may be a few rules of law mentioned in the case excerpt, but usually only one is *the* rule with which the casebook editor is concerned. The techniques used to locate the issue, described below, may also be utilized to find the rule of law. Generally, your best guide is simply the chapter heading. It is a clue to the point the casebook editor seeks to make and should be kept in mind when reading every case in the respective section.

FACTS: A synopsis of only the essential facts of the case, i.e., those bearing upon or leading up to the issue.

The facts entry should be a short statement of the events and transactions that led one party to initiate legal proceedings against another in the first place. While some cases conveniently state the salient facts at the beginning of the decision, in other instances they will have to be culled from hiding places throughout the text, even from concurring and dissenting opinions. Some of the "facts" will often be in dispute and should be so noted. Conflicting evidence may be briefly pointed up. "Hard" facts must be included. Both must be *relevant* in order to be listed in the facts entry. It is impossible to tell what is relevant until the entire case is read, as the ultimate determination of the rights and liabilities of the parties may turn on something buried deep in the opinion.

Generally, the facts entry should not be longer than three to five *short* sentences.

It is often helpful to identify the role played by a party in a given context. For example, in a construction contract case the identification of a party as the "contractor" or "builder" alleviates the need to tell that that party was the one who was supposed to have built the house.

It is always helpful, and a good general practice, to identify the "plaintiff" and the "defendant." This may seem elementary and uncomplicated, but, especially in view of the creative editing practiced by some casebook editors, it is sometimes a difficult or even impossible task. Bear in mind that the *party presently* seeking something from this court may not be the plaintiff, and that sometimes only the cross-claim of a defendant is treated in the excerpt. Confusing or misaligning the parties can ruin your analysis and understanding of the case.

ISSUE: A statement of the general legal question answered by or illustrated in the case. For clarity, the issue is best put in the form of a question capable of a "yes" or "no" answer. In reality, the issue is simply the Rule of Law put in the form of a question (e.g., "May an offer be accepted by performance?").

The major problem presented in discerning what is *the* issue in the case is that an opinion usually purports to raise and answer several questions. However, except for rare cases, only one such question is really the issue in the case. Collateral issues not necessary to the resolution of the matter in controversy are handled by the court by language known as *"obiter dictum"* or merely *"dictum."* While dicta may be included later in the brief, they have no place under the issue heading.

To find the issue, ask *who wants what* and then go on to ask *why did that party succeed or fail in getting it.* Once this is determined, the "why" should be turned into a question.

The complexity of the issues in the cases will vary, but in all cases a single-sentence question should sum up the issue. *In a few cases,* there will be two, or even more rarely, three issues of equal importance to the resolution of the case. Each should be expressed in a single-sentence question.

Since many issues are resolved by a court in coming to a final disposition of a case, the casebook editor will reproduce the portion of the opinion containing the issue or issues most relevant to the area of law under scrutiny. A noted law professor gave this advice: "Close the book; look at the title on the cover." Chances are, if it is Property, you need not concern yourself with whether, for example, the federal government's treatment of the plaintiff's land really raises a federal question sufficient to support jurisdiction on this ground in federal court.

The same rule applies to chapter headings designating sub-areas within the subjects. They tip you off as to what the text is designed to teach. The cases are arranged in a casebook to show a progression or development of the law, so that the preceding cases may also help.

It is also most important to remember to *read the notes and questions* at the end of a case to determine what the editors wanted you to have gleaned from it.

HOLDING AND DECISION: This section should succinctly explain the rationale of the court in arriving at its decision. In capsulizing the "reasoning" of the court, it should always include an application of the general rule or rules of law to the specific facts of the case. Hidden justifications come to light in this entry; the reasons for the state of the law, the public policies, the biases and prejudices, those considerations that influence the justices' thinking and, ultimately, the outcome of the case. At the end, there should be a short indication of the disposition or procedural resolution of the case (e.g., "Decision of the trial court for Mr. Smith (P) reversed").

The foregoing format is designed to help you "digest" the reams of case material with which you will be faced in your law school career. Once mastered by practice, it will place at your fingertips the information the authors of your casebooks have sought to impart to you in case-by-case illustration and analysis.

B. Be as Economical as Possible in Briefing Cases

Once armed with a format that encourages succinctness, it is as important to be economical with regard to the time spent on the actual reading of the case as it is to be economical in the writing of the brief itself. This does not mean "skimming" a case. Rather, it means reading the case with an "eye" trained to recognize into which "section" of your brief a particular passage or line fits and having a system for quickly and precisely marking the case so that the passages fitting any one particular part of

the brief can be easily identified and brought together in a concise and accurate manner when the brief is actually written.

It is of no use to simply repeat everything in the opinion of the court; record only enough information to trigger your recollection of what the court said. Nevertheless, an accurate statement of the "law of the case," i.e., the legal principle applied to the facts, is absolutely essential to class preparation and to learning the law under the case method.

To that end, it is important to develop a "shorthand" that you can use to make margin notations. These notations will tell you at a glance in which section of the brief you will be placing that particular passage or portion of the opinion.

Some students prefer to underline all the salient portions of the opinion (with a pencil or colored underliner marker), making marginal notations as they go along. Others prefer the color-coded method of underlining, utilizing different colors of markers to underline the salient portions of the case, each separate color being used to represent a different section of the brief. For example, blue underlining could be used for passages relating to the rule of law, yellow for those relating to the issue, and green for those relating to the holding and decision, etc. While it has its advocates, the color-coded method can be confusing and time-consuming (all that time spent on changing colored markers). Furthermore, it can interfere with the continuity and concentration many students deem essential to the reading of a case for maximum comprehension. In the end, however, it is a matter of personal preference and style. Just remember, whatever method you use, underlining must be used sparingly or its value is lost.

If you take the marginal notation route, an efficient and easy method is to go along underlining the key portions of the case and placing in the margin alongside them the following "markers" to indicate where a particular passage or line "belongs" in the brief you will write:

N   (NATURE OF CASE)
RL   (RULE OF LAW)
I   (ISSUE)
HL   (HOLDING AND DECISION, relates to
        the RULE OF LAW behind the decision)
HR   (HOLDING AND DECISION, gives the
        RATIONALE or reasoning behind the
        decision)
HA   (HOLDING AND DECISION, APPLIES
        the general principle(s) of law to the facts
        of the case to arrive at the decision)

Remember that a particular passage may well contain information necessary to more than one part of your brief, in which case you simply note that in the margin. If you are using the color-coded underlining method instead of margin notation, simply make asterisks or checks in the margin next to the passage in question in the colors that indicate the additional sections of the brief where it might be utilized.

The economy of utilizing "shorthand" in marking cases for briefing can be maintained in the actual brief writing process itself by utilizing "law student shorthand" within the brief. There are many commonly used words and phrases for which abbreviations can be substituted in your briefs (and in your class notes also). You can develop abbreviations that are personal to you and which will save you a lot of time. A reference list of briefing abbreviations can be found on page xii of this book.

C. Use Both the Briefing Process and the Brief as a Learning Tool

Now that you have a format and the tools for briefing cases efficiently, the most important thing is to make the time spent in briefing profitable to you and to make the most advantageous use of the briefs you create. Of course, the briefs are invaluable for classroom reference when you are called upon to explain or analyze a particular case. However, they are also useful in reviewing for exams. A quick glance at the fact summary should bring the case to mind, and a rereading of the rule of law should enable you to go over the underlying legal concept in your mind, how it was applied in that particular case, and how it might apply in other factual settings.

As to the value to be derived from engaging in the briefing process itself, there is an immediate benefit that arises from being forced to sift through the essential facts and reasoning from the court's opinion and to succinctly express them in your own words in your brief. The process ensures that you understand the case and the point that it illustrates, and that means you will be ready to absorb further analysis and information brought forth in class. It also ensures you will have something to say when called upon in class. The briefing process helps develop a mental agility for getting to the *gist* of a case and for identifying, expounding on, and applying the legal concepts and issues found there. The briefing process is the mental process on which you must rely in taking law school examinations; it is also the mental process upon which a lawyer relies in serving his clients and in making his living.

Abbreviations for Briefs

acceptance	acp	offer	O
affirmed	aff	offeree	OE
answer	ans	offeror	OR
assumption of risk	a/r	ordinance	ord
attorney	atty	pain and suffering	p/s
beyond a reasonable doubt	b/r/d	parol evidence	p/e
bona fide purchaser	BFP	plaintiff	P
breach of contract	br/k	prima facie	p/f
cause of action	c/a	probable cause	p/c
common law	c/l	proximate cause	px/c
Constitution	Con	real property	r/p
constitutional	con	reasonable doubt	r/d
contract	K	reasonable man	r/m
contributory negligence	c/n	rebuttable presumption	rb/p
cross	x	remanded	rem
cross-complaint	x/c	res ipsa loquitur	RIL
cross-examination	x/ex	respondeat superior	r/s
cruel and unusual punishment	c/u/p	Restatement	RS
defendant	D	reversed	rev
dismissed	dis	Rule Against Perpetuities	RAP
double jeopardy	d/j	search and seizure	s/s
due process	d/p	search warrant	s/w
equal protection	e/p	self-defense	s/d
equity	eq	specific performance	s/p
evidence	ev	statute of limitations	S/L
exclude	exc	statute of frauds	S/F
exclusionary rule	exc/r	statute	S
felony	f/n	summary judgment	s/j
freedom of speech	f/s	tenancy in common	t/c
good faith	g/f	tenancy at will	t/w
habeas corpus	h/c	tenant	t
hearsay	hr	third party	TP
husband	H	third party beneficiary	TPB
in loco parentis	ILP	transferred intent	TI
injunction	inj	unconscionable	uncon
inter vivos	I/v	unconstitutional	unconst
joint tenancy	j/t	undue influence	u/e
judgment	judgt	Uniform Commercial Code	UCC
jurisdiction	jur	unilateral	uni
last clear chance	LCC	vendee	VE
long-arm statute	LAS	vendor	VR
majority view	maj	versus	v
meeting of minds	MOM	void for vagueness	VFV
minority view	min	weight of the evidence	w/e
Miranda warnings	Mir/w	weight of authority	w/a
Miranda rule	Mir/r	wife	W
negligence	neg	with	w/
notice	ntc	within	w/i
nuisance	nus	without prejudice	w/o/p
obligation	ob	without	w/o
obscene	obs	wrongful death	wr/d

Table of Cases

Note: There are no principal cases in Chapter 1 of the casebook.

CHAPTER **2**

The Nature of the Federal Judicial Function

Quick Reference Rules of Law

Marbury v. Madison

Appointed federal official (P) v. Secretary of State (D)

5 U.S. (1 Cranch) 137 (1803).

NATURE OF CASE: Petition before the Supreme Court for a writ of mandamus to compel a cabinet secretary to deliver a commission.

FACT SUMMARY: [Facts not stated in casebook excerpt. Congress authorized the Supreme Court to issue writs of mandamus, although the Constitution specifically limits the Court's original jurisdiction to specific areas.]

🏛 RULE OF LAW
The Supreme Court has the power, under the Supremacy Clause and Article III, § 2 of the Constitution, to review acts of Congress that are repugnant to the Constitution and to find them unconstitutional.

FACTS: [Facts not stated in casebook excerpt. Congress authorized the Supreme Court to issue writs of mandamus, although the Constitution specifically limits the Court's original jurisdiction to specific areas.]

ISSUE: Does the Supreme Court have the power, under the Supremacy Clause and Article III, § 2 of the Constitution, to review acts of Congress that are repugnant to the Constitution and to find them unconstitutional?

HOLDING AND DECISION: (Marshall, C.J.) Yes. The Supreme Court has the power, under the Supremacy Clause and Article III, § 2 of the Constitution, to review acts of Congress that are repugnant to the Constitution and to find them unconstitutional. The government of the United States is one of laws, and not men. This appellation is meaningless if the laws furnish no remedy for the violation of a vested right. Clearly, Marbury (P) has a right to have his commission delivered. And furthermore, there is no political question problem here to bar the use of mandamus as a remedy. However, § 13 of the Judiciary Act is unconstitutional. The section gives the Supreme Court original jurisdiction to issue writs of mandamus. The Constitution, on the other hand, limits the Court's original jurisdiction to only designated cases (i.e., affecting ambassadors, other public ministers and consuls, and those in which a state shall be a party); in all other cases, the Supreme Court has only appellate jurisdiction. The Constitution defines and limits the powers of the legislature. The legislature cannot alter the Constitution, which itself provides that it is the "supreme law" of the land, by an ordinary act. To hold otherwise would render the Constitution as only an absurd attempt to limit legislative power. If an act of the legislature is therefore repugnant to the Constitution, and void, does it, notwithstanding its invalidity, bind the courts, and oblige them to give it effect? No. If a law be in opposition to the Constitution, the Court must determine which of these conflicting rules governs the case. The Constitution, if it is to have any meaning at all, must prevail. Article III, § 2 provides that the judicial power of the United States is extended to all cases arising under the Constitution. A case arising under the Constitution cannot be decided without examining the instrument under which it arises. Courts cannot be permitted to look into some parts of the Constitution, and not others. Finally, the Framers of the Constitution contemplated that instrument as a rule for the government of courts, as well as of the legislature. Why else are judges required to take an oath to uphold the Constitution? Thus, since the Supreme Court possesses the power to review acts of Congress, this Court finds that § 13 of the Judiciary Act of 1789 is unconstitutional, and that this Court lacks the authority, under the Constitution, to issue a writ of mandamus in this case.

▶ ANALYSIS

The power of the Court to declare acts of Congress repugnant to the Constitution is not exclusive; other branches of government are not absolved from their responsibility to assess the constitutionality of legislation governing their performance. Nor does *Marbury v. Madison* hold that the act before the Court for review, if found unconstitutional, is void in all contexts. Since the Court is asked to pass on arguments presented by two adverse parties before it, its decision is limited to the facts of the case. However, there may be instances where a law is not only unconstitutional as applied, but is void on its face.

■═■

Quicknotes

SUPREMACY CLAUSE Article VI, ¶ 2 of the U.S. Constitution, which provides that federal action must prevail over inconsistent state action.

WRIT OF MANDAMUS A court order issued commanding a public or private entity, or an official thereof, to perform a duty required by law.

■═■

Hayburn's Case

[Parties not identified.]

2 U.S. (2 Dall.) 408 (1792).

NATURE OF CASE: Motion for a mandamus that the circuit court add petitioner's name to a pension list.

FACT SUMMARY: This case involved a motion for a mandamus to be directed to the circuit court commanding the said court to add Hayburn's (P) name to the pension list of the United States as an invalid pensioner pursuant to an act of Congress.

🏛 RULE OF LAW

Since the branches of the federal government are distinct and independent, Congress cannot constitutionally assign to the judiciary any duties which are not properly judicial.

FACTS: Under a federal statute passed in 1792, disabled veterans of the Revolutionary War desiring to be placed on the pension list of the United States were to apply to the circuit court. The court would determine whether the applicant was qualified and then certify to the Secretary of War that the name be added to the pension list. However, if the Secretary of War suspected that the court had made a mistake, he had the power to withhold the name. The Attorney General made the motion for mandamus on behalf of Hayburn (P), as an interested party, after the court had refused to render an opinion on a writ brought by the Attorney General ex officio without an application from any particular person. The motion directed the circuit court to add Hayburn's (P) name to the pension list as an invalid pensioner, but the court refused to entertain such petitions.

ISSUE: Can Congress constitutionally assign to the judiciary any duties which are not properly judicial?

HOLDING AND DECISION: (Per curiam) No. By the Constitution, the government is divided into three distinct and independent branches. Neither the legislative nor the executive branches can constitutionally assign to the judiciary any duties that are not properly judicial. Under the 1792 Act of Congress, the duties assigned to the circuit courts are not judicial in nature inasmuch as the decisions of the court are subject to consideration and possible suspension by the Secretary of War. The Constitution does not authorize either the Secretary of War or any executive officer to sit as a court of errors on the judicial branch.

▶ ANALYSIS

This was the first case to enunciate the rule that the judiciary would not render advisory opinions. This rule had significance in a modern sense in *Muskrat v. United States*, 219 U.S. 346 (1911), concerning the power of the judiciary to render declaratory judgments. The Court held that in most instances a declaratory judgment is nothing more than an advisory opinion. Eventually, a federal statute was enacted authorizing declaratory judgments.

■═■

Quicknotes

DECLARATORY JUDGMENT A judgment of the court establishing the rights of the parties.

JURISDICTION The authority of a court to hear and declare judgment in respect to a particular matter.

■═■

United States v. Johnson

Federal government (P) v. Landlord (D)

319 U.S. 302 (1943).

NATURE OF CASE: Suit to recover money damages.

FACT SUMMARY: Roach (P) claimed that Johnson (D) had violated a federal regulation fixing the maximum rent that lessors could charge. The United States (P) claimed that the litigation was the product of collusion.

🏛 RULE OF LAW
A court should dismiss any suit which is obviously the product of collusion between the plaintiff and the defendant.

FACTS: Roach (P), a tenant of residential property owned by Johnson (D), brought suit in federal district court alleging that said property was within a "defense rental area," and thus was subject to an applicable rent control regulation. Roach (P), claiming that the rent charged by Johnson (D) exceeded the prescribed maximum, sought treble damages as well as attorney fees. Johnson (D) moved to dismiss the action on the ground that the act pursuant to which the federal regulation had been promulgated was unconstitutional. The United States (P) intervened and filed a brief in support of the constitutionality of the act, but the district court dismissed the complaint on the ground that the act and the regulation were both unconstitutional because Congress had delegated legislative authority to the act's administrator. On appeal, the United States (P) again asserted the constitutionality of the act and regulation and also argued that the district court should have granted a government (P) motion to reopen the case on the ground that the litigation was the result of cooperation and collusion between Roach (P) and Johnson (D).

ISSUE: Should an action be dismissed if it is the result of collusion between the parties?

HOLDING AND DECISION: (Per curiam) Yes. A court should dismiss any suit which is obviously the product of collusion between the plaintiff and the defendant. Such actions are not truly adversarial and therefore do not offer the antagonism which is essential to ensure that rights are vigorously asserted. Especially in cases like the present one, where constitutional issues are involved, a genuine adversarial posture is essential. In this case, it appears that the action was instituted at Johnson's (D) urging and that Roach (P) paid no filing or attorney fees, never met the lawyer who supposedly represented him, did not even read the complaint, and had no knowledge of important aspects of the case. From these facts, it appears that the lawsuit was not adversarial in any real sense, and the district court should have dismissed it as collusive. Judgment vacated.

▶ ANALYSIS

Federal courts refuse to assert jurisdiction over collusive suits, reasoning that such actions do not amount to cases or controversies within the meaning of Article III. Many collusive suits go undetected since neither litigant, obviously, will be inclined to raise the objection that the action is the product of collusion between the parties. As *United States v. Johnson* illustrates, the collusion allegation is sometimes voiced by a third party who has been permitted to intervene in the action. Obviously, the fact that the parties agree on some issues of a suit does not render it collusive. It is the motivation for the commencement of the suit which cannot be the product of collusion.

■═■

Quicknotes

COLLUSION An agreement between two or more parties to engage in unlawful conduct or in other activities with an unlawful goal, typically involving fraud.

JURISDICTION The authority of a court to hear and declare judgment in respect to a particular matter.

■═■

Fairchild v. Hughes

Citizen (P) v. Secretary of State (D)

258 U.S. 126 (1922).

NATURE OF CASE: Appeal in action seeking to declare a constitutional amendment unconstitutional; to enjoin the declaration that the amendment has been ratified; and to enjoin its enforcement.

FACT SUMMARY: Fairchild (P), a citizen, contended that the Nineteenth Amendment, known as the Suffrage Amendment, was unconstitutional because it would not be conclusively valid, but would lead election officers to permit women to vote in states whose constitution limited suffrage to men, which in turn would deprive citizens of their right to have elections where only men could vote, so that the effectiveness of their votes would be diminished, and election expenses would nearly double.

> ## 🏛 RULE OF LAW
> The general right of a citizen to have the government administered according to law and the public moneys not wasted does not entitle him to institute in the federal courts a suit to secure by indirection a determination whether a statute, if passed, or a constitutional amendment about to be adopted, will be valid.

FACTS: Thirty-four states had passed resolutions purporting to ratify the Nineteenth Amendment to the Constitution, known as the Suffrage Amendment, and the Secretary of State (D) had received one certificate to that effect. Once he received one more certificate, the Secretary of State (D) would issue a proclamation declaring that the amendment had been adopted. In addition, a bill had been introduced in the Senate that provided for criminal penalties for any person who refused to permit a woman to vote, and if that bill passed, the Attorney General (D) would be required to enforce its provisions. Fairchild (P), a citizen, brought suit to have the amendment declared unconstitutional, to enjoin the Secretary of State (D) from declaring it adopted, and to enjoin the Attorney General (D) from enforcing it. Fairchild (P) argued that the Secretary of State's (D) threatened proclamation of adoption would not be conclusive of the amendment's validity, but would lead election officers to permit women to vote in states whose constitution limited suffrage to men, which in turn would deprive citizens of their right to have elections where only men could vote, so that the effectiveness of their votes would be diminished, and election expenses would nearly double. The United States Supreme Court granted certiorari.

ISSUE: Does the general right of a citizen to have the government administered according to law and the public moneys not wasted entitle him to institute in the federal courts a suit to secure by indirection a determination

whether a statute, if passed, or a constitutional amendment about to be adopted, will be valid?

HOLDING AND DECISION: (Brandeis, J.) No. The general right of a citizen to have the government administered according to law and the public moneys not wasted does not entitle him to institute in the federal courts a suit to secure by indirection a determination whether a statute, if passed, or a constitutional amendment about to be adopted, will be valid. Fairchild's (P) alleged interests in the issues he raises do not afford a basis for maintaining the action. The action, although in form a suit in equity, does not fall within the meaning of case under section 2 of article 3 of the Constitution, which confers judicial power on the courts. That is because he does not raise any claims before the courts that can be determined by such regular proceedings as are established by law or custom for the protection or enforcement of rights, or the prevention, redress or punishment of wrongs. The Secretary of State's (D) alleged wrongful act is merely threatened, as is that of the Attorney General (D). Fairchild's (P) right to ensure that government is lawfully administered does not entitle him to institute a suit in the federal courts challenging indirectly the validity of statutes or constitutional amendments that have as yet not been passed or adopted. [Disposition not indicated in casebook excerpt.]

▶ ANALYSIS

Although this case does not discuss "standing" per se, it essentially holds that Fairchild (P) lacks Article III standing. Arguably, under the Court's reasoning, Fairchild (P) might have had such standing if he was an election official or a citizen of a state that had not amended its state constitution to permit women to vote.

■■■

Quicknotes

STANDING The right to commence suit against another party because of a personal stake in the resolution of the controversy.

■■■

Allen v. Wright

Parent of black child (P) v. Federal official (D)

468 U.S. 737 (1984).

NATURE OF CASE: Appeal from grant of standing in class action suit.

FACT SUMMARY: In Allen's (P) class action suit against Wright (D) and the Internal Revenue Service (IRS) (D) for the IRS's (D) failure to adopt sufficient standards to fulfill its obligation to deny tax-exempt status to racially discriminatory private schools, Wright (D) contended that Allen (P) lacked standing to sue and that the relief Allen (P) requested was contrary to the will of Congress expressed in a 1979 ban on strengthening IRS (D) guidelines.

🏛 RULE OF LAW
Under Article III of the U.S. Constitution, the principle of separation of powers counsels against recognizing standing in a case brought not to enforce specific legal obligations whose violation works a direct harm, but to seek a restructuring of the apparatus established by the executive branch to fulfill its legal duties.

FACTS: Parents of black children, including Allen (P), brought a nationwide class action suit against Wright (D) and the IRS (D), alleging that the IRS (D) did not adopt sufficient standards and procedures to fulfill its obligation to deny tax-exempt status to racially discriminatory private schools. Allen (P) asserted that the IRS (D) thereby harmed the class directly and interfered with the ability of its children to receive an education in desegregated private schools. The IRS (D) and Wright (D) contended that Allen (P) lacked standing to sue, that the judicial task proposed by Allen (P) was inappropriately intrusive for a federal court, and that the relief requested by Allen (P) would be contrary to the will of Congress expressed in a 1979 ban on strengthening IRS (D) guidelines. The district court granted Wright's (D) motion to dismiss Allen's (P) complaint on the ground that Allen (P) lacked standing and that the relief requested by Allen (P) could be fashioned without large-scale judicial intervention in the administrative process. That court remanded the case to the district court. Certiorari was then granted by the United States Supreme Court.

ISSUE: Under Article III of the U.S. Constitution, does the principle of separation of powers counsel against recognizing standing in a case brought not to enforce specific legal obligations whose violation works a direct harm, but to seek a restructuring of the apparatus established by the executive branch to fulfill its legal duties?

HOLDING AND DECISION: (O'Connor, J.) Yes. Under Article III of the U.S. Constitution, the principle of separation of powers counsels against recognizing standing in a case brought not to enforce specific legal obligations whose violation works a direct harm, but to seek a restructuring of the apparatus established by the executive branch to fulfill its legal duties. Allen (P) here alleged two injuries in his complaint to support class standing to bring this lawsuit. First, he stated that he was harmed directly by the mere fact of government financial aid to discriminatory private schools. Second, Allen (P) et al. contended that the federal tax exemptions to racially discriminatory private schools in their communities impair their ability to have their public schools desegregated. This Court concludes that neither alleged injury suffices to support Allen's (P) standing. The first fails under clear precedents of this Court because it does not constitute judicially cognizable injury. The second fails because the alleged injury is not fairly traceable to alleged unlawful conduct of the IRS (D). The necessity that a plaintiff who seeks to invoke judicial power stand to profit in some personal interest remains an Article III requirement. Allen (P) has not met this fundamental requirement. Reversed.

DISSENT: (Brennan, J.) Here, Allen (P) has alleged at least one type of injury that satisfies the constitutional requirement of distinct and palpable injury. In particular, he has claimed that the IRS's (D) grant of tax-exempt status to racially discriminatory private schools directly injures the class's children's opportunity and ability to receive a desegregated education. It has been consistently recognized throughout the last thirty years that the deprivation of a child's right to receive an education in a desegregated school is a harm of special significance; surely it satisfies any constitutional requirement of injury in fact.

DISSENT: (Stevens, J.) Three propositions are clear here: (1) Allen (P) adequately alleged "injury in fact"; (2) the injury alleged was fairly traceable to the conduct that was claimed to be unlawful; and (3) the "separation of powers" principle does not create a jurisdictional obstacle to the consideration of the merits of Allen's (P) claim.

▶ ANALYSIS

The Supremacy Clause and the decision in *Marbury v. Madison*, 1 Cranch 137 (1803), plainly imply that a litigant always has standing to challenge judicial action claimed to violate his constitutional rights. Thus, in a case involving coercive action against a defendant, there is little question that he may challenge the judicial coercion as violating his rights. The purpose of standing is not only to limit relief to

Continued on next page.

litigants entitled to it, but to ensure that controversies will be concrete and genuine.

■═■

Quicknotes

STANDING TO SUE Plaintiff must allege that he has a legally predictable interest at stake in the litigation.

TAX EXEMPT STATUS Category of property used for educational, religious, or charitable purposes that by law is not subject to assessment for taxes.

■═■

Lujan v. Defenders of Wildlife

Interior Department (D) v. Conservation group (P)

504 U.S. 555 (1992).

NATURE OF CASE: Appeal from denial of summary judgment in an action challenging a rule promulgated under the Endangered Species Act.

FACT SUMMARY: The Defenders of Wildlife (P) sought to establish standing to challenge Interior Department (D) regulations pursuant to the Endangered Species Act based upon members who studied endangered animals.

🏛 RULE OF LAW
A plaintiff must have suffered a concrete and imminent injury in order to establish standing.

FACTS: The Endangered Species Act (ESA) was enacted in 1973 to protect species that were threatened with extinction. Section 7 of the ESA provides that each federal agency must insure that its actions do not jeopardize any species through consultations with the Secretary of Interior (D). In 1979, the Interior Department (D) interpreted the ESA to require consultation only for agency actions taken in the United States. The Defenders of Wildlife (Defenders) (P), an organization devoted to wildlife conservation, sought to challenge this decision. To establish standing to sue, two members of the Defenders (P), Kelly and Skilbred, gave affidavits which stated that they had traveled to foreign countries in the past to study endangered species and intended to do so again in the future. They asserted that projects funded by the Agency for International Development could threaten some species overseas. The Defenders (P) also maintained that the Act specifically provided all citizens with standing. The district court and the court of appeals ruled for the Defenders (P), and the Interior Department (D) appealed and in 1986 the regulation was changed.

ISSUE: Must a plaintiff suffer a concrete and imminent injury in order to establish standing?

HOLDING AND DECISION: (Scalia, J.) Yes. A plaintiff must have suffered a concrete and imminent injury in order to establish standing. Article III of the Constitution requires that the courts decide only cases and controversies. Thus, in order to have the minimum standing to file suit a plaintiff must have suffered an injury in fact, there must be a causal connection between the injury and the conduct complained of, and it must be likely that the injury will be redressed by a favorable decision. When a plaintiff asserts that an injury arises from the government's regulation of a third party, the plaintiff has a more difficult burden to prove standing. The injury must be concrete and particularized and it may not be hypothetical. The injury must be actual or imminent. The Defenders (P) failed to prove imminent injury because the affidavits of Kelly and Skilbred indicated

only a generalized future intention to return to the foreign locations to study. Therefore, their injury is not imminent because they have no definite plans to return. Furthermore, these standing requirements are the minimum necessary to maintain a suit under Article III and Congress cannot provide standing for every citizen with a general grievance about the administration of the law. Accordingly, the suit is dismissed, the court of appeals is reversed, and the case remanded.

CONCURRENCE: (Kennedy, J.) Defenders of Wildlife (P) has failed to demonstrate that its members are "among the injured." Although it has not made a sufficient showing to support its "nexus" theory—whereby anyone who uses any part of a contiguous ecosystem has standing—in different circumstances, a nexus theory might support a claim to standing.

CONCURRENCE: (Stevens, J.) Congress did not intend the consultation requirement of the ESA to apply to activities in foreign countries, so summary judgment must be granted to the Interior Department (D). However, Defenders (P) has suffered an injury sufficient to be granted standing insofar as an injury to an individual's interest in studying a species occurs when someone takes an action to harm that species.

DISSENT: (Blackmun, J.) A reasonable fact-finder could conclude from the affidavits that Kelly or Skilbred would soon return to the foreign sites, thereby satisfying the imminent injury standard. Additionally, Congress intended for the citizen-suit provision of the ESA to augment legal enforcement of the act in this type of situation and it should be given effect.

▶ ANALYSIS

Prior to this decision, many commentators believed that Congress had the power to relax the strict standing requirements of injury, causation, and redressability by inserting a "citizen suit" provision in its statutes. This view was reinforced by a long line of Fair Housing Act cases in which the Court continuously granted standing based primarily on statutory authorization rather than an injury-in-fact. The majority in *Lujan*, however, refused to defer to Congress's grant of environmental standing.

Quicknotes

ARTICLE III, U.S. CONSTITUTION Limits federal judicial power to cases and controversies.

Continued on next page.

INJURY IN FACT   An injury that gives rise to standing to sue.

STANDING   The right to commence suit against another party because of a personal stake in the resolution of the controversy.

■═■

Craig v. Boren

Member of discriminated class and a vendor (P) v. Oklahoma attorney general (D)

429 U.S. 190 (1976).

NATURE OF CASE: Appeal from a federal court decision denying standing to sue.

FACT SUMMARY: When Craig (P) turned 21 and his claim that a gender-based disparity resulted in an unconstitutional liquor statute became moot, Whitener (P), a licensed beer vendor, argued that she had standing to raise the same constitutional issue.

 RULE OF LAW
A vendor has standing to assert the constitutional rights of its vendee.

FACTS: An Oklahoma statute prohibited sale of a low-alcohol beer to males under the age of 21 and to females under the age of 18. Craig (P), a male between the ages of 18 and 21 and Whitener (P), a licensed beer vendor, brought suit to have the statute declared unconstitutional on the grounds that the gender-based disparity violated the Equal Protection Clause. After the Supreme Court noted probable jurisdiction to review the decision upholding the statute, Craig (P) turned 21, and his challenge became nonjusticiable as moot. The remaining question before the Supreme Court then became whether Whitener (P) could rely on the same equal protection objections of males 18-20 years of age to establish her own claim of unconstitutionality of the age-sex differential.

ISSUE: Does a vendor have standing to assert the constitutional rights of its vendee?

HOLDING AND DECISION: (Brennan, J.) Yes. A vendor has standing to assert the constitutional rights of its vendee. Whitener (P), the licensed vendor of the 3.2% beer, having a live controversy against enforcement of the statute, may rely upon the equal protection objections of 18-20-year-old males as the premise of her equal protection challenge to Oklahoma's 3.2% beer law. The vendor of the beer was subject to sanctions and loss of license for violation of the statute, hence was a proper party in interest to object to the enforcement of the sex-based regulatory provision. Article III limitations on a litigant's assertion of jus tertii are not constitutionally mandated, but rather stem from a salutary rule of self-restraint designed to minimize unwarranted intervention into controversies where the applicable constitutional questions are ill-defined and speculative. In this case, such prudential objectives would not be furthered since the lower court had already entertained the relevant constitutional challenge and the parties have sought an authoritative constitutional determination. In such circumstances, a decision to forgo the constitutional merits merely to await the initiation of a new challenge to the statute by injured third parties would be impermissibly to foster repetitive and time-consuming litigation under the guise of caution and prudence. In any event, Whitener (P) has established independently her claim to assert jus tertii standing since the operation of the challenged statutory provisions plainly inflicted "injury in fact" upon her sufficient to guarantee her "concrete adverseness." [The Court went on to hold the statute unconstitutional.]

DISSENT: (Burger, C.J.) Whitener (P) does not have standing arising from her status as a saloon-keeper to assert the constitutional rights of her customers. This case is not controlled by *Griswold v. Connecticut*, 381 U.S. 479 (1965), and "it borders on the ludicrous" to draw a parallel between a vendor of beer and the intimate professional physician-patient relationship which undergirded relaxation of standing rules in that case.

▶ *ANALYSIS*

In the *Craig* case, the Supreme Court observed that the legal duties created by the challenged statutory sanctions were addressed directly to vendors such as Whitener (P) because she was obliged by the legislation either to heed the statutory discrimination, thereby incurring a direct economic injury through the constriction of her buyers' market, or to disobey the statutory command and suffer sanctions and perhaps loss of her license.

■===■

Quicknotes

JUS TERTII Third-party right.

NONJUSTICIABLE Matter which is inappropriate for judicial review.

■===■

Yazoo & Mississippi Valley R.R. v. Jackson Vinegar Co.

Railroad (D) v. Shipper (P)

226 U.S. 217 (1912).

NATURE OF CASE: Suit seeking damages for loss of property.

FACT SUMMARY: Property belonging to Jackson Vinegar Co. (P) was lost while it was being shipped by the Railroad (D). A state law required railroads to settle all claims promptly or pay a penalty.

🏛 RULE OF LAW
A party may not challenge the constitutionality of a statute unless it was unconstitutional as applied against that party.

FACTS: Jackson Vinegar Co. (Jackson) (P) suffered a partial loss of vinegar which was being transported within the state of Mississippi by Yazoo & Mississippi Valley R.R. (D). Jackson (P) notified the Railroad's (D) agent of the loss, claiming that the lost vinegar was worth $4.76. A Mississippi statute required railroads and other common carriers to settle all claims of less than $200 of which they had notice and to pay a $25 penalty when they failed to settle such claims within the time prescribed by the statute. Jackson (P) eventually sued to recover both actual damages and the penalty and won judgment for both in the county circuit court. Since no state court had appellate jurisdiction over the case, the Railroad (D) appealed to the United States Supreme Court challenging the constitutionality of the penalty assessment.

ISSUE: May a party challenge a statute which he believes may, under some circumstances, be unconstitutionally applied?

HOLDING AND DECISION: (Van Devanter, J.) No. A party may not challenge the constitutionality of a statute unless it was unconstitutional as applied against that party. It is possible that the punitive measure would transgress the bounds of constitutionality when applied to a case involving a meritless or inflated claim. But the validity of Jackson's (P) claim was established by the evidence offered at trial. The statute was designed to ensure the prompt settlement of claims of this type and was not unconstitutionally applied against the Railroad (D) in this case. Thus, the Railroad (D) lacks standing to contest the validity of the enactment, notwithstanding the potential for its abuse in other cases. Affirmed.

▶ ANALYSIS

The essence of the standing requirement is that a plaintiff may litigate a matter only if the outcome of the litigation will affect him directly. In this case, the Court held in effect that the Railroad (D) was challenging the validity of the penalty statute only as it might eventually be applied to other common carriers. But the dangers against which the standing requirement is to protect the judicial system were not present in this case. The Railroad (D) truly believed that the statute was invalid in any context, and it could obviously be counted on to pursue all legal remedies to prevent the statute from being applied at all. Thus, the Court probably should have considered the merits of the Railroad's (D) argument that the statute would be unconstitutional under some circumstances, at least.

■═■

Quicknotes

STANDING The right to commence suit against another party because of a personal stake in the resolution of the controversy.

■═■

Board of Airport Commissioners v. Jews for Jesus, Inc.

Municipal commission (D) v. Religious organization (P)

482 U.S. 569 (1987).

NATURE OF CASE: Appeal from judgment holding that a government resolution was facially unconstitutional.

FACT SUMMARY: The Board of Airport Commissioners of Los Angeles (D) contended that its resolution banning all "First Amendment activities" within the Central Terminal Area at Los Angeles International Airport was not constitutionally overbroad.

🏛 RULE OF LAW
A regulation that prohibits all "First Amendment activities" is overbroad and unconstitutional on its face.

FACTS: The Board of Airport Commissioners of Los Angeles (D) adopted a resolution banning all "First Amendment activities" within the Central Terminal Area at Los Angeles International Airport (LAX). Pursuant to the resolution, an airport officer stopped Snyder (P), a minister for the Gospel for Jews for Jesus (Jews for Jesus) (P), a nonprofit religious corporation, from distributing free religious literature at LAX. The officer explained to Snyder (P) that his activities were in violation of the resolution and requested him to leave the terminal; Snyder (P) complied with the request. Snyder (P) and Jews for Jesus (P) brought suit in district court challenging the resolution's constitutionality. On appeal from the district court, the court of appeals held that the resolution was unconstitutional, and the United States Supreme Court granted certiorari.

ISSUE: Is a regulation that prohibits all "First Amendment speech" overbroad and unconstitutional on its face?

HOLDING AND DECISION: (O'Connor, J.) Yes. A regulation that prohibits all "First Amendment speech" is overbroad and unconstitutional on its face. The resolution itself facially violates the First Amendment under the overbreadth doctrine regardless of whether the forum involved is a public or nonpublic forum. The resolution's facial overbreadth is substantial since it prohibits all protected expression such as talking, reading, or wearing a campaign button or symbolic clothes. and does not merely regulate expressive activity that might create problems such as congestion or the disruption of airport users' activities. Under such a sweeping ban, virtually every individual who enters the airport may be found to violate the resolution by engaging in some "First Amendment activit[y]." The ban would be unconstitutional even if the airport were a nonpublic forum because no conceivable governmental interest would justify such an absolute prohibition of speech. Moreover, the resolution's words leave no room for a narrowing, saving construction by state courts. The suggestion that the resolution is not substantially overbroad because it is intended to reach only expressive activity unrelated to airport-related purposes is unpersuasive. Much nondisruptive speech may not be airport related, but is still protected speech even in a nonpublic forum. Moreover, the vagueness of the suggested construction, which would result in giving airport officials the power to decide in the first instance whether a given activity is airport related, presents a great opportunity for abuse. Affirmed.

▶ ANALYSIS

In some cases, the Court abstains or certifies the issue to the state courts where the state courts have not had the opportunity to give the statute under challenge a definite construction. Here, however, the Court determined that neither of these options was viable since California did not have a certification procedure, and because the Court concluded that the resolution could not be subject to an interpretation that would render unnecessary or substantially modify the federal constitutional question. In other words, the Court ruled that as a matter of law the resolution was not susceptible to a limiting construction.

■■■

Quicknotes

OVERBREADTH That quality or characteristic of a statute, regulation, or order which reaches beyond the problem it was meant to solve causing it to sweep within it activity it cannot legitimately reach.

■■■

DeFunis v. Odegaard

Law school applicant (P) v. State education officials (D)

416 U.S. 312 (1974).

NATURE OF CASE: Appeal from reversal of issuance of injunction.

FACT SUMMARY: DeFunis (P), who was admitted to law school while this action was pending, contended that the procedures and criteria employed by the admissions committee insidiously discriminated against him because of his race.

🏛 RULE OF LAW
A case is moot if the controversy between the parties has clearly ceased to be definite and concrete and no longer touches the legal relations of parties having adverse legal interests.

FACTS: DeFunis (P) applied for admission as a first-year student at the University of Washington Law School, a state-operated institution. DeFunis (P) was eventually notified that he had been denied admission. He thereupon sued Odegaard (D) and the University of Washington Law School Admissions Committee (D) for violation of the Equal Protection Clause of the Fourteenth Amendment of the U.S. Constitution. DeFunis (P) contended that the procedures and criteria employed by the University (D) insidiously discriminated against him on account of his race. DeFunis (P) brought suit on behalf of himself alone, and he asked the trial court to issue a mandatory injunction commanding Odegaard (D) to admit him as a member of the first-year law school class on the ground that the admissions policy had resulted in the unconstitutional denial of his application for admission. The trial court agreed with DeFunis (P) and granted the requested relief. DeFunis (P) was admitted to the law school while, at the same time, Odegaard (D) appealed the court's decision. The Washington Supreme Court reversed and held that the law school admissions policy did not violate the Constitution. DeFunis (P) then petitioned the United States Supreme Court for a writ of certiorari, which stayed the judgment of the Washington Supreme Court pending final disposition by the United States Supreme Court. The writ was granted, and DeFunis (P), who had remained in law school, was in the first term of his third and final year when the Court granted his petition.

ISSUE: Is a case moot if the controversy between the parties has clearly ceased to be definite and concrete and no longer touches the legal relations of parties having adverse legal interests?

HOLDING AND DECISION: (Per curiam) Yes. A case is moot if the controversy between the parties has clearly ceased to be definite and concrete and no longer touches the legal relations of the parties having adverse legal interests. Here, DeFunis (P) will complete his law school studies at the end of the term for which he has now registered, regardless of any decision this Court might reach on the merits of the litigation. Because of this fact, the Court cannot, consistently with the limitations of Article III of the U.S. Constitution, consider the substantive constitutional issues tendered by the parties. Accordingly, the judgment of the Supreme Court of Washington is vacated, and the cause is remanded for such proceedings as that court may deem appropriate.

DISSENT: (Douglas, J.) Brennan is correct in saying that this case is not moot, and because of the significance of the issues raised, it is important to reach the merits.

DISSENT: (Brennan, J.) There is a very real chance that DeFunis (P) may not graduate, due to unforeseen circumstances such as illness, and he would again be faced with the University's (D) allegedly unlawful admissions policy. The Court's precedents clearly hold that mere voluntary cessation of allegedly illegal conduct does not moot a case. Avoidance of repetitious litigation serves the public interest, so that mootness determinations, as here, should not be rendered where they not compelled by the record and where it is inevitable that the constitutional issues raised will again be presented for review. Although the Court should, of course, avoid unnecessary decisions of constitutional questions, it should not transform principles of avoidance of constitutional decisions into devices for sidestepping resolution of difficult cases.

▶ ANALYSIS

The doctrine of mootness is closely related to those of standing and ripeness. If a controversy is judged not ripe, the Court is saying that it is too early for a party claiming injury to seek relief. If the controversy is judged to be moot, the Court is saying that it is too late—that because the matter has been resolved, or for other reasons, the party no longer has a claim for redress.

■━■

Quicknotes

MOOT Judgment on the particular issue that has previously been decided or settled.

STANDING The right to commence suit against another party because of a personal stake in the resolution of the controversy.

■━■

United Public Workers v. Mitchell

Union (P) v. Federal official (D)

330 U.S. 75 (1947).

NATURE OF CASE: Suit seeking declaratory and injunctive relief.

FACT SUMMARY: Members of the United Public Workers (P) union wanted to engage in political activity, but Mitchell (D) and the other members of the Civil Service Commission (D) concluded that the Hatch Act precluded such conduct.

🏛 RULE OF LAW
A court should not issue a declaratory judgment in the absence of existing concrete facts or evidence relating to conduct which has already occurred.

FACTS: Various federal civil service employees (P) and members of the United Public Workers of America (P) sued the members of the United States Civil Service Commission (Commission) (D), seeking both a declaratory judgment that a provision of the Hatch Act was unconstitutional and an injunction preventing the Commission (D) from enforcing the provision, which forbade government employees from taking any active part in political management or campaigns. The employees (P) claimed that both that provision and a portion of a Civil Service Rule of similar import violated various provisions of the Constitution. George Poole (P) claimed that he had already violated the challenged provision of the Hatch Act, while the other employees (P) merely alleged that they desired to engage in political management and campaigns. The Commission (D) moved to dismiss the employees' (P) complaint for lack of a justiciable case or controversy. The federal district court denied that motion, but later upheld the validity of the Hatch Act and granted summary judgment for the Commission (D). When the employees (P) appealed to the United States Supreme Court, the Commission (D) again argued that no justiciable controversy was presented since, with the exception of Poole (P), none of the employees (P) had yet engaged in any conduct which was forbidden by the Act.

ISSUE: Should a court issue a declaratory judgment in the absence of existing concrete facts or evidence relating to conduct which has already occurred?

HOLDING AND DECISION: (Reed, J.) No. A court should not issue a declaratory judgment in the absence of existing concrete facts or evidence relating to conduct which has already occurred. The employees (P), with the exception of Poole (P), have not yet acted and have not had the Hatch Act applied against them. In effect, the employees (P) allege a hypothetical threat and seek an advisory opinion concerning the propriety of conduct which may never occur. In this situation, neither declaratory nor injunctive relief should be afforded. Poole (P), on the other hand, has pre-sented facts which amount to a justiciable controversy, but Poole (P) is entitled to no relief because the record shows that he violated the Act and that, as applied to him, the Act was valid.

DISSENT: (Black, J.) All the complaints state a case or controversy, and the Act, as applied in all cases, is invalid.

DISSENT: (Douglas, J.) It is clear that these employees (P) desired to engage in a specified type of conduct and that that conduct would, under the Hatch Act, have resulted in their dismissal. Their complaint clearly presents a justiciable controversy, and it will harm them irreparably and defeat the purpose of the declaratory judgment procedure if they are required to risk their jobs in order to test the validity of the Hatch Act.

▶ ANALYSIS

Article III of the Constitution directs the federal courts to exercise jurisdiction over "cases and controversies." From this mandate, the concepts of ripeness and mootness have evolved, as has the prohibition against collusive suits. A case is not deemed ripe for adjudication unless the activity from which relief is sought has already occurred, or at least commenced. Otherwise, the courts lack a factual frame of reference upon which to base a decision. It is often difficult to evaluate, in the abstract, the propriety of conduct which has not yet taken place, and if courts adjudicated controversies which were not yet ripe they would run the risk of rendering ill-considered decisions which would prove detrimental to subsequent litigants. However, if a threatened harm is sufficiently imminent and identifiable, there would seem to be no reason for invoking the ripeness doctrine, even if the anticipated activity has not yet commenced.

■═■

Quicknotes

COLLUSION An agreement between two or more parties to engage in unlawful conduct or in other activities with an unlawful goal, typically involving fraud.

HATCH ACT Legislation enacted in 1887 which restricted the political activity of executive branch employees of the federal government, the District of Columbia government and certain state and local agencies.

RIPENESS A doctrine precluding a federal court from hearing or determining a matter unless it constitutes an actual and present controversy warranting a determination by the court.

■═■

Abbott Laboratories v. Gardner

Drug manufacturer (P) v. Federal official (D)

387 U.S. 136 (1967).

NATURE OF CASE: Review of decision that case was not ripe.

FACT SUMMARY: Abbott Laboratories (Abbott) (P) sued to declare an FDA (D) regulation invalid.

🏛 RULE OF LAW
Ripeness requires fitness of the issues for judicial decision and hardship to the parties if court consideration is withheld.

FACTS: Congress amended the Federal Food, Drug, and Cosmetic Act in 1962 to require drug manufacturers to list a generic name, if available, along with the drug's brand name on labels and printed material. The Act's purpose was to inform doctors and the public of less expensive generic drugs. The FDA (D), headed by Gardner (D), promulgated a regulation that required drug manufacturers to print the generic name each time the brand name was used on labels and advertisements. Abbott (P) and others sought injunctive and declaratory relief against the regulation's requirement that a generic name be listed each time the brand name was used. Abbott (P) argued that the regulation exceeded the FDA's (D) authority. The lower court granted Abbott (P) injunctive and declaratory relief. However, the appellate court held that the case was not ripe for adjudication. Abbott (P) appealed.

ISSUE: Is the doctrine of ripeness satisfied when the issues are ripe for determination and hardship to the parties would result if court consideration were withheld?

HOLDING AND DECISION: (Harlan, J.) Yes. Ripeness is satisfied when the issues are fit for judicial determination and the parties would suffer hardship if a judicial determination were withheld. Courts must avoid premature adjudication of cases to prevent entanglement in abstract disagreements. The only issue here depends on a matter of law. If the regulation properly construes the statute, it is valid. Additionally, since the regulation was a final agency action, Abbott (P) would suffer hardship if adjudication were withheld because Abbott (P) would have to incur substantial costs or challenge the regulation after prosecution and risk penalties. Accordingly, the case is ripe enough for determination. Reversed and remanded.

DISSENT: (Fortas, J.) Those challenging the regulations have a remedy and there are no special reasons to relieve them of the necessity of deferring their challenge to the regulations until enforcement is undertaken. The courts do not and should not pass on these complex problems in the abstract because these regulations peculiarly depend for their quality and substance upon the facts of particular situations.

▶ ANALYSIS

The ripeness doctrine is very closely related to the problem of advisory opinions. When a case is not ripe, the court does not have an adequate record from which to base its decision. Although a litigant need not suffer actual harm before a claim is ripe, generally, a litigant must allege that there is a reasonable probability that the litigant will suffer specific harm that is imminent.

∎≡∎

Quicknotes

RIPENESS A doctrine precluding a federal court from hearing or determining a matter unless it constitutes an actual and present controversy warranting a determination by the court.

∎≡∎

O'Shea v. Littleton

State attorney (D) v. African American citizen (P)

414 U.S. 488 (1974).

NATURE OF CASE: Appeal from injunction against racially discriminatory conduct.

FACT SUMMARY: In Littleton's (P) action against O'Shea (D) for discriminatory practices of conduct in the administration of the criminal justice system, depriving Littleton (P) of rights secured by the First, Sixth, Eighth, Thirteenth, and Fourteenth Amendments and by 42 U.S.C. §§ 1981, 1982, 1983, and 1985, Littleton (P) contended that O'Shea (D) and Alexander County, Illinois, selectively discriminated in enforcement and administration of criminal justice in Alexander County on the basis of race, as well as against poor persons.

RULE OF LAW

Those who seek to invoke the power of federal courts must allege some threatened or actual injury resulting from putatively illegal action before a federal court may assume jurisdiction.

FACTS: Littleton (P) brought suit against O'Shea (D), the States Attorney for Alexander County, Illinois, for discriminating practices of conduct in the administration of the criminal justice system, which deprived Littleton (P) of rights secured by the First, Sixth, Eighth, Thirteenth, and Fourteenth Amendments and by 42 U.S.C. §§ 1981, 1982, 1983, and 1985. Littleton (P) contended that O'Shea (D) selectively discriminated in enforcement and administration of criminal justice in Alexander County on the basis of race, as well as against financially poor persons. Littleton (P) also contended that O'Shea (D) deliberately applied state criminal laws and procedures more harshly to black residents of Alexander County and inadequately applied those same laws and procedures against whites who victimized blacks, to deter blacks from engaging in their lawful attempts to achieve equality. The district court dismissed the case for want of jurisdiction to issue the injunctive relief prayed for and on the ground that O'Shea (D) was immune from suit respecting acts done in the course of his duties. The court of appeals reversed, holding that injunctions could be issued against judicial officers if it was alleged and proved that they knowingly engaged in conduct intended to discriminate against a cognizable class of persons on the basis of race. O'Shea (D) petitioned for certiorari from the United States Supreme Court.

ISSUE: Must those who seek to invoke the power of federal courts allege some threatened or actual injury resulting from putatively illegal action before a federal court may assume jurisdiction?

HOLDING AND DECISION: (White, J.) Yes. Those who seek to invoke the power of federal courts must allege some threatened or actual injury resulting from a putatively illegal action before a federal court may assume jurisdiction. Here, the judgment of the court of appeals must be reversed because Littleton's (P) complaint failed to satisfy the threshold requirement imposed by Article III of the Constitution that those who seek to invoke the power of federal courts must allege an actual case or controversy. Abstract injury is not enough. It must be alleged that the plaintiff has sustained or is immediately in danger of sustaining some direct injury as the result of the challenged official conduct. Here, Littleton (P) seeks an injunction aimed at controlling or preventing the occurrence of specific events that might take place in the course of future state criminal trials. That is not sufficient to establish the basic requisites of the issuance of equitable relief, here in the form of an injunction. In these circumstances, those basic requisites are the likelihood of substantial and immediate irreparable injury and the inadequacy of remedies at law. If Littleton (P) is ever prosecuted and faces trial, or if he is illegally sentenced, then state and federal procedures will be available to provide relief from the wrongful conduct alleged. Reversed.

CONCURRENCE: (Blackmun, J.) The complaint failed to satisfy the threshold requirement imposed by Article III of the Constitution that those who seek to invoke the power of the federal courts must allege an actual case or controversy.

DISSENT: (Douglas, J.) The allegations in this case of past and continuing wrongdoings clearly state a case or controversy in the Article III sense. Specificity of proof may not be forthcoming, but specificity of charges is clear. If this case does not present a "case or controversy" involving Littleton (P), then that concept has been so watered down as to no longer be recognizable.

ANALYSIS

In a case like *O'Shea*, in which matters complained of consist of official practices in law enforcement, it is especially difficult to identify the individuals who are likely to be harmed by those practices in the future. Such cases often involve requests for "structural relief"—that is, the shaping of a decree designed to modify the way in which an arm of government conducts its affairs. The Court's reluctance to become enmeshed in those affairs, especially when state

Continued on next page.

institutions are at the bar, has been expressed, in part, in terms of justiciability doctrine—notably, ripeness and standing.

■━■

Quicknotes

ARTICLE III, U.S. CONSTITUTION   Limits federal judicial power to cases and controversies.

JUSTICIABILITY   An actual controversy that is capable of determination by the court.

■━■

Nixon v. United States

Former federal judge (P) v. Federal government (D)

506 U.S. 224 (1993).

NATURE OF CASE: Review of case dismissal.

FACT SUMMARY: Nixon (P), a former federal judge, sought judicial review of the Senate trial procedure used to convict him.

⚖ RULE OF LAW

The political question doctrine dictates that the court abstain from making judgments on controversies committed to another branch of government.

FACTS: Nixon (P), a former Chief District Judge, was convicted for giving false testimony regarding a monetary bribe he was alleged to have accepted. Nixon (P) refused to resign his position as a judge and continued to draw salary and benefits. The Senate initiated proceedings under Senate Rule XI, which allowed a committee to conduct hearings and the full senate to vote. The Senate voted to convict Nixon (P) by more than the requisite two-thirds majority after receiving the full trial transcript and summaries of the evidence. Nixon (P) sought a declaratory judgment, arguing that he was not properly tried by the Senate in violation of the Impeachment Clause, Article I, § 3, cl. 6 of the Constitution. The federal court dismissed the case pursuant to the political question doctrine. Nixon (P) appealed.

ISSUE: Does the political question doctrine dictate that courts abstain from making judgments on controversies committed to another branch of government?

HOLDING AND DECISION: (Rehnquist, C.J.) Yes. The political question doctrine dictates that the court abstain from making judgments on controversies committed to another branch of government. Article I, § 3, cl. 6 grants to the Senate the sole power to impeach. The framers of the Constitution expressly rejected a judicial role in impeachments due to the possibility of bias. Review of these proceedings would raise the same problem. Also, impeachment was designed to be the only check on judicial power by the legislature. The impeachment procedure already contains adequate protections against abuse without judicial review. Affirmed.

CONCURRENCE: (White, J.) The Constitution does not forbid consideration of a judge's contention that the method by which the Senate convicted him has violated the impeachment trial clause, and, therefore, the merits should have been reached in this case. However, the Senate in this case fulfilled its duty to try Nixon (P). The political question doctrine applies to cases in which a coordinate political branch is given final responsibility, and here the majority has determined that the Constitution's use of the word "sole" in the phrase "the Senate shall have the sole Power to try all impeachments" gives the Senate such final responsibility. However, the use of the word "sole" can also be interpreted to emphasize the division of labor between the Senate and the House in the impeachment process. Thus, the majority wrongly identifies the judiciary, rather than the House, as the source of potential interference with which the Framers were concerned. It is thus "perplexing" that the majority is willing to abandon its obligation to review the constitutionality of legislative acts merely on the strength of the word "sole," as such abandonment goes against the principles of separation of power, checks and balances, and the Constitution's history. Further, the majority's notion that one simply cannot ascertain the sense of "try" which the Framers employed and hence cannot undertake judicial review, is untenable. The word "try" is used in its legal sense, and the majority's conclusion that "try" is incapable of meaningful judicial construction is not without irony. One might think that if any class of concepts would fall within the definitional abilities of the judiciary, it would be that class having to do with procedural justice. It is also historically clear that the Founders intended the Senate to conduct its proceedings in a manner that resembled a judicial proceeding, but that would not preclude the use of factfinding committees, since the Constitution grants the Senate ample discretion on how best to try impeachments.

CONCURRENCE: (Souter, J.) Although the political question doctrine applies in the present case, if the Senate were to abuse its discretion in trying an impeachment, the Court should review.

▶ ANALYSIS

Generally, the Court considers many factors when determining whether a nonjusticiable political question is involved. Three factors routinely considered include: (1) is the issue textually committed to another branch of government? (2) is there a lack of identifiable standards upon which the court may make a ruling? and (3) what effect would a judicial decision would have on the political process if the prior decision is not final?

Quicknotes

POLITICAL QUESTION An issue that is more appropriately left to the determination of another governmental branch and which the court declines to hear.

CHAPTER 3

The Original Jurisdiction of the Supreme Court

Quick Reference Rules of Law

Louisiana v. Mississippi

State (P) v. State (D)

488 U.S. 990 (1988).

NATURE OF CASE: Motion for leave to file a bill of complaint.

FACT SUMMARY: Louisiana (P) claimed that land on an island in the Mississippi River was in Louisiana (P) rather than in Mississippi (D).

🏛 RULE OF LAW
[There was no majority opinion other than to deny the motion.]

FACTS: Louisiana (P), intervening on behalf of private parties, claimed that land on an island in the Mississippi River was located in Louisiana (P) rather than Mississippi (D), and moved to file a bill of complaint in the United States Supreme Court. The majority denied the motion.

ISSUE: [There was no issue other than whether the court would grant the motion.]

HOLDING AND DECISION: [The Court denied the motion without an opinion.]

DISSENT: (White, J.) Louisiana's (P) complaint is clearly within the Court's original jurisdiction, and involves exactly the kind of border dispute that the Court has previously accepted and adjudicated. Although Louisiana (P) intervened in a private dispute, and resolution of that action might settle the dispute among the parties and Louisiana (P), a judgment will not bind Mississippi (D). It is possible that the private action will result in a judgment unfavorable to Louisiana (P), and, if so, the Court's preference to have disputes within its original jurisdiction adjudicated in other fora will be vindicated, but "this is no way to treat a sovereign State that wants its dispute with another State settled in this Court." Leave to file should have been granted.

▶ ANALYSIS

18 U.S.C. § 1251(a) prescribes that the United States Supreme Court has exclusive jurisdiction over controversies between States. Other than such controversies, it has been assumed that the Supreme Court's original jurisdiction is concurrent with the jurisdiction of the lower federal courts or state courts, and this assumption has been codified in § 1251(b), which permits concurrent jurisdiction by permitting the operation of any jurisdiction otherwise granted.

■===■

Quicknotes

JURISDICTION The authority of a court to hear and declare judgment in respect to a particular matter.

■===■

CHAPTER 4

Congressional Control of the Distribution of Judicial Power Among Federal and State Courts

Quick Reference Rules of Law

Sheldon v. Sill

Obligor (D) v. Assignee (P)

49 U.S. (8 How.) 441 (1850).

NATURE OF CASE: Action to recover on a bond and mortgage.

FACT SUMMARY: Sheldon (D) executed a bond and mortgage. Hastings assigned both to Sill (P), a citizen of another state, who then sued in federal court to recover on the bond and mortgage.

🏛 RULE OF LAW
Congress has the power to remove a case or controversy from the jurisdiction of the federal courts.

FACTS: Sheldon (D), a Michigan citizen, executed a bond and mortgage obligating him to the Bank of Michigan. Hastings, president of the bank, assigned the obligations to Sill (P), a resident of New York, who sued Sheldon (D) in federal court to recover on the bond and mortgage. By way of defense, Sheldon (D) cited a provision of the Judiciary Act that denied federal courts the jurisdiction to consider suits by assignees of choses in action unless the assignor could also have sued in federal court. Sill (P) countered with the observation that Article III of the Constitution vests the federal courts with jurisdiction to decide "controversies between citizens of different states." The trial court rendered judgment in favor of Sill (P), but Sheldon (D) appealed.

ISSUE: May a federal statute restrict the jurisdiction that is conferred on the federal courts by Article III of the Constitution?

HOLDING AND DECISION: (Grier, J.) Yes. Congress has the power to remove a case or controversy from the jurisdiction of the federal courts. The lower federal courts were created by Congress, not by the Constitution. Since Congress established these courts, it has the power to determine the scope of their jurisdiction. It has long been recognized that it has the right to do so by restricting the authority conferred by Article III of the Constitution, which may be construed as applying only to the Supreme Court anyway since the Constitution set up no system of subordinate federal courts. Therefore, the cited provision of the Judiciary Act requires reversal of the judgment in favor of Sill (P) since he satisfies the Act's definition of an assignee of a chose of action. Reversed.

▶ ANALYSIS

Surprisingly, some of the earliest constitutional scholars argued that Article III required Congress to vest the inferior federal courts with jurisdiction to resolve all suits enumerated in the Article. This view, however, never achieved preeminence. Today, the authority of Congress to enact laws circumscribing the jurisdiction of the federal courts is seldom questioned. In fact, Congress has frequently acted to deprive the federal courts of jurisdiction over suits that they would otherwise have the authority to decide. One way that Congress accomplishes this objective is to confer original jurisdiction to resolve certain cases upon the Supreme Court.

■■■

Quicknotes

ARTICLE III, U.S. CONSTITUTION Limits federal judicial power to cases and controversies.

CHOSE IN ACTION The right to recover, or the item recoverable, in a lawsuit.

■■■

Ex parte McCardle

[Parties not identified.]

74 U.S. (7 Wall.) 506 (1869).

NATURE OF CASE: Appeal from denial of habeas corpus.

FACT SUMMARY: McCardle (D) appealed from a denial of habeas corpus to the Supreme Court, but Congress passed an act forbidding the court jurisdiction.

🏛 RULE OF LAW
Congress has the power, under the Constitution, to make exceptions to the appellate jurisdiction of the Supreme Court.

FACTS: After the Civil War, Congress imposed military government on many former Confederate States under authority of the Civil War Reconstruction Acts. McCardle (D), a Mississippi newspaper editor, was held in military custody on charges of publishing libelous and incendiary articles. McCardle (D) brought a habeas corpus writ based on a congressional act passed on February 5, 1867. The act authorized federal courts to grant habeas corpus to persons held in violation of constitutional rights, and also gave authority for appeals to the Supreme Court. The circuit court denied McCardle's (D) habeas corpus writ, but the Supreme Court sustained jurisdiction for an appeal on the merits. However, after arguments were heard, Congress passed an act on March 27, 1868, that repealed that much of the 1867 act that allowed an appeal to the Supreme Court from the circuit court and the exercise by the Supreme Court by jurisdiction on any such appeals, past or present.

ISSUE: Does Congress have the power, under the Constitution, to make exceptions to the appellate jurisdiction of the Supreme Court?

HOLDING AND DECISION: (Chase, C.J.) Yes. Congress has the power, under the Constitution, to make exceptions to the appellate jurisdiction of the Supreme Court. The appellate jurisdiction of the Supreme Court is not derived from acts of Congress, but is conferred by the Constitution with such exceptions and regulations as Congress shall make. And though Congress has affirmatively described in the act of 1789 the regulations governing the exercise of the Supreme Court's appellate jurisdiction with the implication that any exercise of that jurisdiction not within the purview of the act would be negated, the exception to the appellate jurisdiction in the present case is not to be inferred from such affirmations. The exceptions in this case are express. That part of the 1867 act giving the Court appellate jurisdiction in habeas corpus cases is expressly repealed. The effect is to take away the Court's jurisdiction, dismissing the cause. When a legislative act is repealed, it is as if it had never existed except to transactions past and closed. Thus, no judgment can be rendered in a suit after repeal of the act under which it was brought. But this does not deny forever the Court's appellate power in habeas corpus cases. The act of 1868 affects only such appeals from circuit courts brought under the act of 1867. Appeal dismissed.

▶ ANALYSIS

McCardle is clearly an example of judicial restraint. The authority of Congress to control the jurisdiction of the Supreme Court is not unlimited. This was proved in *Marbury v. Madison*, 5 U.S. (1 Cranch) 137 (1803), where the Court, faced with an extension by Congress of its original jurisdiction as granted under the Constitution, refused to accept the constitutionality of the congressional act. While this specifically limited the Supreme Court's original jurisdiction, it provided Marshall with the ideal arena to assert the doctrine of judicial review. But in *McCardle*, the Court backed away from confrontation with Congress due to current-day political crises that followed the Civil War. Thereafter, the Court sought to limit congressional power by the power of judicial review announced in *Marbury*. The Court held on several occasions that certain congressional attempts to delimit its jurisdiction were unconstitutional attempts to invade the judicial province. Such congressional actions were considered a violation of the separation of powers. Today, it is doubtful that *McCardle* would be sustained.

■▬■

Quicknotes

APPELLATE JURISDICTION The power of a higher court to review the decisions of lower courts.

■▬■

Battaglia v. General Motors Corp.

Employee (P) v. Employer (D)

169 F.2d 254 (2d Cir. 1948).

NATURE OF CASE: Appeal from dismissal of actions under the Fair Labor Standards Act (FLSA) for overtime pay and damages.

FACT SUMMARY: Employees (P) who brought actions against their employer, General Motors (D), under the Fair Labor Standards Act (FLSA) for overtime pay and damages contended that the Portal-to-Portal Act of 1947 (the "Act"), 29 U.S.C. §§ 251-62, which removed employer liability for overtime pay for preliminary and incidental (portal-to-portal) work under the FLSA, and which took away jurisdiction from courts to hear actions for such overtime pay, was unconstitutional.

 RULE OF LAW
The Portal-to-Portal Act of 1947 is constitutional.

FACTS: The FLSA, 29 U.S.C. §§ 201-219, provides that employees be paid time-and-a-half for hours worked in excess of a 40-hour work week. Such pay is known as overtime pay. FLSA also provides that employers are liable to their employees for overtime pay as well as liquidated damages in an equal amount if they violate FLSA. FLSA did not define "work week." In 1946, the United States Supreme Court interpreted "work week" to include preliminary and incidental (portal-to-portal) work, which previously had not been considered compensable. Consequently, under this definition, many employees' work weeks exceeded 40 hours, resulting in employer liability under the FLSA. Numerous lawsuits were filed in response to the Supreme Court's decisions, and, in response, Congress enacted the Portal-to-Portal Act of 1947 (the "Act"), 29 U.S.C. §§ 251-62. Sections 2(a) and (b) of this Act removed employer liability under the FLSA for overtime pay related to preliminary and incidental work, and § 2(d) provided that "No court of the United States, of any State, Territory, or possession of the United States, or of the District of Columbia, shall have jurisdiction of any action or proceeding, whether instituted prior to or after May 14, 1947, to enforce liability or impose punishment for or on account of the failure of the employer to pay . . . overtime compensation under the Fair Labor Standards Act of 1938 . . ." as related to preliminary and incidental work. Four cases brought by employees (P) of General Motors (D) under the FLSA seeking overtime pay and damages were consolidated in the district court. The Portal-to-Portal Act was passed while the cases were pending, and General Motors (D) moved to dismiss the cases on the grounds that no cause of action was alleged and that the court's jurisdiction had been removed by operation of the Act. The employees (P) then challenged the constitutionality of the Act. Ultimately, the

district court granted the motions to dismiss, and the court of appeals granted review.

ISSUE: Is the Portal-to-Portal Act of 1947 constitutional?

HOLDING AND DECISION: (Chase, J.) Yes. The Portal-to-Portal Act of 1947 is constitutional. First, Congress may remove jurisdiction it has conferred provided due process is not violated and there is no deprivation of property without just compensation. Here, Congress conferred jurisdiction in the FLSA, and took it away in the Act. The issue then is whether § 2(d) of the Act deprives employees (P) of property without due process or just compensation. The answer depends on how the employees' (P) rights to compensation for preliminary and incidental (portal-to-portal) activities are viewed. There are three ways of looking at these rights: first, as wholly statutory up to the time the Act was enacted; second, as purely statutory up to the time of the Supreme Court decisions and contractual thereafter; and finally, as wholly contractual from the beginning. If the rights were purely statutory, there is no question the Act is constitutional because it is well established that rights derived from a statute are extinguished by its repeal, and are subject to Congress's action. If the rights were statutory up to the time of the Supreme Court cases, but contractual thereafter, or if they were contractual from the time the FLSA was enacted, the issue is more complex, because there is precedent that holds that due process is violated where a person is deprived of previously vested contract rights. The answer, however, is that even if the rights were contractual under such circumstances, it was the FLSA that made the contracts include the right to overtime pay for portal-to-portal activities, so that the Act negated that aspect of the contracts. Thus, the contracts were made subject to Congress's exercise of its power to regulate commerce. This reasoning is sound, because otherwise, persons could contractually insulate themselves from Congress's regulation—but no power of Congress can be restricted in this manner. Further, the Act does not violate Article III or encroach on the judiciary's power as an independent branch of government. The Act did not change the Supreme Court's decisions (even though it was enacted in response thereto), and it did not undo any final judgments based on those precedents. Nor did the Act impose on the courts any rule of decision. On the contrary, it left express private contracts and those implied in fact untouched and enforceable in the courts. Merely because the Act prevented the courts from following the Supreme Court's decisions does not ipso facto mean it is unconstitutional. Affirmed.

Continued on next page.

▶ *ANALYSIS*

This decision uses the Fifth Amendment to reject preclusion of judicial review of Congress's control over jurisdiction. Under this view, regardless of whether § 2(d) of the Act had an independent end in itself, if one of its effects would be to deprive employees (P) of property without due process or just compensation, it would be invalid, and subdivision (d) on the one hand and subdivisions (a) and (b) on the other would have to stand or fall together. Of course, after engaging in judicial review, the court concludes that the Fifth Amendment is not violated.

■■■

Quicknotes

FIFTH AMENDMENT Provides that no person shall be compelled to serve as a witness against himself, or be subject to trial for the same offense twice, or be deprived of life, liberty, or property without due process of law.

■■■

Crowell v. Benson

Government official (P) v. Employer (D)

285 U.S. 22 (1932).

NATURE OF CASE: Suit to enjoin enforcement of an award made by an administrative agency.

FACT SUMMARY: Crowell (P), deputy commissioner of a government agency, ordered Benson (D) to compensate Knudsen (P) for an injury allegedly suffered by Knudsen (P) while in Benson's (D) employ.

▥ RULE OF LAW
Although Congress may, by a specific statute, vest fact-finding authority in a tribunal other than a court, the facts that purportedly establish the applicability of such a statute to a particular case may be reviewed de novo by a federal court.

FACTS: Knudsen (P) filed a claim under the Longshoremen's and Harbor Workers' Compensation Act, claiming that he had been injured while in the employ of Benson (D). Crowell (P), as deputy commissioner of the U.S. Employees' Compensation Commission, made an award in Knudsen's (P) favor, but Benson (D), contending that Knudsen (P) had not been in his employ at the time of the injury, brought suit to enjoin the enforcement of the award. The federal district court granted a hearing de novo upon both the law and the facts. That court eventually determined that Knudsen (P) had not been in Benson's (D) employ, and restrained the enforcement of the award. The circuit court of appeals affirmed. Crowell (P) petitioned for certiorari to the United States Supreme Court, and Benson (D) argued that the Compensation Act, which gave judicial authority to Crowell (P) as deputy commissioner, was violative of the constitutional guarantees of due process and trial by jury as well as the provisions of Article III of the Constitution pertaining to the judicial power of the United States. Crowell (P) argued that the award in favor of Knudsen (P) should not have been overturned, and that the court should not have conducted a de novo review of the facts upon which Knudsen's (P) claim was based.

ISSUE: Although Congress may, by a specific statute, vest fact-finding authority in a tribunal other than a court, may the facts that purportedly establish the applicability of such a statute to a particular case be reviewed de novo by a federal court?

HOLDING AND DECISION: (Hughes, C.J.) Yes. Although Congress may, by a specific statute, vest fact-finding authority in a tribunal other than a court, the facts that purportedly establish the applicability of such a statute to a particular case may be reviewed de novo by a federal court. There are sound reasons why Congress might have desired the deputy commissioner's (P) factual conclusions to be final. On the other hand, the issue of whether or not Knudsen (P) was in Benson's (D) employ was "jurisdictional" in the sense that, unless that fact could be established, the Compensation Act could not have become operative and the deputy commissioner (P) could not have conducted the judicial hearing in the first place. Review of this factual determination was within the purview of the court, from which it follows that it was proper for the district court to conduct a hearing de novo. Moreover, the evidence adduced at the hearing amply supports the conclusion that the award in Knudsen's (P) favor should not have been made because he was not in Benson's (D) employ at the time of his injury. Affirmed.

DISSENT: (Brandeis, J.) There is no constitutional impediment to denying a de novo review of the deputy commissioner's (P) findings. The Constitution does not require that a judicial finding of fact in a civil proceeding not be based on evidence introduced at an administrative hearing, or deem that a determination made on the basis of such evidence is not an independent judicial finding. The deputy commissioner (P) necessarily determined that an employer-employee relationship existed. However, that determination is not jurisdictional, but quasi-jurisdictional, and in that respect should be accorded finality. Nothing in Article III requires that a controversy be determined in the first instance in the federal district courts, the jurisdiction of which is subject to Congress's control. In those instances where a controversy may not be decided in the first instance by an administrative tribunal, it is because due process requires the matter to be judicially determined. But, in civil cases involving property rights disputes, as here, the determination of facts may be made administratively, as no due process concerns require that such determinations be made judicially. Thus, Article III has no bearing on the question presented here.

▌ ANALYSIS

Crowell v. Benson illustrates the principle that Congress may, by the enactment of a particular statute, deprive the federal courts of jurisdiction over types of cases that would otherwise be within the ambit of their authority. Legislative functions are frequently conferred upon administrative agencies, although the Administrative Procedure Act generally accords a right to judicial review of administrative decision. In addition, Congress sometimes passes over the lower federal courts and gives the Supreme Court exclusive jurisdiction over matters that would otherwise be cognizable in a federal district court, and other courts are also occasionally given jurisdiction over matters after Congress has

Continued on next page.

specifically removed them from the authority of the lower federal courts.

■■■■■■

Quicknotes

ARTICLE III, U.S. CONSTITUTION   Limits federal judicial power to cases and controversies.

DE NOVO   The review of a lower court decision by an appellate court, which is hearing the case as if it had not been previously heard and as if no judgment had been rendered.

■■■■■■

Commodity Futures Trading Comm'n v. Schor

Independent agency (D) v. Broker's customer (P)

478 U.S. 833 (1986).

NATURE OF CASE: Appeal from court ruling limiting administrative jurisdiction.

FACT SUMMARY: In Schor's (P) action against the Commodity Futures Trading Commission (CFTC) (D) for redress stemming from a violation of the Commodity Exchange Act by Schor's (P) stockbroker, Schor (P) contended that the CFTC (D) had no power to adjudicate a counterclaim made against Schor (P) by his broker.

🏛 RULE OF LAW
The broad grant of power in 7 R.S.C. § 12a(5), the Commodity Exchange Act, clearly authorizes promulgation of regulations providing for adjudication of common law counterclaims arising out of the same transaction as a reparations complaint.

FACTS: Under the Commodity Exchange Act, 7 U.S.C. § 1 et seq., fraudulent and manipulative conduct in connection with commodity futures transactions may be prosecuted. The CFTC (D) was created as an independent agency with authority to implement the Act. Among the duties assigned the CFTC (D) was administration of a reparation procedure through which customers of professional brokers could seek redress for the broker's violations of the Act or CFTC (D) regulations. The CFTC (D) then promulgated a regulation that allowed it to adjudicate counterclaims arising out of the transaction set forth in the original complaint. This regulation also allowed a counterclaimant the option, in a reparations proceeding, to seek relief against the reparations complainant in another forum. Schor (P) filed a complaint against his futures broker, Conti, with the CFTC (D). Schor (P) had an account with Conti which contained a debit balance because Schor's (P) net futures trading losses and expenses exceeded the funds deposited in Schor's (P) account. Schor (P) alleged that the debit balance was the result of Conti's violations of the Act. Conti brought a counterclaim against Schor (P) in the CFTC (D) and denied violating the Act, insisting that the debit balance resulted from Schor's (P) trading and was, therefore, a simple debt owed by Schor (P). The judge in the CFTC (D) proceeding ruled in Conti's favor on all claims and counterclaims. Schor (P) then challenged the CFTC's (D) statutory authority to adjudicate Conti's counterclaim, contending that the CFTC (D) had no power to adjudicate the counterclaim made against Schor (P). The CFTC (D) judge rejected Schor's (P) challenge, and the CFTC (D) declined to review the ruling. Schor (P) then filed a petition for review with the court of appeals. The court dismissed Conti's counterclaims, basing its decision on the reasoning that Congress had no explicit intention of giving the CFTC (D) constitutionally questionable jurisdiction over state common law counterclaims. The CFTC (D) appealed.

ISSUE: Does the broad grant of power in 7 U.S.C. § 12a(5), the Commodity Exchange Act, clearly authorize promulgation of regulations providing for adjudication of common law counterclaims arising out of the same transaction as a reparations complaint?

HOLDING AND DECISION: (O'Connor, J.) Yes. The broad grant of power in 7 U.S.C. § 12a(5), the Commodity Exchange Act, clearly authorizes promulgation of regulations providing for adjudication of common law counterclaims arising out of the same transactions as a reparations complaint. Here, under the court of appeals approach, the entire dispute may not be resolved in the administrative forum. Consequently, the entire dispute will typically end up in court, for when the broker files suit to recover the debit balance, the customer will normally be compelled, either by compulsory counterclaim rules or by the expense or inconvenience of litigating the same issues in two forums, to forgo his reparations remedy and to litigate his claim in court. In sum, as Schor (P) himself aptly summarized, to require a bifurcated examination of the single dispute "would be to emasculate, if not destroy, the purpose of the Commodity Exchange Act to provide an efficient and relatively inexpensive forum for the resolution of disputes in futures trading." Thus, the CFTC's (D) long-held position that it has the power to take jurisdiction over counterclaims such as Conti's is eminently reasonable and well within the scope of its delegated authority. Reversed and remanded.

DISSENT: (Brennan, J.) By sanctioning the adjudication of state law counterclaims by a federal administrative agency, the Court far exceeds the analytic framework of its precedents. Perhaps the resolution of claims such as Schor's (P) may be accomplished more conveniently under the Court's decision than under an approach that does not abdicate responsibility to legislative convenience, but the framers of the U.S. Constitution foreswore this sort of convenience in order to preserve freedom. Our Constitution unambiguously enunciates a fundamental principle—that the judicial power of the United States be reposed in an independent judiciary.

▶ ANALYSIS

After the *Schor* decision, the black-letter law would appear to be that the validity of statutes giving legislative or

Continued on next page.

administrative tribunals the power to adjudicate cases arising under federal law will depend on a "balancing" of the concerns that moved Congress to choose such a tribunal against the values embodied in Article III of the U.S. Constitution. It is obvious that this test gives Congress much latitude. Thus, the choice of a legislative or administrative tribunal is valid if Congress has made a reasoned judgment that it is necessary and proper, in connection with a valid statutory enterprise, to delegate an adjudicative function to a special or temporary tribunal or agency that is constituted without regard to the restrictions and guarantees of Article III.

■══■

Quicknotes

ARTICLE III, U.S. CONSTITUTION   Limits federal judicial power to cases and controversies.

LEGISLATIVE RULE   The promulgation of a rule by an administrative agency, acting within the scope of its power pursuant to statute, enacting a law governing a particular activity.

■══■

Tafflin v. Levitt

Unpaid depositor (P) v. Savings and loan officer (D)

493 U.S. 455 (1990).

NATURE OF CASE: Review of federal court abstention.

FACT SUMMARY: A state court claimed the right to try RICO claims.

🏛 RULE OF LAW
State courts have concurrent jurisdiction over federal claims, unless a statute states otherwise, the legislative history indicates otherwise, or the interests of the state and federal government are incompatible.

FACTS: Racketeer Influenced and Corrupt Organizations Act (RICO) claims were brought in federal court by the holders of unpaid certificates of deposit against the officers and directors (D) of a state-chartered savings and loan that had failed. The officers (D) argued that the federal court should abstain from hearing the RICO claims because state courts had concurrent jurisdiction and the RICO claim had already been raised in state court. The federal court abstained from hearing the case. The court of appeals agreed.

ISSUE: Do state courts have concurrent jurisdiction over federal actions, unless a federal statute states otherwise, the legislative history indicates otherwise, or the interests of the state and federal government are incompatible?

HOLDING AND DECISION: (O'Connor, J.) Yes. State courts have concurrent jurisdiction over federal claims, unless a federal statute indicates otherwise, the legislative history indicates otherwise, or the interests of the state and federal government are incompatible. State courts possess concurrent jurisdiction over all claims, subject to limitation only by the Supremacy Clause. In *Gulf Offshore v. Mobil Oil Corp.*, 453 U.S. 473 (1981), this Court held that the desirability of uniform interpretation, the expertise of federal judges and the greater hospitality of federal courts to federal claims were the key factors in determining in compatibility. There does not appear to be any incompatibility between state court jurisdiction over RICO claims and federal interests. Affirmed.

CONCURRENCE: (Scalia, J.) The Supremacy Clause requires an affirmative act. Unmistakable implication in the legislative history alone is not sufficient to prevent state concurrent jurisdiction, implication in the text of the statute is required. Additionally, incompatible interests of the state and federal government may not always be sufficient to bar state concurrent jurisdiction.

▶ ANALYSIS

Many cases involve both state and federal claims. As noted previously, federal courts must be granted authority to hear a claim; thus, some cases are exclusive to state court jurisdiction by default. Additionally, although federal law may textually exclude state court jurisdiction, the more difficult cases involve determining whether exclusive federal jurisdiction is implied. Another complex jurisdictional issue arises when a plaintiff asserts a federal claim, and the defendant seeks to remove the claim to federal court.

■■■

Quicknotes

CONCURRENT JURISDICTION Authority by two or more different courts over the subject matter of a proceeding; the case may be heard and determined by either.

LEGISLATIVE HISTORY The process by which a bill is enacted into law, which reflects the legislature's intention enacting that law.

RICO Racketeer Influenced and Corrupt Organization laws; federal and state statutes enacted for the purpose of prosecuting organized crime.

■■■

Tennessee v. Davis

State (P) v. Federal revenue agent indicted for murder (D)

100 U.S. (10 Otto) 257 (1880).

NATURE OF CASE: Criminal prosecution for murder.

FACT SUMMARY: Davis (D), a federal revenue agent, was indicted for murder and scheduled for trial before a Tennessee (P) court. A federal law allowed prosecutions of revenue agents to be removed to federal court.

🏛 RULE OF LAW

Congress has the power to enact statutes directing that certain state criminal prosecutions be removed to federal court.

FACTS: Davis (D), a federal revenue agent, was charged with murder in Tennessee (P). Prior to his trial before a state court, Davis (D) petitioned for removal to federal court, citing a federal law authorizing removal of any civil suit or criminal prosecution commenced against a revenue agent for conduct that occurred while acting under color of his office. Davis (D) claimed that the incident resulting in his indictment had occurred when he defended himself against shots fired at him while he was fulfilling his duty to confiscate an illegal distillery. Tennessee (P) opposed the petition for removal, claiming that the Constitution did not authorize Congress to enact the removal statute.

ISSUE: Does Congress have the constitutional authority to pass a law allowing certain state suits to be removed to federal court?

HOLDING AND DECISION: (Strong, J.) Yes. Congress has the power to enact statutes directing that certain state criminal prosecutions be removed to federal court. The "necessary and proper" clause of the Constitution empowers Congress to pass laws facilitating the exercise of federal authority, including the judicial power. This latter power extends to all cases arising under the Constitution, the laws of the United States, and federal treaties. The right of Congress to authorize removal of state civil cases to federal court has long been recognized, and there is no reason why it should not have the same right with respect to criminal prosecutions. Removal statutes cannot be criticized as invasions of the sovereignty of the states, because the formation of the United States and the ratification of the Constitution contemplated a sacrifice of state autonomy. The statute enacted by Congress is not in conflict with the Constitution. Therefore, Davis's (D) petition for removal should be granted.

▌ ANALYSIS

At one time, it was recognized that Congress could authorize the removal of a state court action, but not prior to judgment. As *Tennessee v. Davis* illustrates, the right to authorize removal at even the earliest stages of litigation has long been acknowledged. Since 1815, federal officials have had a right to insist upon removal of state court actions that promise to be influenced by local bias. Today's removal statutes have been accorded a liberal construction by the courts, and Congress has provided for removal in numerous specific contexts.

■■■

Quicknotes

NECESSARY AND PROPER CLAUSE, ART I, § 8 OF THE CONSTITUTION Enables Congress to make all laws that may be "necessary and proper" to execute its other, enumerated powers.

REMOVAL Petition by a defendant to move the case to another court.

■■■

Tarble's Case

[Parties not identified.]

80 U.S. (13 Wall.) 397 (1872).

NATURE OF CASE: Petition for a writ of habeas corpus.

FACT SUMMARY: Tarble, a minor, enlisted in the Army of the United States (D) without his father's (P) consent. The father (P) then petitioned for a writ of habeas corpus to obtain the minor's release from the service.

🏛 RULE OF LAW
A state court has no jurisdiction to issue a writ of habeas corpus releasing a person held by the United States or one of its officers.

FACTS: Edward Tarble enlisted in the Army of the United States (D), although he was allegedly a minor and had failed to obtain his father's (P) consent to enlist. Asserting these facts, Tarble's father (P) petitioned the Dane County, Wisconsin, court for a writ of habeas corpus directing the federal government (D) to release his son. A commissioner of that court granted the writ, and the Supreme Court of Wisconsin ultimately affirmed the validity of its issuance. The federal government (D) then brought a writ of error, challenging the jurisdiction of the state court to issue the writ in question.

ISSUE: May a state court issue a writ of habeas corpus releasing a person from the custody of the U.S. government?

HOLDING AND DECISION: (Field, J.) No. A state court has no jurisdiction to issue a writ of habeas corpus releasing a person held by the United States or one of its officers. State and local government conflict in some spheres, but the Constitution provides that when jurisdictional confrontations occur, it is the federal government that reigns supreme. The harmonious interrelating of the two levels of government requires that the authority of one yield to the other, and it is the state that must give way. The federal government has plenary authority to maintain and regulate the military, and if state judicial officers had the power to secure the release of soldiers, the effectiveness of the army would be drastically undermined. To deprive states of the power to issue writs of habeas corpus against the United States in no way threatens civil liberties, because the federal government is as jealous a protector of individual rights as are the governments of the states. If, however, the relief sought in this case were permitted, the federal government (D) would face endless challenges to its authority, and would continually have to involve itself in protracted legal proceedings in order to preserve the effectiveness of the military. For these reasons, the Dane County court had no jurisdiction to issue the writ of habeas corpus releasing Tarble. Reversed.

DISSENT: (Chase, C.J.) The Constitution gives state courts the right to issue writs of habeas corpus against the U.S. government, although their decisions to do so are, of course, ultimately reviewable by the Supreme Court. If state courts are denied the power to issue such writs, many injustices and errors in judgment will go unrectified.

▶ ANALYSIS

Prior to *Tarble*'s *case*, state courts had frequently asserted a right to issue writs of habeas corpus to release individuals from the custody of the United States. Some state courts appear to have continued the practice even after the *Tarble* decision. The reasoning of *Tarble*'s *case* has been expanded to apply to other writs as well. For example, in *McClung v. Siliman*, 6 Wheat. 598 (U.S. 1821) it was held that a writ of mandamus could not issue from a state court to compel action on the part of a register of the U.S. land office. The *McClung* decision was premised on the fact that the United States had not even given federal courts the power to issue writs of mandamus against an executive official, but the case has traditionally been interpreted as barring state mandamus under any circumstances.

■■■

Quicknotes

WRIT OF HABEAS CORPUS A proceeding in which a defendant brings a writ to compel a judicial determination of whether he is lawfully being held in custody.

■■■

Testa v. Katt

Buyer (P) v. Seller (D)

330 U.S. 386 (1947).

NATURE OF CASE: Appeal from reversal of an award of damages under the Emergency Price Control Act.

FACT SUMMARY: Testa (P) sought treble damages in Rhode Island State Court for Katt's (D) violation of the Federal Emergency Price Control Act for selling him an auto for more than the ceiling price.

RULE OF LAW
A state court cannot refuse to enforce a right arising from federal law for reasons of conflict with state policy or "want of wisdom" on the part of Congress.

FACTS: Under the Emergency Price Control Act, anyone who sold goods for more than the price ceiling on those goods was liable to the buyer for treble the overcharge plus attorney's fees. The federal act created a right of action not only in federal court, but in state court as well. Testa (P) purchased a car in 1944 from Katt (D), a dealer, for $1,100, $210 above the ceiling price. Testa (P) brought suit under the act in Providence, Rhode Island, in the state district court. He was awarded the full amount of damages possible under the act. On appeal to the state superior court, damages were reduced to the amount of overcharge plus fees. The state supreme court reversed on grounds that the federal statute was penal, and that it need not enforce penal laws of a government foreign in the international sense. It held that as the United States was foreign in the "private international" sense, it need not enforce the federal act. Testa (P) appealed.

ISSUE: Can a state court refuse to enforce a right arising from federal law for reasons of conflict with state policy or "want of wisdom" on the part of Congress?

HOLDING AND DECISION: (Black, J.) No. A state court cannot refuse to enforce a right arising from federal law for reasons of conflict with state policy or "want of wisdom" on the part of Congress. The Supremacy Clause of the Constitution provides that the Constitution, federal laws, and treaties are the supreme law of the land, that the judges in every state are bound by that supreme law—any state law, constitution, or policy to the contrary notwithstanding: "The obligation of states to enforce federal laws is not lessened by reason of the form in which they are cast or the remedy which they provide." For a state to say that federal policy being in conflict with its own proscribes enforcement of a federal act is to ignore the policy espoused by Congress for all the people and all the states. Rhode Island's failure to enforce the federal act violated the supremacy clause and necessitates reversal. Reversed and remanded.

ANALYSIS

A state court must entertain a cause of action created under federal law providing jurisdiction in state courts. States may not discriminate against rights that arise under federal laws. Despite the rule of this case, the question left unanswered is: Where did Congress obtain the power to require state courts to exercise jurisdiction? Some suggest the Necessary and Proper Clause as the source for such power while others have inferred it to come from Congress's power to establish inferior courts.

Quicknotes

JURISDICTION The authority of a court to hear and declare judgment in respect to a particular matter.

TREBLE DAMAGES An award of damages triple the amount awarded by the jury, provided for by statute for violation of certain offenses.

Dice v. Akron, Canton & Youngstown R.R.

Railroad fireman (P) v. Railroad (D)

342 U.S. 359 (1952).

NATURE OF CASE: Negligence action under the Federal Employers' Liability Act.

FACT SUMMARY: Dice (P), a railroad fireman, was injured in an accident involving a train of the Railroad (D).

RULE OF LAW
Though federal claims may be adjudicated by state courts, state laws are never controlling on the question of what the incidents of any federal right may be.

FACTS: Dice (P), a railroad fireman, was injured when an engine of the Railroad (D) jumped the track. He sued in an Ohio state court under the Federal Employers' Liability Act, charging negligence. At trial, the Railroad (D) offered in defense a document signed by Dice (P) that purported to release the Railroad (D) of all liability over and above $924.63, which Dice (P) had already received. Dice (P) contended that he had not read the statement before signing it, relying on fraudulent representations of the Railroad (D) that the document was merely a receipt for the $924.63. The jury found for Dice (P), but the trial court entered "judgment notwithstanding the verdict" for the Railroad (D) on the grounds that under Ohio state law Dice (P) could not escape responsibility for signing the release. Under Ohio law, he was under a duty to read the document before signing it. The Ohio Court of Appeals reversed the trial judge on the grounds that federal law (that a finding of fraud will preclude the use of a release such as the one in this case) should have been applied. The Ohio Supreme Court reversed again and this appeal followed.

ISSUE: In adjudicating a claim arising out of federal law, may a state court properly apply state law?

HOLDING AND DECISION: (Black, J.) No. Though federal claims may be adjudicated by state courts, state laws are never controlling on the question of what the incidents of any federal right may be. Federal rights according relief to injured railroad employees could be defeated if states were permitted to have the final say as to what defenses could and could not be interposed here. It is true that Ohio normally allows the judge in an action to resolve all issues of fraud in a negligence action, and that, in itself, is a perfectly acceptable procedure. But it is well settled that the federal right to a jury trial is an essential one, which Ohio may not infringe upon. Judgment of the Ohio Court of Appeals is reversed and remanded.

DISSENT: (Frankfurter, J.) Requiring federal standards for the determination of fraud does not unconstitutionally invade the states' reserved power to maintain the common-law division between law (i.e., negligence determined by a jury) and equity (i.e., fraud relieved by a judge).

ANALYSIS

This case points up the general rule for the treatment of federal rights in state courts. In short, they are always governed by federal law. The Seventh Amendment right to a civil jury trial is an exclusively federal right. It is not a fundamental right incorporated in the Fourteenth Amendment and extended to the states. As such, states may properly provide that certain issues are to be determined by judges. When a federal right is involved, however, such discretion ceases. The federal standard of the Seventh Amendment must prevail.

Quicknotes

FEDERAL EMPLOYERS' LIABILITY ACT Permits federal employees to file suit for injuries sustained as a result of their employer's negligent conduct.

JUDGMENT NOTWITHSTANDING THE VERDICT A judgment entered by the trial judge reversing a jury verdict if the jury's determination has no basis in law or fact.

CHAPTER 5

Review of State Court Decisions by the Supreme Court

Quick Reference Rules of Law

Martin v. Hunter's Lessee

Purported owner of land (D) v. Purported owner of land (P)

14 U.S. (1 Wheat.) 304 (1816).

NATURE OF CASE: Appeal from an action of ejectment.

FACT SUMMARY: Hunter (P), alleging ownership of the disputed property from the State of Virginia pursuant to legislation forfeiting the property of British subjects, instituted an action of ejectment against Martin (D), a British subject and devisee of the original owner, after the Supreme Court reversed a Virginia Court of Appeals ruling that had held that Martin (D) had lost title to land to the state.

RULE OF LAW
Federal courts may hear appeals from state court decisions.

FACTS: This was an action of ejectment instituted by Hunter (P) in the Superior Court of Virginia against Martin (D), a British subject who inherited land from Lord Fairfax. Hunter (P) claimed under a grant from the State of Virginia made in 1789 pursuant to state legislation forfeiting property belonging to British subjects. Originally, Martin (D) was granted a writ of ejectment against Hunter's (P) lessee by a Virginia district court on the basis of the Treaty of Peace with Great Britain of 1783 providing that no further confiscations would be made. The Virginia Court of Appeals reversed on the ground that a 1796 act between Virginia and those claiming under grant by Lord Fairfax relinquished their claims to his estate and that the state's title was perfected before the Treaties of Peace. The Supreme Court reversed holding that the Jay Treaty of 1794 established that British subjects who then held lands in the United States would continue to hold them. The Virginia court on remand held that the Supreme Court's appellate jurisdiction did not extend to state court decisions and that if the Judiciary Act purported to so extend the Court's appellate jurisdiction it was unconstitutional. Martin (D) appealed to the Supreme Court.

ISSUE: May federal courts hear appeals from state court decisions?

HOLDING AND DECISION: (Story, J.) Yes. Federal courts may hear appeals from state court decisions. The appellate power of the Supreme Court is not limited by the terms of the Third Article of the Constitution. The language of Article III extends judicial power to cases and not to courts. It is plain that the Framers of the Constitution did contemplate that cases within the judicial cognizance of the United States not only might, but would, arise in the state courts, in the exercise of their original jurisdiction. This view can be seen by the wording of the Supremacy Clause which makes the Constitution, treaties, and laws of the United States applicable to every state. A motive of another kind, perfectly compatible with the most sincere respect for state tribunals, might induce the grant of appellate power over their decisions. That motive is the importance, and even necessity, of uniformity of decisions throughout the United States upon all subjects within the purview of the Constitution. Therefore, the court concludes that the appellate power of the United States does extend to cases pending in state courts; and that the 25th Section of the Judiciary Act, which authorizes the exercise of this jurisdiction in the specified cases, by a writ of error, is supported by the letter and spirit of the Constitution. Reversed.

DISSENT: (Johnson, J.) In this act there is nothing that amounts to an assertion of the inferiority or dependence of the state tribunals. The presiding judge of the state court is himself authorized to issue the writ of error, if he will, and thus give jurisdiction to the Supreme Court; and if he thinks proper to decline it, no compulsory process is provided by law to oblige him. The aggrieved party can then apply to a judge of the United States for writ compelling the opposite party to appear before this Court. Therefore, appellate jurisdiction of the Supreme Court applies to cases and persons, not to state courts.

ANALYSIS

The Constitution was ordained and established, not by the states in their sovereign capacities, but by the people of the United States. Therefore, the Constitution was not necessarily carved out of existing state sovereignties, nor out of a surrender of powers already existing in state institutions, for the powers of the states depend on their own constitutions. On the other hand, the sovereign powers vested in the state governments remain unaltered only so far as they are not granted to the government of the United States. These deductions are recognized by the Constitution that declares that the powers not delegated to the United States by the Constitution, nor prohibited by it to the states, are reserved to the states. Such was the reasoning brought out in the instant case.

Quicknotes

EJECTMENT An action to oust someone in unlawful possession of real property and to restore possession to the party lawfully entitled to it.

JURISDICTION The authority of a court to hear and declare judgment in respect to a particular matter.

Murdock v. City of Memphis

Grantors' descendant (P) v. Municipality (D)

87 U.S. (20 Wall.) 590 (1875).

NATURE OF CASE: Appeal from an action for breach of a deed of trust.

FACT SUMMARY: Murdock (P) sued the city of Memphis (D) in a state court of Tennessee, alleging that under an 1844 deed, the ancestors of Murdock (P) had deeded land to the city to be held in trust for the purpose of establishing a naval depot and that since no such use was made of the land it should revert back to Murdock (P).

🏛 RULE OF LAW
The Supreme Court will not review a suit resting on an adequate and independent state ground that supports a state court decision, even when the case contains a federal question.

FACTS: In July 1844, the ancestors of Murdock (P), by ordinary deed of bargain and sale, conveyed to the city of Memphis (D) land for the location of a congressionally authorized naval depot. By the same deed both the ancestors of Murdock (P) and the City (D) conveyed the land to one Wheatley, in trust for the grantor's heirs in case the land was not appropriated by the United States for the purpose of building thereon a naval depot. The United States paid $20,000 to the city of Memphis (D) for the land and the City (D) conveyed the land. Although the United States took possession of the land and erected several structures, it never actually built a naval depot. Ten years later, it transferred the land back to the City (D). Murdock (P) brought suit against the City (D) alleging that by the failure of the United States to appropriate the land for a naval depot the land came within the clause of the 1844 deed, conveying it to Wheatley in trust for the grantor's heirs, that is, Murdock (P). Murdock (P) also argued that the land was held in trust by the City (D). The City (D) contended that since the United States had actually appropriated the land as a naval depot within the meaning of the 1844 deed, the land did not revert back to Murdock (P). The lower state court held for the City (D) and the Supreme Court of Tennessee affirmed. Murdock (P) appealed to the United States Supreme Court.

ISSUE: May the Supreme Court review a suit resting on an adequate and independent state ground that supports a state court decision even if a federal question is involved?

HOLDING AND DECISION: (Miller, J.) No. Section 25 of the Judiciary Act of 1789 amended in 1867 lays down two fundamental propositions. One is that the Supreme Court does not have jurisdiction to review state court decisions that rest on an adequate and independent state ground, even when a federal issue is involved. The other is that the Supreme Court will accept as binding upon itself the state court's decisions as to matters of state law. However, this does not preclude the federal courts from considering state and federal questions together if a case is originally brought first in a federal court. Even if there is error in the state court's decision it does not rate review if the state case can still stand on adequate state grounds. In the case at bar the federal question involved was the Act of 1854 whereby Congress conveyed the land in question back to the city of Memphis. This Act did not recognize any trust but rather cedes the property to the mayor and aldermen for use of the city. This court is, therefore, of the opinion that this, the only federal question in the case, was rightly decided by the Supreme Court of Tennessee and that no further review of the case is necessary. Affirmed.

DISSENT: (Clifford, J.) This court has jurisdiction to determine the whole case, including questions of state law, where it appears that the record presents a federal question erroneously decided against the plaintiff in error.

DISSENT: (Bradley, J.) This court had no jurisdiction to hear the case at all since there was no federal question involved. But if the court had jurisdiction it was jurisdiction to consider the whole case and not merely one issue in it.

▶ ANALYSIS

The Supreme Court can review a state court decision if that case is decided entirely in light of a federal question. This is true even if there existed an adequate state ground upon which the state court could have relied. In cases of this sort, where the state court erroneously decides the federal question, the Supreme Court will remand the case to the state court for resolution of the state issues. Carried even further, it has been held that if a state statute incorporates by reference federal law, the Supreme Court has jurisdiction to review a state decision involving the statute but only as to the federal question, after which the case will be remanded to the state court.

■=■

Quicknotes

JURISDICTION The authority of a court to hear and declare judgment in respect to a particular matter.

■=■

Fox Film Corp. v. Muller

Contracting party (P) v. Contracting party (D)

296 U.S. 207 (1935).

NATURE OF CASE: Suit seeking damages for breach of contract.

FACT SUMMARY: Fox Film Corp. (P) sued Muller (D) in state court, alleging breach of contract. In another action, a federal court had already ruled that the contracts sued on were invalid.

🏛 RULE OF LAW
A state court decision that arguably involved a federal question may not be reviewed by the Supreme Court if the decision also rested upon an independent, nonfederal basis that was adequate to support the state court's judgment.

FACTS: Fox Film Corp. (Fox) (P) sued for damages in state court, alleging that Muller (D) had breached two contracts pertaining to the exhibiting of films belonging to Fox (P). The contracts sued on were virtually identical to agreements that a federal court, in another action involving Fox (P), had ruled were violative of the Sherman Antitrust Act. The objectionable portion of the contracts consisted of an arbitration clause that the federal court had concluded was so integrally related to the remainder of each agreement as to render the instruments completely invalid. The trial court dismissed the suit against Muller (D), and the Supreme Court of Minnesota eventually entered a final judgment affirming the dismissal. Fox (P) petitioned for certiorari, and alleged that the case at least partially involved issues of state law.

ISSUE: Does the Supreme Court have appellate jurisdiction over a state court decision that was based partially on nonfederal grounds that were adequate to support the state court's judgment?

HOLDING AND DECISION: (Sutherland, J.) No. A state court decision that arguably involved a federal question may not be reviewed by the Supreme Court if the decision also rested upon an independent, nonfederal basis that was adequate to support the judgment of the state court. In this case, even if a federal question was also involved, the state court's conclusion that the contract provisions were nonseverable was alone dispositive of the case, and that determination required no resolution of federal issues. Fox (P) argued that the Supreme Court may exercise jurisdiction where state and federal questions are inextricably interwoven, but in this case the issues were clearly independent, and resolution of the nonfederal question was determinative of the entire case. Therefore, the Supreme Court has no jurisdiction over the Fox (P) appeal. Writ dismissed.

▶ ANALYSIS

The various courts that comprise the federal system are alike in their reluctance to intrude upon the functions of the state courts. The Framers of the Constitution contemplated a separate system of federal courts, complementary to, but separate from, the state tribunals which were to follow. Even the federal legislative scheme is designed to serve only as an adjunct to state law. Hence, Congress has left it to the individual states to formulate statutes of broad scope, with federal statutory enactments primarily filling in whatever gaps remain after the various state legislatures have acted. This approach reflects the attitude that a decentralized scheme of lawmaking permits greater attention to be paid to the differences among states and among regions.

━━■

Quicknotes

JURISDICTION The authority of a court to hear and declare judgment in respect to a particular matter.

SHERMAN ANTITRUST ACT Prohibits unreasonable restraint of trade.

SUBSTANTIVE LAW Law that pertains to the rights and interests of the parties and upon which a cause of action may be based.

━━■

Michigan v. Long

State (P) v. Convicted marijuana possessor (D)

463 U.S. 1032 (1983).

NATURE OF CASE: Review of a decision reversing a criminal conviction.

FACT SUMMARY: Long (D) asserted that the United States Supreme Court was without jurisdiction to review the Michigan Supreme Court's decision reversing his criminal conviction, his claim being that the decision below rested on an adequate and independent state ground.

🏛 RULE OF LAW
When a state court decision fairly appears to rest primarily on federal law, or to be interwoven with federal law, and when the adequacy and independence of any possible state law ground is not clear from the face of the opinion, the United States Supreme Court will accept as the most reasonable explanation that the state court decided the case the way it did because it believed that federal law required it to do so, but if the state court decision indicates clearly and expressly that it is alternatively based on bona fide separate, adequate, and independent state grounds, the Court will not review the decision.

FACTS: Long (D) was convicted for possession of marijuana, but the Michigan Supreme Court reversed his conviction in an opinion that stated the search of Long's (D) vehicle was proscribed by the United States and Michigan constitutions. Michigan (P) sought review by the United States Supreme Court, but Long (D) insisted it had no jurisdiction to decide the case because the decision below rested on an adequate and independent state ground.

ISSUE: When a state court decision fairly appears to rest primarily on federal law, or to be interwoven with federal law, and when the adequacy and independence of any possible state law ground is not clear from the face of the opinion, will the United States Supreme Court accept as the most reasonable explanation that the state court decided the case the way it did because it believed that federal law required it to do so, but if the state court decision indicates clearly and expressly that it is alternatively based on bona fide separate, adequate, and independent state grounds, will the Court not review the decision?

HOLDING AND DECISION: (O'Connor, J.) Yes. When a state court decision fairly appears to rest primarily on federal law, or to be interwoven with federal law, and when the adequacy and independence of any possible state law ground is not clear from the face of the opinion, the United States Supreme Court will accept as the most reasonable explanation that the state court decided the case the way it did because it believed that federal law required

it to do so, but if the state court decision indicates clearly and expressly that it is alternatively based on bona fide separate, adequate, and independent state grounds, the Court will not review the decision. In this case, apart from two citations to the State Constitution, the court below relied exclusively on its understanding of federal law. Because of respect for the independence of state courts and the need to avoid rendering advisory opinions, this Court, in determining whether state court references to state law constitute adequate and independent state grounds, will no longer look beyond the opinion under review, or require state courts to reconsider cases to clarify the grounds of their decisions. Taking this approach here, the Court does not lack jurisdiction to decide the case. Reversed and remanded.

CONCURRENCE IN PART: (Blackmun, J.) The majority errs in the part of its opinion that fashions a new presumption of jurisdiction over cases coming here from state courts since there is little efficiency and an increased danger of advisory opinions in this new approach.

DISSENT: (Stevens, J.) There are four ways to resolve the question of whether the state law ground, which is clearly adequate to support the judgment, is independent of the Michigan Supreme Court's understanding of federal law. First, the Court could ask the Michigan Supreme Court directly. Second, the Court could attempt to infer from all possible sources of state law what the Michigan Supreme Court meant. Third, the Court could presume that adequate state grounds are independent unless it clearly appears otherwise. Fourth, the Court could presume that adequate state grounds are not independent unless it clearly appears otherwise. While this Court has, on different occasions, employed each of the first three approaches, never until today has it even hinted at the fourth. While the majority's rejection of the first approach as inefficient and unduly burdensome for state courts is defensible, and the second approach is an inappropriate expenditure of the Court's resources, the majority is wrong to choose the fourth approach over the third. When left with a choice between two presumptions, one in favor of jurisdictions and one against it, the latter presumption has always prevailed historically. In reviewing decisions of state courts, the primary role of this Court is to make sure that persons who seek to vindicate federal rights have been fairly heard. Until recently, the Court has had virtually no interest in cases of this type, but priorities have shifted during the past decade and the result has been a docket swollen with requests by states to reverse judgments that their courts have rendered in favor of their citizens.

Continued on next page.

ANALYSIS

There were instances in the past in which a case was remanded to the state's highest court for purposes of clarifying whether its decision had been based on an independent state ground. However, in addition to the inefficiency of this method and the burden it places on state courts, another problem with this approach was illustrated in *Duxon v. Duffy*, 344 U.S. 143 (1952). In that instance, the United States Supreme Court continued the case twice for the purpose of obtaining just such a clarification from the California Supreme Court. No such clarification was ever made. The California Supreme Court informally advised the petitioner's counsel that "it doubted its jurisdiction to render such a determination." As a result the United States Supreme Court had to go back and vacate the judgment of the California Supreme Court and remand the case.

Quicknotes

FEDERAL COURT JURISDICTION The authority of the federal courts to hear and determine in the first instance matters pertaining to the federal Constitution, federal law, or treaties of the United States.

JURISDICTION The authority of a court to hear and declare judgment in respect to a particular matter.

SUBSTANTIVE LAW Law that pertains to the rights and interests of the parties and upon which a cause of action may be based.

Indiana ex rel. Anderson v. Brand

Teacher (P) v. School official (D)

303 U.S. 95 (1938).

NATURE OF CASE: Petition for a writ of mandate.

FACT SUMMARY: Anderson (P), a public school teacher, enjoyed tenure under Indiana law. However, the statute that conferred tenure was later made inapplicable to Anderson (P), and Brand (D) sought her dismissal.

🏛 RULE OF LAW
A federal court may prevent a state from acting pursuant to a statute that impairs the contractual rights of its citizens.

FACTS: Anderson (P) commenced employment as a public school teacher in Indiana in 1924. Three years later, Indiana enacted the Teachers' Tenure Law, and the employment contracts signed by Anderson (P) for 1931 through 1933 specifically stated that they were subject to the provisions of the act. In 1933, however, the act as applied to teachers in township schools was repealed. Brand (D) then notified Anderson (P) of his intent to terminate her employment, and conducted a hearing at which his grounds for that decision were considered. The cancellation of Anderson's (P) contract was approved by the county commissioner and, although she was permitted to teach during the 1933-34 school year, Anderson (P) was threatened with termination at the conclusion of that period. Anderson (P) then petitioned for a writ of mandate to compel Brand (D) to continue her in her employment. Brand (D) demurred, arguing that he and the county commissioner had already decided the matter. The demurrer also cited the repeal of the tenure legislation as it related to township schools. The state court sustained Brand's (D) demurrer and the Supreme Court of Indiana affirmed. On certiorari to the United States Supreme Court, Anderson (P) argued that repeal of the Teachers' Tenure Law impaired an existing contract right in violation of the Constitution.

ISSUE: May a federal court prevent a state from acting pursuant to a statute that impairs the contractual rights of its citizens?

HOLDING AND DECISION: (Roberts, J.) Yes. A federal court may prevent a state from acting pursuant to a statute that impairs the contractual rights of its citizens. A legislative enactment, when acted upon by individuals, may give rise to a contract between those persons and the state or one of its subdivisions. The 1927 Teachers' Tenure Law repeatedly uses the word "contract" in describing the arrangement that exists between teachers and the municipalities that employ them. Thus, Anderson (P) enjoyed a contractual right to continue teaching until she engaged in some type of conduct that constituted a ground for removal of a tenured teacher. The 1927 law had conferred this contractual right upon Anderson (P), and the state legislature was not entitled to impair that right by enacting the subsequent law repealing provisions of the 1927 legislation. Therefore, the judgment below must be reversed and the case remanded for consideration of only that portion of Brand's (D) demurrer that presents no issues of federal law.

DISSENT: (Black, J.) The right of tenured teachers to serve until removed for cause was conferred by statute rather than by contract. The Indiana legislature has the right to pass laws relating to education, and has the continuing right to modify those laws according to the dictates of changing circumstances. That right to amend or repeal existing statutes was not, and could not be, surrendered by the legislature through the creation of the vested and in-alienable contractual right.

▶ ANALYSIS

In preventing abrogation of the contract clause of the federal Constitution, the Supreme Court is usually protecting against the impairment of a right created by the laws of a state. In recognition of this fact, the court generally accords considerable deference to the state court's resolution of the issue of whether or not a contractual right existed and was later impaired. Some cases, in fact, favor the view that even if contractual rights are held to have been impaired, the Supreme Court has an obligation to seek an alternative ground for the state court's decision that would not rest on a statute that runs afoul of the contract clause.

■=■

Quicknotes

DEMURRER The assertion that the opposing party's pleadings are insufficient and that the demurring party should not be made to answer.

IMPAIRMENT The weakening or diminishing in power of a right.

WRIT OF MANDATE The written order of a court directing a particular action.

■=■

Cardinale v. Louisiana

Convicted murderer (D) v. State (P)

394 U.S. 437 (1969).

NATURE OF CASE: Appeal of conviction for murder.

FACT SUMMARY: Cardinale (D) failed to raise and preserve a federal question in the trial court record.

🏛 RULE OF LAW
Federal constitutional issues must be raised and decided in the state court before the federal courts may rule on the issue.

FACTS: Cardinale (D) confessed to a brutal murder, and the entire confession was used to convict him. A Louisiana statute required that confessions be heard in their entirety. No federal question was raised at trial. The Louisiana Supreme Court affirmed the conviction. Cardinale (D) sought federal review of the murder conviction arguing that parts of the confession were prejudicial and irrelevant to his murder conviction.

ISSUE: Must federal constitutional issues be raised and decided in state courts before the federal courts may rule?

HOLDING AND DECISION: (White, J.) Yes. Constitutional issues must be raised and decided in state courts before the federal courts may rule. This policy, established in 1936, gives the state an opportunity to review its own statute and interpret its meaning in light of a constitutional challenge. Also, questions not raised below are likely to have an inadequate record. Cardinale (P) failed to raise constitutional questions about the admissibility of his confession at the state court level. Therefore, federal courts may not decide the issue. Writ dismissed.

CONCURRENCE: (Black, J.) The writ was correctly dismissed because it had been improvidently granted.

▶ ANALYSIS

The question of whether a constitutional issue was presented to the state court is itself a constitutional question that the Supreme Court may review. The Court distinguishes cases in which a new claim is made for the first time upon review and cases in which a new argument is being made. Once a federal claim is made in state court, the party may raise any argument in support of that claim to the Supreme Court.

■■■

Quicknotes

CLAIM The demand for a right to payment or equitable relief; the fact or facts giving rise to such demand.

■■■

Staub v. City of Baxley

Convicted solicitor (D) v. Municipality (P)

355 U.S. 313 (1958).

NATURE OF CASE: Appeal from state court conviction for solicitation.

FACT SUMMARY: Staub (D) was convicted of solicitation in violation of a city ordinance which required her to first obtain a permit.

🏛 RULE OF LAW
A state court decision based upon a state procedural rule that lacks fair and substantial support does not constitute adequate state grounds to bar Supreme Court review.

FACTS: Staub (D), an employee of the International Ladies' Garment Workers Union, sought to unionize employees who resided in the City of Baxley (P). Staub (D), without a permit, went to the home of one of the employees and discussed the benefits of unionization, distributed literature, and collected membership cards. Staub (D) was arrested for solicitation for violating a city ordinance that required the purchase of a permit before a person could solicit membership for any organization that required membership fees. Staub (D) attacked the validity of the ordinance on First and Fourteenth Amendment grounds in the Baxley Mayor's Court. Staub (D) was convicted of solicitation and sentenced to imprisonment for thirty days or fined $300. Staub (D) appealed her conviction in superior court, raising both constitutional defenses, but the conviction was affirmed. Next, Staub (D) appealed to the appellate court, which refused to consider the constitutional defenses because Staub (D) failed to attack specific sections of the ordinance on constitutional grounds; instead, Staub (D) attacked the entire ordinance. The Georgia Supreme Court declined review. Staub (D) appealed.

ISSUE: Does a state court decision based upon a state procedural rule that lacks fair and substantial support constitute adequate state grounds to bar Supreme Court review?

HOLDING AND DECISION: (Whittaker, J.) No. A state court decision based upon a state procedural rule that lacks fair and substantial support does not constitute adequate state grounds to bar Supreme Court review. Although the Supreme Court may not review a state case based upon an "adequate nonfederal ground," a decision based upon a state procedural rule that lacks fair and substantial support is not an adequate nonfederal ground and is reviewable. In the present case, the rule forcing states to count off the particular provisions of the ordinance is an arid ritual of meaningless form. Thus, it is not an adequate state ground to justify her conviction. Reversed.

DISSENT: (Frankfurter, J.) As long as state rules do not discriminate against raising federal claims, they should not be disturbed.

▶ ANALYSIS

As *Staub* indicates, in order to bar Supreme Court review, the state court's basis for decision must be adequate. Thus, adequacy of the state court's grounds for decision becomes a federal question. The Supreme Court must determine whether the state decision is based upon fair and substantial support according to the facts.

Quicknotes

FEDERAL COURT JURISDICTION The authority of the federal courts to hear and determine in the first instance matters pertaining to the federal Constitution, federal law, or treaties of the United States.

FIRST AMENDMENT RIGHTS Rights conferred by the First Amendment to the United States Constitution prohibiting Congress from enacting any law respecting an establishment of religion, prohibiting the free exercise of religion, abridging freedom of speech or the press, the right of peaceful assembly and the right to petition for a redress of grievances.

FOURTEENTH AMENDMENT Declares that no state shall make or enforce any law that shall abridge the privileges and immunities of citizens of the United States. No state shall deny to any person within its jurisdiction the equal protection of the laws.

Cox Broadcasting Corp. v. Cohn

Public broadcasting company (D) v. Parent of rape victim (P)

420 U.S. 469 (1975).

NATURE OF CASE: Appeal from an action for damages for invasion of privacy.

FACT SUMMARY: Cohn (P) sued Cox Broadcasting Corp. (Cox) (D) for damages for invasion of privacy under a Georgia statute that made it a misdemeanor to publish or broadcast the name or identity of a rape victim when Cox (D) reported on criminal court proceedings concerning the rape and death of Cohn's (P) daughter.

🏛 **RULE OF LAW**
The Constitution bars a civil action against the press for publishing true information disclosed in public court documents open to public inspection.

FACTS: Cox (D), reporting on the court proceedings in a prosecution for rape, gave the name of the rape victim that it had learned from public records. Cohn (P), the rape victim's father, sued Cox (D) for damages for invasion of privacy under a Georgia statute that made it a misdemeanor to publish or broadcast the name or identity of a rape victim. Cox (D) claimed that its use of the name was privileged under the First and Fourteenth Amendments. The trial court gave summary judgment for Cohn (P). Cox (D) appealed and the Georgia Supreme Court held that the Georgia statute was inapplicable since it created no civil cause of action. Consequently, continued the court, it need not consider the issue of the constitutionality of the statute. Instead, it reversed the summary judgment holding that Cohn (P) has a common law tort claim for invasion of privacy and that the trier of fact must determine whether the public disclosure of the daughter's name actually invaded the father's zone of privacy. On rehearing, the Georgia trial court relied on the misdemeanor statute as an authoritative declaration of state policy and held that the name of a rape victim is not a matter of public concern. It then held the Georgia statute was a legitimate limitation on the right of freedom of expression contained in the First Amendment. Cox (D) appealed to the United States Supreme Court, invoking jurisdiction under 28 U.S.C. § 1257 that states that the court's appellate jurisdiction with respect to state litigation can be granted only after the highest state court in which judgment could be had has rendered a final judgment or decree. The Supreme Court reversed the state court decision and held for Cox (D).

ISSUE: Does the Constitution bar a civil action against the press for publishing true information disclosed in public documents open to public inspection?

HOLDING AND DECISION: (White, J.) Yes. The Constitution bars a civil action against the press for publishing true information disclosed in public court documents open to public inspection. Although the ultimate issue was one of the constitutionality of civil actions against the press, initially this Court must resolve two questions of jurisdiction arising under 28 U.S.C. § 1257. First, was the constitutional validity of the Georgia statute drawn into issue and upheld by the Georgia Supreme Court? Second, was the decision from which this appeal has been taken a final judgment or a decree? Historically, this Court has appellate jurisdiction with respect to state litigation only after the highest state court in which judgment could be had has rendered a final judgment or decree. However, there are cases in which the highest state court has finally determined the federal issue present, but in which there are further proceedings in lower state courts. In these cases the Supreme Court has taken jurisdiction and such is the case at bar. Consequently, we conclude that this Court has jurisdiction to review the judgment of the Georgia Supreme Court rejecting the challenge under the First and Fourteenth Amendments to the state law authorizing damage suits against the press for publishing the name of a rape victim whose identity is revealed in the course of a public prosecution. The Georgia Supreme Court's judgment is plainly final on the federal issue and is not subject to further review in the state courts. Although the trial court's decision as to which party might prevail is still unsettled, if the Georgia Supreme Court erroneously upheld the statute, there should be no trial at all. Moreover, delaying the final decision of the First Amendment claim until after trial will leave unanswered an important question of freedom of the press that could only further harm the operation of a free press. Given these factors, that the litigation could be terminated by a decision on the merits now and that a failure to decide the issue will leave the operation of the press in Georgia hampered by civil and criminal sanctions, this Court finds it necessary to reach the merits. On the merits this Court holds that the Constitution bars a civil action against the press for publishing true information disclosed in public court documents open to public inspection. Reversed.

DISSENT: (Rehnquist, J.) The decision that is the subject of this appeal is not a final judgment as that term is used in 28 U.S.C. § 1257. The appeal should be dismissed for want of jurisdiction. The finality requirement should not be disturbed, except in very few situations, where intermediate rulings may carry serious public consequences. The Court here, far from eschewing a constitutional holding in advance of the necessity for one, construes § 1257 so that it may

Continued on next page.

virtually rush out and meet the prospective constitutional litigant as he approaches our doors.

▶ *ANALYSIS*

As the Supreme Court enunciated in the case at bar there are times when it is not feasible to wait for a final decision. For example, there are cases in which an important right may be destroyed if a party is not able to secure immediate review. In other cases, the issue that needs review is capable of being separated from the rest of the case and prompt review will prevent the entire trial court proceeding from being held in abeyance. For these reasons, as well as others, the decisions of the Supreme Court concerning the finality of the issue are not altogether harmonious. Indeed, the Court has stated that there is not even a sure test as to what constitutes a final decision that can be applied universally to all cases.

■━■

Quicknotes

APPELLATE JURISDICTION The power of a higher court to review the decisions of lower courts.

FIRST AMENDMENT RIGHTS Rights conferred by the First Amendment to the United States Constitution prohibiting Congress from enacting any law respecting an establishment of religion, prohibiting the free exercise of religion, abridging freedom of speech or the press, the right of peaceful assembly and the right to petition for a redress of grievances.

FOURTEENTH AMENDMENT Declares that no state shall make or enforce any law that shall abridge the privileges and immunities of citizens of the United States. No state shall deny to any person within its jurisdiction the equal protection of the laws.

■━■

CHAPTER 6

The Law Applied in Civil Actions in the District Courts

Quick Reference Rules of Law

Sibbach v. Wilson & Co., Inc.

Alleged tort victim (P) v. Alleged tortfeasor (D)

312 U.S. 1 (1940).

NATURE OF CASE: Appeal from an action to recover damages for personal injuries.

FACT SUMMARY: When Sibbach (P) refused to submit to a district court order requiring a physical examination pursuant to Fed. R. Civ. P. 35, the court adjudged Sibbach (P) guilty of contempt.

🏛 RULE OF LAW
Although, under Federal Rules of Civil Procedure, a federal court has the right to compel a party to submit to a physical examination, it does not have the authority to punish noncompliance with a contempt citation.

FACTS: Sibbach (P) brought an action against Wilson & Co. (D) in the federal district court of Illinois to recover damages for bodily injuries inflicted in Indiana. Wilson (D) denied the allegations of the complaint, and moved for an order requiring Sibbach (P) to submit to a physical examination pursuant to Rule 35 of the Federal Rules of Civil Procedure to determine the nature and extent of Sibbach's (P) injuries. The district court ordered that Sibbach (P) submit to such an examination. Sibbach (P) refused to comply with the court order, challenging its validity. It appeared that the courts of Indiana, the state where the cause of action arose, held such an order proper, whereas the courts of Illinois, the state in which the trial court sat, held that such an order could not be made. The district court adjudged Sibbach (P) guilty of contempt and directed that she be committed until compliance with the court order could be had. Sibbach (P) appealed and the court of appeals decided that Rule 35 was valid and affirmed the lower court's judgment. The Supreme Court granted certiorari.

ISSUE: Although the Federal Rules of Civil Procedure grant to the federal courts the authority to compel a party to submit to a physical examination pursuant to Rule 35, do they also permit punishment as contempt for the refusal to obey such an order?

HOLDING AND DECISION: (Roberts, J.) No. Sibbach (P) contended that Rules 35 and 37 are not within the mandate of Congress to this court. Congress has undoubted power to regulate the practice and procedure of federal courts, and may exercise that power by delegating to this or other federal courts authority to make rules not inconsistent with the statutes or Constitution of the United States. However, Congress has never attempted to declare the substantive state law. Therefore, in deciding whether a rule falls within the mandate of Congress to the federal courts, the test must be whether it regulates procedure—the judicial process for enforcing rights and duties recognized by a substantive law. That the rules in question are procedural is admitted. Sibbach (P) further alleged that Rule 35 offends the important right to freedom from invasion of the person. Yet, this contention ignores the fact that no invasion of freedom from personal restraint attaches to refusal to comply with Rule 35's provisions. The district court treated Sibbach's (P) refusal to comply with its order as an act of contempt and committed Sibbach (P) therefor. Neither in the court of appeals nor here was this action assigned as error. However, under Rule 37, there is an explicit exemption from punishment as for contempt for the refusal to obey an order that a party submit to a physical or mental examination. Thus, the district court erred in holding Sibbach (P) in contempt. The judgment of the court of appeals is reversed and the case remanded.

DISSENT: (Frankfurter, J.) That disobedience of an order under Rule 35 cannot be visited with punishment as for contempt does not mitigate its intrusion into an historic immunity of the privacy of the person.

▶ ANALYSIS

Rule 35 is used only where the physical or mental condition of a person is the direct issue in an action. If the physical condition of a person is an indirect or collateral issue the federal courts may not apply Rule 35. Also, the Rule can be used only in relation to a party plaintiff or defendant. In order to invoke Rule 35, a party must make a motion and show good cause. However, good cause may be shown from the pleadings if a plaintiff has claimed physical or mental injuries or if a defendant uses mental or physical conditions as a defense to a claim.

■━■

Quicknotes

CONTEMPT OF COURT Conduct that is intended to obstruct the court's effective administration of justice or to otherwise disrespect its authority.

GOOD CAUSE Sufficient justification for failure to perform an obligation imposed by law.

SUBSTANTIVE LAW Law that pertains to the rights and interests of the parties and upon which a cause of action may be based.

■━■

Swift v. Tyson

Bill's endorsee (P) v. Bill's acceptor (D)

41 U.S. (16 Pet.) 1 (1842).

NATURE OF CASE: Certified question presented on a certificate of division from the Circuit Court in action for payment on a bill of exchange.

FACT SUMMARY: Swift (P), the endorsee of a bill of exchange from Norton & Keith, sued Tyson (D), the bill's acceptor, for payment when the bill was dishonored.

🏛 RULE OF LAW
The decisions of state courts, especially in questions of general commercial law, cannot be said to constitute "laws" so as to be binding on federal courts in forming their decisions.

FACTS: Swift (P) was the endorsee of a bill of exchange issued in Maine in the amount of $1,540.30, which he had taken in payment of a promissory note due him by Norton & Keith. Tyson (D) had accepted the bill in the city of New York and, as acceptor, was responsible for its payment to Swift (P). However, the bill was dishonored at its maturity. Therefore, Swift (P) brought this suit to compel payment by Tyson (D). While acknowledging that Swift (P) was a bona fide holder without knowledge of any defects in the bill, Tyson (D) offered to prove that Tyson (D) had himself originally accepted the bill from Norton & Keith as partial consideration for the purchase of Maine lands which Norton & Keith fraudulently and falsely claimed title to. Tyson (D) therefore argued: (1) that there was failure of consideration for the obligation; (2) that since the acceptance was made in New York, the federal court, according to the 34th section of the Judiciary Act of 1789, must apply the New York laws; and (3) that according to New York laws, as expounded by its courts, a pre-existing debt does not constitute, in the sense of a general rule, a valuable consideration applicable to negotiable instruments. The trial judges were divided in their opinions regarding this and certain other questions of law and the question was certified to the higher court.

ISSUE: Do the decisions of state courts constitute "laws" so as to be binding upon the federal courts in forming their decisions?

HOLDING AND DECISION: (Story, J.) No. The decisions of state courts, especially in questions of general commercial law, cannot be said to constitute "laws" so as to be binding on federal courts in forming their decisions. The "laws" of a state consist of rules and enactments promulgated by the legislature or long-established local customs having the force of laws. The 34th section is limited to positive state statutes and the construction thereof adopted by local courts, and to rights and titles to things having a permanent locality, such as rights and titles to real estate, etc. Court decisions are not "laws," but are only evidence of what the laws are. Such decisions are frequently reversed and qualified as incorrect. The 34th section has never applied to questions of a general nature as, for example, to the construction of ordinary contracts or to questions of general commercial law. The decisions of local courts will receive the attention and respect of this court, but they cannot furnish positive rules, or conclusive authority by which our own judgments are bound and governed. The question certified is answered in the negative.

▶ ANALYSIS

Determining that a federal district court has jurisdiction to hear a case does not actually determine what law it should look to in deciding the case. This problem is ordinarily referred to as the "*Erie* problem" after the following case of *Erie Railroad Co. v. Tompkins*, 304 U.S. 64 (1938). The starting place in the consideration of the question whether state law or federal law is to be applied is the organization of our federal system. Broadly speaking, it can be said that federal substantive law operates in relation to state law in two principal ways. As to certain matters, federal law assumes basic responsibility of the states and seeks simply to regulate the exercise of state authority (e.g., by the Due Process Clause of the Fourteenth Amendment). In others, federal law displaces state law and itself takes over.

Quicknotes

CERTIFIED QUESTION A question that is taken from federal court to the state supreme court so that the court may rule on the issue, or that is taken from a federal court of appeals to the United States Supreme Court.

***ERIE* DOCTRINE** Federal courts must apply state substantive law and federal procedural law.

JURISDICTION The authority of a court to hear and declare judgment in respect to a particular matter.

Erie Railroad Co. v. Tompkins

Alleged tortfeasor (D) v. Alleged tort victim (P)

304 U.S. 64 (1938).

NATURE OF CASE: Action to recover damages for personal injury allegedly caused by negligent conduct.

FACT SUMMARY: In a personal injury suit a federal district court trial judge refused to apply applicable state law because such law was "general" (judge-made) and not embodied in any statute.

RULE OF LAW
In diversity actions, federal courts must apply to substantive issues state law, whether statutory, case law, or common law, unless the Constitution or a federal statute is on point.

FACTS: Tompkins (P) was walking in a right of way parallel to some railroad tracks when an Erie Railroad (Erie) (D) train came by. Tompkins (P) was struck and injured by what he would, at trial, claim to be an open door extending from one of the rail cars. Under Pennsylvania case law (the applicable law since the accident occurred there), state courts would have treated Tompkins (P) as a trespasser in denying him recovery for other than wanton or willful misconduct on Erie's (D) part. Under "general law," recognized in federal courts, Tompkins (P) would have been regarded as a licensee and would only have been obligated to show ordinary negligence. Because Erie (D) was a New York corporation, Tompkins (P) brought suit in a federal district court in New York, where he won a judgment for $30,000. Upon appeal to a federal circuit court, the decision was affirmed.

ISSUE: In diversity actions, must federal courts apply to substantive issues state law, whether statutory, case law, or common law, unless the Constitution or a federal statute is on point?

HOLDING AND DECISION: (Brandeis, J.) Yes. In diversity actions, federal courts must apply to substantive issues state law, whether statutory, case law, or common law, unless the Constitution or a federal statute is on point. The Court's opinion is in four parts: (1) *Swift v. Tyson*, 41 U.S. (16 Pet.) 1 (1842), which held that federal courts exercising jurisdiction on the ground of diversity of citizenship need not, in matters of general jurisprudence, apply the unwritten law of the state as declared by its highest court, is overruled. Section 34 of the Federal Judiciary Act of 1789, c. 20, 28 U.S. § 725 requires that federal courts, in all matters except those where some federal law is controlling, apply as their rules of decision the law of the state, unwritten as well as written. Up to this time, federal courts had assumed the power to make "general law" decisions even though Congress was powerless to enact

"general law" statutes; (2) *Swift* had numerous political and social defects. The hoped-for uniformity among state courts had not occurred; there was no satisfactory way to distinguish between local and general law. On the other hand, *Swift* introduced grave discrimination by noncitizens against citizens. The privilege of selecting the court for resolving disputes rested with the noncitizen who could pick the more favorable forum. The resulting far-reaching discrimination was due to the broad province accorded "general law" in which many matters of seemingly local concern were included. Furthermore, local citizens could move out of the state and bring suit in a federal court if they were disposed to do so; corporations, similarly, could simply reincorporate in another state. More than statutory relief is involved here; the unconstitutionality of *Swift* is clear. (3) Except in matters governed by the federal Constitution or by acts of Congress, the law to be applied in any case is the law of the state. There is no federal common law. The federal courts have no power derived from the Constitution or by Congress to declare substantive rules of common law applicable in a state whether they be "local" or "general" in nature. (4) The federal district court was bound to follow the Pennsylvania case law that would have denied recovery to Tompkins (P).

CONCURRENCE: (Reed, J.) *Swift v. Tyson* is correctly overturned, but the reasoning of the majority in so far as it relies upon the unconstitutionality of the "course pursued" by the federal courts is erroneous.

ANALYSIS

Erie can fairly be characterized as the most significant and sweeping decision on civil procedure ever handed down by the United States Supreme Court. As interpreted in subsequent decisions, *Erie* held that while federal courts may apply their own rules of procedure, issues of substantive law must be decided in accord with the applicable state law—usually the state in which the federal court sits. Note, however, how later Supreme Court decisions have made inroads into the broad doctrine enunciated here.

◼▬◼

Quicknotes

DIVERSITY ACTION An action commenced by a citizen of one state against a citizen of another state or against an alien, involving an amount in controversy set by statute, over which the federal court has jurisdiction.

Continued on next page.

PERSONAL INJURY Harm to an individual's person or body.

SUBSTANTIVE LAW Law that pertains to the rights and interests of the parties and upon which a cause of action may be based.

■═■

Guaranty Trust Co. v. York

Trustee (D) v. Noteholder (P)

326 U.S. 99 (1945).

NATURE OF CASE: Class action alleging fraud and misrepresentation.

FACT SUMMARY: York (P), barred from filing suit in state court because of the state statute of limitations, brought an equity action in federal court based upon diversity of citizenship jurisdiction.

🏛 RULE OF LAW
Where a state statute that would completely bar recovery in state court has significant effect on the outcome-determination of the action, even though the suit be brought in equity, the federal court is bound by the state law.

FACTS: Van Swerigen Corporation, in 1930, issued notes and named Guaranty Trust Co. (Guaranty) (D) as trustee with power and obligations to enforce the rights of the noteholders in the assets of the corporation and the Van Swerigens. In 1931, when it was apparent that the corporation could not meet its obligations, Guaranty (D) cooperated in a plan for the purchase of the outstanding notes for 50% of the notes' face value and an exchange of twenty shares of the corporation's stock for each $1,000 note. In 1934, York (P) received some cash, her donor not having accepted the rate of exchange. In 1940, three accepting noteholders sued Guaranty (D), charging fraud and misrepresentation, in state court. York (P) was not allowed to intervene. Summary judgment in favor of Guaranty (D) was affirmed. In 1942, York (P) brought a class action suit in federal court based on diversity of citizenship and charged Guaranty (D) with breach of trust. Guaranty (D) moved for and was granted summary judgment on the basis of the earlier state decision. The court of appeals reversed on the basis that the earlier state decision did not foreclose this federal court action, and held that even though the state statute of limitations had run, the fact that the action was brought in equity releases the federal court from following the state rule.

ISSUE: Where a state statute that would completely bar recovery in state court has significant effect on the outcome-determination of the action, even though the suit be brought in equity, is the federal court bound by the state law?

HOLDING AND DECISION: (Frankfurter, J.) Yes. Where a state statute that would completely bar recovery in state court has significant effect on the outcome-determination of the action, even though the suit be brought in equity, the federal court is bound by the state law. *Erie Railroad Co. v. Tompkins,* 304 U.S. 64 (1938), overruled a particular way of looking at law after its inadequacies had been laid bare. Federal courts have traditionally given state-created rights in equity greater respect than rights in law since the former are more frequently defined by legislative enactment. Even though federal equity may be thought of as a separate legal system, the substantive right is created by the state, and federal courts must respect state law which governs that right. While state law cannot define the remedies that a federal court must give simply because a federal court in diversity jurisdiction is available as an alternative, a federal court may afford an equitable remedy for a substantive right recognized by a state even though a state court cannot give it. Federal courts enforce state-created substantive rights if the mode of proceeding and remedy were consonant with the traditional body of equitable remedies, practice, and procedure. Matters of "substance" and of "procedure" turn on different considerations. Here, since the federal court is adjudicating a state-created right solely because of diversity of citizenship of the parties, it is, in effect, only another court of the state, and it cannot afford recovery if the right to recovery is made unavailable by the state. The question is not whether a statute of limitations is "procedural," but whether the statute so affects the result of litigation as to be controlling in state law. It is, therefore, immaterial to make a "substantive-procedure" dichotomy—*Erie Railroad Co. v. Tompkins* was not an endeavor to formulate scientific legal terminology, but rather an expression of a policy that touches the distribution of judicial power between state and federal courts. *Erie* insures that insofar as legal rules determine the outcome of litigation, the result should not be any different in a federal court extending jurisdiction solely on the basis of diversity of citizenship. Through diversity jurisdiction, Congress meant to afford out-of-state litigants another tribunal, and not another body of law. Reversed.

DISSENT: (Rutledge, J.) History and tradition have consistently held that statutes of limitations are not absolute barriers to equity actions, and that tradition should be viewed as having been incorporated into those acts of Congress that have conferred equity jurisdiction on the federal courts. The majority now removes this principle from those acts, but it is not the Court's place to make such a change; that is Congress's role.

▶ ANALYSIS

Guaranty Trust, which clarified *Erie,* may itself be in the process of being slowly eroded by modern courts. *Hanna v. Plumer,* 380 U.S. 460 (1965), held that where state law conflicts with the Federal Rules of Civil Procedure, the

Continued on next page.

latter prevails regardless of the effect on the outcome of the litigation. And in *Byrd v. Blue Ridge Elec. Cooperative*, 356 I/S/ 525 (1958), the Court suggested that some constitutional doctrines (here, the right to a jury trial in federal court) are so important as to be controlling over state law—once again, the outcome notwithstanding.

■━■

Quicknotes

DIVERSITY JURISDICTION The authority of a federal court to hear and determine cases involving a statutory sum and in which the parties are citizens of different states, or in which one party is an alien.

DIVERSITY OF CITIZENSHIP Parties are citizens of different states, or one party is an alien.

EQUITABLE REMEDY A remedy that is based upon principles of fairness as opposed to rules of law.

STATUTE OF LIMITATIONS A law prescribing the period in which a legal action may be commenced.

■━■

Hanna v. Plumer

Car accident victim (P) v. Executor of alleged tortfeasor's estate (D)

380 U.S. 460 (1965).

NATURE OF CASE: Appeal of summary judgment in federal diversity tort action.

FACT SUMMARY: Hanna (P) filed a tort action in federal court in Massachusetts, where Plumer (D) resided, for an auto accident that occurred in South Carolina.

🏛 RULE OF LAW
The *Erie* doctrine mandates that federal courts are to apply state substantive law and federal procedural law, but where matters fall roughly between the two and are rationally capable of classification as either, the Constitution grants the federal court system the power to regulate their practice and pleading (procedure).

FACTS: Hanna (P), a citizen of Ohio, filed a tort action in federal court in Massachusetts against Plumer (D), the executor of the estate of Louise Plumer Osgood, a Massachusetts citizen. It was alleged that Mrs. Osgood caused injuries to Hanna (P) in an auto accident in South Carolina. Service on Plumer (D) was accomplished pursuant to Fed. R. Civ. P. 4(d)(1) by leaving copies of the summons with Plumer's (D) wife. At trial, motion for summary judgment by Plumer (D) was granted on the grounds that service should have been accomplished pursuant to Massachusetts law (by the *Erie* doctrine) which requires service by hand to the party personally. On appeal, Hanna (P) contended that *Erie* should not affect the application of the Federal Rules of Civil Procedure to this case. Plumer (D), however, contended that (1) a substantive law question under *Erie* is any question in which permitting application of federal law would alter the outcome of the case (the so-called outcome determination test); (2) the application of federal law here (i.e., 4(d)(II)) would necessarily affect the outcome of the case (from a necessary dismissal to litigation); and, therefore, (3) *Erie* required that the state substantive law requirement of service by hand be upheld along with the trial court's summary judgment.

ISSUE: The *Erie* doctrine mandates that federal courts are to apply state substantive law and federal procedural law, but where matters fall roughly between the two and are rationally capable of classification as either, does the Constitution grant the federal court system the power to regulate their practice and pleading (procedure)?

HOLDING AND DECISION: (Warren, C.J.) Yes. The *Erie* doctrine mandates that federal courts are to apply state substantive law and federal procedural law, and, where matters fall roughly between the two and are rationally capable of classification as either, the Constitution grants the federal court system the power to regulate their practice and pleading (procedure). It is well settled that the Enabling Act for the Federal Rules of Civil Procedure

requires that a procedural effect of any rule on the outcome of a case be shown to actually "abridge, enlarge, or modify" the substantive law in a case for the *Erie* doctrine to come into play. Article III and the Necessary and Proper Clause provide that Congress has a right to provide rules for the federal court system such as Fed. R. Civ. P. 4(d)(1). Here, the question applies only to procedural requirements, i.e., service of summons, and so a dismissal for improper service would not alter the substantive right of Hanna (P) to serve Plumer (D) personally and refile or effect the substantive law of negligence in the case. "Outcome determination analysis was never intended to serve as a talisman" for the *Erie* doctrine. The judgment of the trial court must be reversed.

CONCURRENCE: (Harlan, J.) The majority is correct to reject the outcome determination test. However, the majority is wrong that anything arguably procedural is constitutionally placed within the province of the federal government to regulate. Instead, the test for what is "substantive" should be whether "the choice of rule would substantially affect those primary decisions respecting human conduct which our constitutional system leaves to state regulation."

⏐ ANALYSIS

This case points up a return to the basic rationales of *Erie Railroad Co. v. Tompkins*. First, the Court asserts that one important consideration in determining how a particular question should be classified (substantive or procedural) is the avoidance of "forum shopping" (the practice of choosing one forum, such as federal, to file in, in order to gain the advantages of it), which permits jurisdictions to infringe upon the substantive law defining powers of each other. Second, the Court seeks to avoid inequitable administration of the laws that would result from allowing jurisdictional consideration to determine substantive rights. Here, Justice Warren, in rejecting the "outcome determination" test, asserts that any rule must be measured ultimately against the Federal Rules Enabling Act and the Constitution.

■=■

Quicknotes

ERIE **DOCTRINE** Federal courts must apply state substantive law and federal procedural law.

SUBSTANTIVE LAW Law that pertains to the rights and interests of the parties and upon which a cause of action may be based.

■=■

Railway Co. v. Whitton's Administrator

Alleged tortfeasor (D) v. Administrator of alleged tort victim's estate (P)

80 U.S. (13 Wall.) 270 (1871).

NATURE OF CASE: Writ of error challenging the jurisdiction of the federal court.

FACT SUMMARY: Railway Co. (D) challenged the jurisdiction of the federal court to hear a case brought by Whitton (P) under a Wisconsin statute which required that the case be heard in a Wisconsin state court.

🏛 RULE OF LAW
Federal courts cannot be deprived of their proper jurisdiction by state statute in those cases wherein a general right or rule as to property or personal rights— or injuries to either—has been established by state legislation.

FACTS: Whitton (P), the administrator of his wife's Wisconsin estate, brought suit in a Wisconsin state court to recover damages for his wife's death which was allegedly caused by Railway's (D) negligence. The action was brought under a Wisconsin statute which, after first creating such a right of action, required that it be brought only in a Wisconsin state court as a necessary condition for obtaining relief. However, while the case was pending, Congress passed an act that permitted such a suit to be removed to the federal circuit court. Whitton (P) accordingly removed the case to the federal court where he received a $5,000 judgment. Railway (D) challenged the jurisdiction of the federal court on writ of error. Railway (D) argued that the remedy granted by the state statute could be enforced only when the condition that the case be tried in a state court was complied with.

ISSUE: Can federal courts be deprived of their proper jurisdiction by state statute in those cases wherein a general right or rule as to property or personal rights, or injuries to either, has been established by state legislation?

HOLDING AND DECISION: (Field, J.) No. Federal courts cannot be deprived of their proper jurisdiction by state statute in those cases wherein a general right or rule as to property or personal rights, or injuries to either, has been established by state legislation. Virtually every state has statutes providing for the institution of numerous suits, such as partition, foreclosure, and the recovery of real property in particular courts and in the counties where the land is situated. Nevertheless, it has never been pretended that such limitations could ever affect, in any respect, the jurisdiction of the federal court over such suits where the citizenship of one of the parties was otherwise sufficient. Decision not stated in casebook.

▶ ANALYSIS

It is important to be aware that the rule of the *Whitton* case is merely a normal and not a universal one. Federal courts do not always sit in the role of courts of coordinate competence, given federal jurisdiction, to enforce state-created rights. A state may create a right of action, entailing, for example, the exercise of discretion by a specialized administrative tribunal, of a kind which a federal court will regard as nonnegotiable, as it were, and thus outside the *Whitton* principle. In addition, certain traditional types of claims upon the courts in the field of decedents' estates and family law have been regarded as involving matters of such special camera to the states as to be inappropriate for determination by any separate, even though coordinate, system of courts.

■■■

Quicknotes

FEDERAL COURT JURISDICTION The authority of the federal courts to hear and determine in the first instance matters pertaining to the federal Constitution, federal law, or treaties of the United States.

■■■

CHAPTER 7

Federal Common Law

Quick Reference Rules of Law

United States v. Hudson & Goodwin

Federal government (P) v. Individuals convicted of criminal libel (D)

11 U.S. (7 Cranch) 32 (1812).

NATURE OF CASE: Certified question to the United States Supreme Court in criminal libel action.

FACT SUMMARY: Following the issuance of an indictment for libel against individuals (D) who were accused of libeling the President and Congress of the United States, the circuit court divided upon the question of whether circuit courts have common-law jurisdiction over libel and therefore certified that question to the United States Supreme Court.

RULE OF LAW
Exercise of criminal jurisdiction in common-law cases is not within the implied powers of the U.S. circuit courts.

FACTS: The United States (P) sought an indictment for libel against individuals (D) who were accused of libeling the President and Congress by falsely stating that the President and Congress secretly voted $2,000,000 as a present to Bonaparte, for permission to make a treaty with Spain. Upon argument of a general demurrer to the indictment, the District of Connecticut Circuit Court divided on the question whether the circuit court of the United States had common-law jurisdiction in cases of libel. That question was certified to the United States Supreme Court.

ISSUE: Do the implied powers of the U.S. circuit courts include the exercise of criminal jurisdiction in common-law cases?

HOLDING AND DECISION: (Johnson, J.) No. Exercise of criminal jurisdiction in common-law cases is not within the implied powers of the U.S. circuit courts. First, the powers of the general government consist of concessions from the states. As such, whatever is not given to the government is reserved to the states—they are vested with jurisdiction in those areas. Although the judicial power of the United States is among those concessions, nevertheless it is only the United States Supreme Court that derives its power directly from the Constitution. All other courts are created by the general government and exercise only that power conferred thereby. Their jurisdiction is thus clearly limited. Circuit courts do have certain implied powers as, for example, that of preserving their existence and promoting the purposes for their creation. However, jurisdiction of crimes against the state is not one of those implied powers. The legislative authority of the Union must first make the act a crime, affix a punishment, and then declare that the court shall have jurisdiction of the offense. The proposition is thus answered in the negative.

ANALYSIS

Many eminent judges and lawyers have maintained that such jurisdiction over crimes at common law and under the law of nations was intended to be vested in the federal courts. In an article, "New Light on the History of the Federal Judiciary Act of 1789," 37 Harvard Law Review 49, 73 (1923), Charles Warren argues that the original draft bill shows that the Framers clearly intended to exclude federal courts from such jurisdiction. That position—urged by the Jeffersonians—finally prevailed.

Quicknotes

CERTIFIED QUESTION A question that is taken from federal court to the state supreme court so that the court may rule on the issue, or that is taken from a federal court of appeals to the United States Supreme Court.

COMMON LAW CRIME An activity that has been defined as a crime not by legislative enactment but by the courts through case law.

IMPLIED POWERS Powers delegated to the various branches of government that, while not expressly stated in the Constitution, are necessary to effectuate the enumerated powers.

Clearfield Trust Co. v. United States

Presenter of forged check (D) v. Federal government (P)

318 U.S. 363 (1943).

NATURE OF CASE: Appeal from an action to recover money on a check.

FACT SUMMARY: The federal government (P) brought suit in the federal district court against the Clearfield Trust Co. (Clearfield) (D) seeking reimbursement of a forged Works Progress Administration check which Clearfield (D) cashed and expressly guaranteed by prior endorsements.

🏛 RULE OF LAW
The rights and duties of the United States on commercial paper which it issues are governed by federal rather than local law.

FACTS: A check drawn on the Treasurer of the United States and made payable to Claire Barner was cashed by an unknown party who endorsed the check in the name of Barner and transferred it to J.C. Penney Co. J.C. Penney Co. endorsed the check over to Clearfield Trust Co. (D). Clearfield (D) collected on the check from the government (P), expressly guaranteeing it by prior endorsements. Barner then informed the WPA that he had not received the check. Over a year later, Clearfield (D) received notice that the government (P) was seeking reimbursement. Suit was instituted over another year later by the government (P) in the federal district court based on the express guarantee of prior endorsements made by Clearfield (D). The district court dismissed the complaint on the ground that the rights of the parties were to be determined by the law of Pennsylvania, the place of the transaction, and that, since the federal government (P) unreasonably delayed in giving notice of the forgery to Clearfield (D), it was barred from recovery. The court of appeals reversed.

ISSUE: Are the rights and duties of the United States on commercial paper which it issues governed by federal rather than local law?

HOLDING AND DECISION: (Douglas, J.) Yes. The rights and duties of the United States on commercial paper which it issues are governed by federal rather than local law. When the United States disburses its funds or pays its debts, it is exercising a constitutional function. This check was issued for services performed under the Federal Emergency Relief Act of 1935. The authority to issue the check had its origin in the Constitution and the statutes of the United States and was in no way dependent on the laws of Pennsylvania or any other state. In absence of an applicable act of Congress, it is for the federal courts to fashion the governing rule of law according to their own standards. Although in our choice of the applicable federal rule we have occasionally selected state law, the reasons that make state law at times the appropriate federal rule are inappropriate in the instant case. The issuance of commercial paper by the United States is on a vast scale, commonly occurring in several states. Therefore, the application of state law would subject the rights and duties of the United States to exceptional uncertainty. The desirability of a uniform rule is plain. As to the issue of prompt notice, this Court holds that lack of such notice will be a defense. If it is shown that the drawee, on learning of the forgery, did not give prompt notice of it and that damage resulted, recovery by the drawee is barred. But the damage must be established and not left to conjecture as was done in the case at bar. No such damage has been shown by Clearfield (D), who can still recover from J.C. Penney Co. Consequently, the decision of the court of appeals is affirmed.

▶ ANALYSIS

Justice Jackson, in the case of *D'Oench, Duhme & Co.*, stated that "a federal court sitting in a nondiversity case does not sit as a local tribunal. In some cases it may see fit for special reasons to give the law of a particular state highly persuasive or even controlling effect, but in the last analysis its decision turns upon the law of the United States. Federal law is no judicial chameleon changing complexion to match that of each state wherein lawsuits happen to be commenced because of the accidents of service of process and of the application of the venue statutes."

■■■

Quicknotes

COMMERCIAL PAPER A negotiable instrument; a written promise, signed by the promisee, to pay a specified sum of money to the promisor either on demand or on a specified date.

■■■

Boyle v. United Technologies Corp.

Parent of killed helicopter pilot (P) v. Helicopter manufacturer (D)

487 U.S. 500 (1988).

NATURE OF CASE: Appeal of award of damages for wrongful death.

FACT SUMMARY: The Sikorsky Division (D) of United Technologies sought immunity from tort actions relating to the helicopters it built for the United States Navy.

🏛 RULE OF LAW
Liability for design defects in military equipment cannot be imposed when the equipment conforms to specifications approved by the government.

FACTS: The Sikorsky Division (Sikorsky) (D) of United Technologies built the CH-53D helicopter for the United States military. Boyle's (P) son, a Marine helicopter co-pilot, was killed when the CH-53D helicopter he was flying crashed into the ocean during a training exercise; he survived the impact but drowned when he was unable to escape the helicopter. Boyle (P) brought suit against Sikorsky (D), contending that it had defectively repaired a device in the automatic flight control system and had defectively designed the emergency escape system. A jury awarded Boyle (P) $725,000. The court of appeals reversed, ruling that Sikorsky (D) could not be held liable for defective design since it was entitled to the "military contractor defense." Boyle (P) appealed, and certiorari was granted.

ISSUE: May a military contractor be held liable for defective design relating to a product which was built for the U.S. government and conforms to government specifications?

HOLDING AND DECISION: (Scalia, J.) No. Liability for design defects in military equipment cannot be imposed when the equipment was built for the U.S. government and conforms to specifications approved by the government. The procurement of equipment by the U.S. government is an area of uniquely federal interest. Where uniquely federal interests are involved, the federal common law preempts state law to the extent that there is a conflict. A state-imposed duty of care is in direct conflict with a government contract which specifies a certain design. Therefore, federal law displaces state tort law with regard to the procurement of equipment by the federal government. The Federal Tort Claims Act exempts discretionary functions of the government from liability. The selection of the appropriate design for military equipment is a discretionary function; thus, federal law provides immunity to military contractors. The scope of this immunity covers equipment which conforms to specifications which have been approved by the United States. The supplier must

also warn the government about the dangers of use since there would be incentive to withhold information because of the immunity. Sikorsky (D) supplied the CH-53D helicopters to the U.S. military after the design had been approved by the Navy. Therefore, Sikorsky (D) was entitled to the immunity provided by federal law, and Boyle's (P) award was properly reversed. Affirmed.

DISSENT: (Brennan, J.) State laws should not be displaced by federal law except where Congress has explicitly decided to supersede them or in a few narrow circumstances. Military contractors have long lobbied unsuccessfully for immunity in Congress. Furthermore, the category of "uniquely federal interests" has never before been extended to the conduct of non-government employees such as government contractors.

DISSENT: (Stevens, J.) Where an entirely new doctrine such as the military contractor defense is created, the proper decision maker should be Congress because only the legislature has the proper means to balance the conflicting interests which are involved.

▶ ANALYSIS

Since the decision, Congress extended the Federal Tort Claims Act immunity to cover all conduct by federal officials within the scope of their employment, whether discretionary or not. In *Trevino v. General Dynamics Corp.*, 865 F.2d 1474 (5th Cir. 1989), which was decided subsequent to *Boyle*, the court ruled that a government employee's signature on each page of a contractor's design drawings wasn't necessarily the approval required by *Boyle*.

■=■

Quicknotes

DEFECTIVE DESIGN A product that is manufactured in accordance with a particular design; however, such design is inherently flawed so that it presents an unreasonable risk of injury.

IMMUNITY Exemption from a legal obligation.

■=■

Chelentis v. Luckenbach S.S. Co.

Injured seaman (P) v. Ship company (D)

247 U.S. 372 (1918).

NATURE OF CASE: Appeal from a federal court of appeal's upholding of dismissal of a seaman's common-law injuries claim.

FACT SUMMARY: When Chelentis (P), a seaman, was injured while performing duties aboard a ship owned by Luckenbach S.S. Co. (Luckenbach) (D), he brought a common law negligence suit against Luckenbach (D) for full indemnity for amputation of his leg.

🏛 RULE OF LAW
States lack the power to abolish the well-recognized maritime rule as to measure of recovery and substitute therefor the full indemnity rule of the common law.

FACTS: Chelentis (P), a seaman, injured while performing duties aboard a ship owned by Luckenbach (D), brought a common law negligence suit in state court against Luckenbach (D) for full indemnity for amputation of his leg. Chelentis (P) did not question seaworthiness of the ship, and made no claim for maintenance, cure, or wages. On diversity grounds, the case was removed to the federal district court which directed a verdict for Luckenbach (D). The federal court of appeals affirmed, and Chelentis (P) appealed to the United States Supreme Court.

ISSUE: Do states lack the power to abolish the well-recognized maritime rule as to measure of recovery and substitute therefor the full indemnity rule of the common law?

HOLDING AND DECISION: (McReynolds, J.) Yes. States lack the power to abolish the well-recognized maritime rule as to measure of recovery and substitute therefor the full indemnity rule of the common law. Such a substitution would distinctly and definitely change or add to the settled maritime law. It would be destructive of the "uniformity and consistency" at which the Constitution aimed on all subjects of a commercial character affecting the intercourse of the states with each other or with foreign nations. Chelentis (P) is not provided a right of full indemnity under the common law by the Judiciary Act of 1789 because such legislation gave no authority to the states that would work material prejudice to the characteristic features of the general maritime law or interfere with the proper harmony and uniformity of that law in its international and interstate relations. Such legislation only provides to litigants the right of a common-law remedy where the common law is competent to give it. Here, Chelentis's (P) rights are to be measured by the law of the sea. Affirmed.

▶ ANALYSIS

In *Chelentis*, the Supreme Court noted that the distinction between rights and remedies is fundamental. A right is a well-founded or acknowledged claim; a remedy is the means employed to enforce a right or redress an injury. The Court went on to explain that while a right sanctioned by the maritime law may be enforced through any appropriate remedy recognized at common law, a complaining party does not have the election to determine whether the defendant's liability is to be measured by common-law standards rather than those of the maritime law.

Quicknotes

DIVERSITY ACTION An action commenced by a citizen of one state against a citizen of another state or against an alien, involving an amount in controversy set by statute, over which the federal court has jurisdiction.

Banco Nacional de Cuba v. Sabbatino

Creditor (P) v. Receiver for Cuban corporation (D)

376 U.S. 398 (1964).

NATURE OF CASE: Appeal by receiver of a Cuban corporation from a summary judgment in favor of a creditor.

FACT SUMMARY: When Banco Nacional de Cuba (Banco Nacional) (P) brought a diversity action in federal district court against Sabbatino (D), the receiver for a Cuban corporation, for conversion of proceeds to which Banco Nacional (P) claimed it was entitled, the federal district court, relying on the act of state doctrine, granted summary judgment in favor of Banco Nacional (P).

🏛 **RULE OF LAW**
Courts will not examine the validity of a taking of property within its own territory by a foreign sovereign government, recognized by this country at the time of suit, in the absence of a treaty or other unambiguous agreement regarding controlling legal principles, even if the complaint alleges that the taking violates customary international law.

FACTS: A New York corporation contracted to buy sugar from a subsidiary of a Cuban corporation, whose stock was owned primarily by Americans. The Cuban government expropriated the sugar under a decree that passed title to a Cuban governmental agency. The New York corporation secured a Cuban export license for the sugar by promising to pay the proceeds to Banco Nacional (P), but after export it refused to honor this promise and transferred the funds to Sabbatino (D), a receiver for the Cuban corporation that had sold the sugar. Banco Nacional (P) brought a diversity action in federal district court against the purchaser for conversion of the proceeds. Proceeding on the basis that a taking invalid under international law does not convey good title, the federal district court found the Cuban expropriation decree to violate such law and granted summary judgment against Sabbatino (D). The federal court of appeals affirmed. Sabbatino (D) appealed to the United States Supreme Court.

ISSUE: Will courts examine the validity of a taking of property within its own territory by a foreign sovereign government, recognized by this country at the time of suit, in the absence of a treaty or other unambiguous agreement regarding controlling legal principles, even if the complaint alleges that the taking violates customary international law?

HOLDING AND DECISION: (Harlan, J.) No. Courts will not examine the validity of a taking of property within its own territory by a foreign sovereign government, recognized by this country at the time of suit, in the absence of a treaty or other unambiguous agreement regarding controlling legal principles, even if the complaint

alleges that the taking violates customary international law. If the act of state doctrine is a principle of decision binding on federal and state courts alike, but compelled by neither international law nor the Constitution, its continuing vitality depends on its capacity to reflect the proper distribution of functions between the judicial and political branches of the government on matters bearing upon foreign affairs. The greater the degree of codification or consensus concerning a particular area of international law, the more appropriate it is for the judiciary to render decisions regarding it since the courts can then focus on the application of an agreed principle to circumstances of fact rather than on the sensitive task of establishing a principle not inconsistent with the national interest or with international justice. The possible adverse consequences of a conclusion to the contrary is highlighted by contrasting the practices of the political branch with the limitations of the judicial process in matters of this kind. In sum, the act of state doctrine is here compelled neither by the inherent nature of sovereign immunity or by some principle of international law. While historic notions of sovereign authority do bear upon the wisdom of employing the act of state doctrine, they do not dictate its existence. Reversed.

DISSENT: (White, J.) The act of state doctrine does not require American courts to disregard international law and the rights of litigants to a full determination on the merits. While political matters in the realm of foreign affairs are within the exclusive domain of the Executive Branch, this is far from saying that the Constitution vests in the executive exclusive absolute control of foreign affairs or that the validity of a foreign act of state is necessarily a political question. It cannot be contended that the Constitution allocates this area to the exclusive jurisdiction of the executive since the judicial power is expressly extended by that document to controversies between aliens and citizens or states, aliens and aliens, and foreign states and American citizens or states.

▶ *ANALYSIS*

In *Banco Nacional*, the Supreme Court noted that some aspects of international law touch much more sharply on national nerves than do others, and that the less important implications of an issue are for American foreign relations, the weaker the justification for exclusivity in the political branches. Furthermore, the balance of relevant considerations may also be shifted if the government which

Continued on next page.

perpetuated the challenged act of state is no longer in existence.

■━■

Quicknotes

CONVEYANCE OF TITLE   Any transfer or conveyance having an effect on title to an interest in real property.

DIVERSITY ACTION   An action commenced by a citizen of one state against a citizen of another state or against an alien, involving an amount in controversy set by statute, over which the federal court has jurisdiction.

SOVEREIGN   A state or entity with independent authority to govern its affairs.

■━■

Cannon v. University of Chicago

Female student applicant (P) v. University (D)

441 U.S. 677 (1979).

NATURE OF CASE: Review of dismissal for failure to state a claim.

FACT SUMMARY: Cannon (P) sued to compel admission to the University of Chicago (UC) (D), claiming a private cause of action for sexual discrimination under Title IX.

🏛 RULE OF LAW
An implied remedy for a federal statutory violation may be found if Congress intended to make a remedy available.

FACTS: Cannon (P) was denied admission to the UC medical school (D), which received federal funds. Cannon (P) sued to compel admission under Title IX, claiming that the UC (R) denied her admission based upon her sex. Although Title IX barred educational programs or activities that received federal funds from excluding participants based upon their sex, it did not expressly authorize a private cause of action. The UC (D) successfully argued that Cannon (P) failed to state a claim upon which relief may be granted, and the district court dismissed the case. Cannon (P) appealed, and the appellate court affirmed. Cannon (P) now appeals.

ISSUE: Does an implied remedy for a statutory violation exist if Congress intended to make a remedy available?

HOLDING AND DECISION: (Stevens, J.) Yes. An implied remedy for a statutory violation may be found if Congress intended to make a remedy available. The Court must balance the four factors to determine if Congress intended an implied remedy. The four factors include: (1) whether the statute was enacted for the benefit of a special class of which the plaintiff is a member; (2) whether the legislative history denies intention to create a private cause of action; (3) whether an implied remedy would frustrate the underlying purpose of the statute; and (4) whether the federal remedy would interfere with the state's police power. Title IX was enacted for women. The legislative history shows no hostility to private remedies. A private remedy under Title IX would not frustrate the purpose of Title IX or the state's authority. Accordingly, Cannon (P) should be allowed to pursue her claim. Reversed and remanded.

CONCURRENCE: (Rehnquist, J.) The Court in the future should be very reluctant to imply a cause of action and should return this function to Congress where it belongs.

DISSENT: (Powell, J.) It is clear that no private action should be implied here. Under Article III, Congress alone has the responsibility for determining the jurisdiction of the lower federal courts, and, as the legislative branch, should also determine when private parties are to be given causes of action under legislation it adopts. Congress knows how to provide for a private remedy in a federal statute if it intends to include one. If it does not provide such a remedy, the federal courts should not assume the legislative role of creating such a remedy. In other words, the Court should refrain from legislating. The remedy adopted here by the majority is an open invitation to the federal courts to legislate causes of action not authorized by Congress. Implying such remedies from a regulatory statute is the rare exception and the Court in the past repeatedly turned away private plaintiffs seeking to imply causes of action from federal statutes. Moreover, in those rare instances where the Court upheld the implication of private causes of action, the decisions were either aberrant, or were rendered to avoid ruling that a statute was precatory in the absence of alternative enforcement mechanisms. The factors the majority uses for implying a private cause of action give courts too much leeway for independent judicial lawmaking, without focusing sufficiently on congressional intent. This also invites Congress to avoid resolution of the often controversial question of whether a new regulatory statute should be enforced through private litigation. By implying a cause of action, the Court violates the separation of powers and denigrates the democratic process.

▶ ANALYSIS

Implied common law remedies for federal statutory violations are rare. Courts are reluctant to grant a remedy when the legislature fails to include one. Justice Powell's view, which adheres to strict separation of powers, has dominated the Court in recent years.

■▬■

Quicknotes

CAUSE OF ACTION A fact or set of facts the occurrence of which entitles a party to seek judicial relief.

REMEDY Compensation for violation of a right or for injuries sustained.

■▬■

Alexander v. Sandoval

Alabama state agency (D) v. Member of allegedly discriminated class (P)

532 U.S. 275 (2001).

NATURE OF CASE: Appeal from a federal court decision holding that private individuals were not precluded from bringing a private enforcement suit under Title VI of the Civil Rights Act of 1964.

FACT SUMMARY: When Sandoval (P) brought a class action to enjoin the Alabama Department of Public Safety from administering driver's license examinations only in English, the lower federal courts held that Title VI of the Civil Rights Act of 1964 did not preclude private individuals from bringing enforcement actions under the Act.

🏛 RULE OF LAW
Private individuals may not sue to enforce disparate-impact regulations under Title VI of the Civil Rights Act of 1964.

FACTS: Sandoval (P) brought a class suit to enjoin the Alabama Department of Public Safety from administering driver's license examinations only in English. The Alabama Constitution had been amended to declare English "the official language of the state." The federal court and court of appeals agreed with Sandoval's position that the English-only policy violated federal Department of Justice antidiscrimination regulations because its *effect* was to subject non-English speakers to discrimination based on national origin. Both courts also held that Title VI of the Civil Rights Act of 1964 did not preclude private individuals from bringing enforcement actions under the Act. Alabama (D) appealed to the Supreme Court.

ISSUE: May private individuals sue to enforce disparate-impact regulations under Title VI of the Civil Rights Act of 1964?

HOLDING AND DECISION: (Scalia, J.) No. Private individuals may not sue to enforce disparate-impact regulations under Title VI of the Civil Rights Act of 1964. While Section 602 of Title VI authorizes federal agencies to effectuate the provisions of the Civil Rights Act, the methods which Section 602 provides for enforcing its authorized regulations manifest no intent to create a private remedy. If anything, they suggest the opposite. Section 602 empowers agencies to enforce their regulations either by terminating funding to the "particular program, or part thereof," that has violated the regulations or "by any other means authorized by law." No enforcement action may be taken, however, until the department or agency concerned has advised the appropriate person of the failure to comply with the requirement and has determined that compliance cannot be secured by voluntary means. Every agency enforcement action is subject to judicial review. Furthermore,

if an agency attempts to terminate program funding, still more restrictions apply. Whatever these elaborate restrictions on agency enforcement may imply for the private enforcement of rights created *outside* of Section 602, they tend to contradict a congressional intent to create privately enforceable rights through Section 602 itself. The express provision of one method of enforcing a substantive rule suggests that Congress intended to preclude others. Reversed.

DISSENT: (Stevens, J.) On its own terms, the statute supports an action challenging policies of federal grantees that explicitly or unambiguously violate antidiscrimination norms such as, for example, policies that on their face limit benefits or services to certain races. With regard to more subtle forms of discrimination, such as schemes that limit benefits or services on ostensibly race-neutral grounds but have the predictable and perhaps intended consequence of materially benefiting some races at the expense of others, the statute does not establish a static approach, but instead empowers the relevant agencies to evaluate social circumstances to determine whether there is a need for stronger measures.

▶ ANALYSIS

In *Alexander*, the Sandoval class argued that the *regulations* contained right-creating language thus must be privately enforceable. Such argument, however, said the Supreme Court, skips an analytical step, pointing out that language in a regulation may invoke a private right of action that Congress through statutory text created, but it may not create a right that Congress has not.

■=■

Quicknotes

DISPARATE TREATMENT Unequal treatment of employees or of applicants for employment without justification.

■=■

Ward v. Love County

Native American (P) v. County (D)

253 U.S. 17 (1920).

NATURE OF CASE: Suit to recover taxes paid under protest.

FACT SUMMARY: Land allotted to Ward (P) and other American Indians (P) was exempted from taxation by federal law. Later, Congress permitted the land to be taxed, and Love County (D) taxed the land which Ward (P) owned.

🏛 RULE OF LAW
The United States Supreme Court may review state court decisions that, to any extent, involve issues of federal law.

FACTS: Land allotted to Coleman Ward (P) and other American Indians (P) was nontaxable, according to the laws and Constitution of the United States, for twenty-one years following the date of the patent, provided that the land remained in the possession of the original allottees. Ten years after the land was allotted, Congress provided that it was henceforth subject to taxation as if it were the land of persons other than the allottees. Love County (D), Oklahoma, thereafter assessed taxes on the land owned by Ward (P) and sixty-six other Choctaw Indians (P). The Indians (P) opposed the levy, claiming that the exemption their lands had enjoyed was a vested property right of which they could not constitutionally be deprived. At the time that Love County (D) assessed its tax, various suits were pending in which Oklahoma Indians had challenged the elimination of the tax-exempt status of their lands, and the United States Supreme Court ultimately ruled that removal of the exemption violated the Fifth Amendment and that Oklahoma authorities had no power to tax the Indians' lands. Love County (D) nevertheless demanded that Ward (P) and the others (P) pay the tax, and threatened to advertise and sell the property of all who refused. Land belonging to others actually was sold pursuant to the county's (D) threat. Ward (P) and the other Indians (P) eventually paid their taxes to avoid the sale of their lands and the imposition of an 18% penalty. A suit was then filed in state court to recover the amounts paid, allegedly under coercion. The trial court granted the relief sought, but the Oklahoma Supreme Court reversed, holding that the taxes had been paid voluntarily and that, in any event, the county (D) could not be ordered to repay the tax money because some of it had already been paid over to the state and to various municipal governments. Ward (P) and the others (P) then asked the United States Supreme Court to review the decision of the highest Oklahoma court. The county (D) moved to dismiss the writ of certiorari, claiming that the Supreme Court lacked appellate jurisdiction

because the judgment of the Oklahoma court had been based solely on state law.

ISSUE: May decisions of state courts be reviewed by the United States Supreme Court?

HOLDING AND DECISION: (Van Devanter, J.) Yes. The United States Supreme Court may review state court decisions which, to any extent, involve issues of federal law. If a state court's holding is premised entirely on its resolution of state law issues, the Supreme Court has no appellate jurisdiction. But, the tax exemption involved in this case was clearly a federal right, and the legitimacy of its elimination presents an issue of federal law. The argument that the Oklahoma Supreme Court avoided all federal questions by concluding that the taxes were paid voluntarily is unpersuasive. That factual conclusion cannot be accepted in view of the coercive measures employed to compel the comparatively unsophisticated Indians (P) to pay the taxes. The state supreme court also erred in concluding that Love County's (D) subsequent dispersal of the tax monies to other governmental entities relieved it of its obligation to repay the funds. Since disposition of the case necessarily involves the resolution of issues of federal law, the United States Supreme Court has authority to reverse the judgment of the Oklahoma court. Accordingly, that judgment is reversed, and the cause is remanded for further proceedings.

▶ ANALYSIS

The appellate jurisdiction of the United States Supreme Court includes the authority to review the decisions of a state court of last resort. However, the Supreme Court may review a state court decision only if it is based upon federal law. This means that any state law decision that is not premised entirely on the resolution of purely state law issues is reviewable. If the Supreme Court could review decisions based solely on state law, the state courts would have no final authority at all. Thus there would be no true separation of the state and federal judicial systems.

■═■

Quicknotes

APPELLATE JURISDICTION The power of a higher court to review the decisions of lower courts.

■═■

Bivens v. Six Unknown Named Agents of the Federal Bureau of Narcotics

Arrestee (P) v. Federal agents (D)

403 U.S. 388 (1971).

NATURE OF CASE: Appeal from an action seeking damages for unreasonable search and seizure.

FACT SUMMARY: Bivens (P), arrested and searched in his home by agents of the Federal Bureau of Narcotics (D), brought suit for damages in federal district court asserting that the arrest and search were effected without a warrant, that unreasonable force was employed, and that the arrest was made without probable cause in derogation of his Fourth Amendment rights.

RULE OF LAW
Violation of a person's Fourth Amendment rights against unreasonable searches and seizures by a federal agent acting under color of his authority gives rise to a cause of action for damages consequent upon his unconstitutional conduct.

FACTS: Bivens (P) brought this action for damages in federal district court against six agents of the Federal Bureau of Narcotics (D) alleging that they entered his home under claim of federal authority and arrested him for narcotics violations. Bivens (P) further contended that the arrest and search were effected without a warrant, that unreasonable force was employed in making the arrest, and that the arrest was made without probable cause. From these actions on the part of the federal agents, Bivens (P) claimed to have suffered humiliation, embarrassment, and mental suffering, and sought $15,000 in damages from each of them. The agents (D) moved for dismissal of the complaint on the ground that it failed to state a cause of action. The district court granted the motion. The court of appeals affirmed.

ISSUE: Does a cause of action for damages arise when a federal agent, acting under color of his authority, violates the Fourth Amendment guarantee against unreasonable searches and seizures?

HOLDING AND DECISION: (Brennan, J.) Yes. Violation of a person's Fourth Amendment rights against unreasonable searches and seizures by a federal agent acting under color of his authority gives rise to a cause of action for damages consequent upon his unconstitutional conduct. The Fourth Amendment operates as a limitation upon the exercise of federal power, regardless of whether the state in whose jurisdiction that power is exercised would prohibit or penalize the identical act if engaged in by a private citizen. And where federally protected rights have been invaded, courts will be alert to adjust their remedies so as to grant the necessary relief. Our cases have long since rejected the notion that the Fourth Amendment proscribes only such conduct as would, if engaged in by private persons, be condemned by state law. Therefore, the agents' (D) argument that the Fourth Amendment serves only as a limitation on federal defenses to a state law claim, and not as an independent limitation upon the exercise of federal power, must be rejected. For just as state law may not authorize federal agents to violate the Fourth Amendment, neither may state law undertake to limit the extent to which federal authority can be exercised. The inevitable consequence of this dual limitation on state power is that the federal question becomes not merely a possible defense to the state law action, but an independent claim sufficient to make out Bivens's (P) cause of action. Since Bivens's (P) complaint states a cause of action under the Fourth Amendment, he is entitled to recover money damages for any injury he has suffered as a result of the agents' (D) violation of the amendment. Although the Fourth Amendment does not in so many words provide for its enforcement by an award of money damages, where legal rights have been invaded, and a federal statute provides for a general right to sue for such invasion, federal courts may use any available remedy to make good the wrong done. Reversed.

CONCURRENCE: (Harlan, J.) The contention that the federal courts are powerless to accord a litigant damages for a claimed invasion of his federal constitutional rights, until Congress expressly authorizes the remedy, cannot rest on the notion that the decision to grant compensatory relief involves a resolution of policy considerations not susceptible to judicial discernment. Thus, in suits for damages based on violations of federal statutes lacking any express authorization of a damages remedy, this Court has authorized such relief where damages are necessary to effectuate the congressional policy underlying the substantive provisions of the statute.

DISSENT: (Black, J.) There can be no doubt that Congress could create a federal cause of action for damages for an unreasonable search in violation of the Fourth Amendment. Although Congress has created such a federal cause of action against state officials acting under color of state law, it has never created such a cause of action against federal officials.

DISSENT: (Burger, C.J.) The majority violates the separation of powers by prescribing a remedy that usurps the legislative function.

Continued on next page.

DISSENT: (Blackmun, J.) The Court's "judicial legislation" will produce an avalanche of new federal cases.

ANALYSIS

Constitutional or statutory federal law, while defining substantive rights, often leaves undetermined the remedies applicable in case the substantive rights are violated. Many cases, of which the *Bivens* case is but one, raise the complex issue of whether constitutional violations are to be solved by state law or by judge-made federal remedies. Such questions often arise when federal regulatory statutes define new rights and duties without creating new remedies which are available for violations of these rights.

■══■

Quicknotes

CAUSE OF ACTION A fact or set of facts the occurrence of which entitles a party to seek judicial relief.

FOURTH AMENDMENT Provides that persons be secure as to their person and private belongings against unreasonable searches and seizures.

REMEDY Compensation for violation of a right or for injuries sustained.

SEARCH AND SEIZURE An inspection conducted in order to obtain evidence to be utilized for the prosecution of a crime and the subsequent taking of such evidence.

■══■

The Federal Question Jurisdiction of the District Courts

Quick Reference Rules of Law

Osborn v. Bank of the United States

State official (D) v. Bank (P)

22 U.S. (9 Wheat) 738 (1824).

NATURE OF CASE: Appeal in action for injunction.

FACT SUMMARY: The Bank of the United States (P) seeks to enjoin Osborn (D), the Ohio state auditor, from enforcing an Ohio law taxing the bank's (P) actions in that state.

🏛 RULE OF LAW
Congress is capable of granting to federal district courts original jurisdiction in any case involving the Constitution, laws or treaties of the United States.

FACTS: On February 8, 1819, the Ohio legislature passed an act that accused the Bank of the United States (P) of operating contrary to Ohio law. The act levied an annual tax of $50,000 on each of the bank's (P) offices of discount and deposit in that state. The bank (P) therefore brought suit in the Ohio federal district court to restrain Osborn (D), the Ohio auditor, from proceeding against the bank (P) under the act. A writ of injunction was issued. However, an amended bill was then brought by the bank (P) charging that Osborn (D) and his employee, Harper (D), had violated the injunction by taking $100,000 from one of the bank's Ohio offices. The circuit court ordered Osborn (D) to return the money with interest. Osborn (D) appealed, arguing that the circuit court had no jurisdiction because: (1) the act of Congress had not given it and (2) under the Constitution, Congress cannot give it. Osborn (D) also argued that the case relied primarily on contract—not on questions of the U.S. Constitution, laws, or treaties—and, as such, only the state court has jurisdiction.

ISSUE: Is Congress capable, under the Constitution, of granting original jurisdiction to federal district courts in any case involving the Constitution, laws, or treaties of the United States?

HOLDING AND DECISION: (Marshall, C.J.) Yes. Congress is capable of granting to federal district courts original jurisdiction in any case involving the Constitution, laws, or treaties of the United States. This principle seems clear from Article III which declares "that the judicial power shall extend to all cases in law and equity arising under this Constitution, the laws of the United States and treaties . . ." But this suit does, in fact, arise under a law of the United States, namely, the act of Congress incorporating the bank (P) and enabling it "to sue and be sued . . . in every circuit court of the United States." As to Osborn's (D) argument that jurisdiction is lacking since this case involves several questions depending on general principles of law—and only on the act incorporating the bank (P)—were that argument valid then the federal court would hardly ever have jurisdiction since few cases totally depend upon the Constitution, laws, or treaties of the United States. With the exception of cases in which original jurisdiction has been given exclusively to the United States Supreme Court, Congress may bestow original or appellate jurisdiction as it chooses. Despite the fact that this case may involve several questions of fact and law depending on general principles—and not on U.S. law—the federal circuit court still has jurisdiction. This is because the law of the United States forms an ingredient in this case. The law in question is the act incorporating the bank (P). That law is deeply involved here since every act of the bank (P) arises from, and is regulated by, that law. The circuit court's order is affirmed as to restitution, but reversed as to interest.

DISSENT: (Johnson, J.) As regards jurisdiction, the Constitution does not confer jurisdiction in cases such as this simply because it is possible that it might give rise to a question involving a U.S. law. Instead, jurisdiction should be found only in those actions—such as patent-right violations—that thoroughly involve U.S. laws. However, in other cases that are primarily founded on general principles—involve U.S. laws—original jurisdiction is not present. To hold otherwise will result in the federal circuit courts having almost unlimited jurisdiction.

▶ ANALYSIS

The basic premise of *Osborn* is described by commentators as being that every case in which a federal question might arise must be capable of being initiated in the federal courts since the issue of jurisdiction must be determined at the outset of the case. And, despite the fact that the federal question might never be actually raised, the case, having been commenced in the federal court, may also be concluded there. The criticism is that there are numerous cases, actually only involving state law, of which it may be said that there is a remote connection with a federal question. It is suggested that Justice Marshall's holding in *Osborn* was greatly influenced by his belief that the bank (P) would receive hostile treatment in state courts.

■=■

Quicknotes

JURISDICTION The authority of a court to hear and declare judgment in respect to a particular matter.

ORIGINAL JURISDICTION The power of a court to hear an action upon its commencement.

■=■

Textile Workers Union v. Lincoln Mills

Union (P) v. Employer (D)

353 U.S. 448 (1957).

NATURE OF CASE: Petition for writ of certiorari in a suit to compel arbitration of a labor-management grievance.

FACT SUMMARY: Textile Workers Union (P) sued in federal court under the Taft-Hartley Act, § 301(a), to compel Lincoln Mills (D), an employer, to submit to arbitration of grievances as provided for in a collective bargaining agreement between the parties.

🏛 RULE OF LAW
The federal courts may fashion a federal substantive law regarding labor contracts in those labor disputes involving federal rights.

FACTS: Textile Workers Union (P) sued in federal court under the Taft-Hartley Act, § 301(a), to compel Lincoln Mills (D), an employer, to submit to arbitration of grievances as provided for in a collective bargaining agreement between the parties. Section 301(a) confers jurisdiction on federal courts to hear actions for violations of labor-management agreements that affect commerce. The issue was whether this grant of jurisdiction was constitutional. The United States Supreme Court granted certiorari.

ISSUE: May the federal courts fashion a federal substantive law regarding labor contracts in those labor disputes involving federal rights?

HOLDING AND DECISION: (Douglas, J.) Yes. The federal courts may fashion a federal substantive law regarding labor contracts in those labor disputes involving federal rights. Therefore, the grant of jurisdiction in § 301(a) is constitutional because it applies to cases governed by federal common law and by definition that arise under federal law.

CONCURRENCE: (Burton, J.) Although, contrary to the majority's conclusion, federal law is not the substantive law to be applied in a suit under § 301 of the Taft-Huntley Act, some federal rights may necessarily be involved, and hence the constitutionality of § 301 can be upheld as a congressional grant to the federal district courts of "protective jurisdiction."

DISSENT: (Frankfurter, J.) Under the concept of so-called "protective jurisdiction," the majority suggests that in any case for which Congress has the constitutional power to prescribe federal rules of decision and thus confer true federal question jurisdiction, it may, without so doing, enact a jurisdictional statute, which will provide a federal forum for the application of state statute and decisional law. Under the protective jurisdiction theory the "arising under the laws of the United States" jurisdiction conferred

by Article III of the Constitution would vastly extend the jurisdiction of federal courts. For example, every contract or tort arising out of a contract affecting commerce might be a potential cause of action in the federal courts, even though only state law was involved in the decision of the case. "Protective jurisdiction," once the label is discarded, cannot be justified under any view of the allowable scope to be given to Article III. Consequently, the suggestion that § 301 permits the federal courts to work out, without more, a federal code governing collective-bargaining contracts must be rejected. There is nothing in Article III that supports the view that original jurisdiction over cases involving federal questions must extend to every case in which there is the potentiality of appellate jurisdiction.

▶ ANALYSIS

The above case is one of the three most celebrated instances of assumption of law-making power by the federal courts based on jurisdictional grants. The second is the power to create federal admiralty law implied from Article III's grant of admiralty jurisdiction. This implication is the source not only of judge-made law but also of Congress's power to legislate on admiralty matters. The third is the law governing litigation between the states: law-making power is there implied from the jurisdictional grant over interstate controversies and justified by the inappropriateness of using any one state's law.

■=■

Quicknotes

JURISDICTION The authority of a court to hear and declare judgment in respect to a particular matter.

LABOR UNION A group of employees formed for the purpose of obtaining more favorable working conditions or wages.

SUBSTANTIVE LAW Law that pertains to the rights and interests of the parties and upon which a cause of action may be based.

■=■

Louisville & Nashville R.R. Co. v. Mottley

Contracting party (D) v. Contracting party (P)

211 U.S. 149 (1908).

NATURE OF CASE: Suit to compel specific performance of a contract.

FACT SUMMARY: The Mottleys (P) were injured in a collision of Louisville & Nashville (D) trains. In exchange for lifetime passes, the Mottleys (P) released the railroad (D) from all claims for damages.

RULE OF LAW
A federal court may not exercise jurisdiction over a case merely because an anticipated defense or the response thereto will involve a federal question.

FACTS: In September of 1871, the Mottleys (P) were injured when the Louisville & Nashville R.R. (D) train in which they were traveling collided with another train owned by the railroad (D). The Mottleys (P) agreed to release the railroad (D) from all potential damage claims, in exchange for which the railroad (D) issued free passes, renewable annually, to both of the Mottleys (P). The railroad (D) sent the passes each year until 1907, when the passes were not renewed, apparently because Congress had enacted a law that precluded common carriers from granting free transportation. The Mottleys (P), who were citizens of Kentucky, sued the railroad (D), also a Kentucky citizen, in federal court. Their suit prayed for specific performance of the railroad's (D) agreement to provide lifetime passes, and asserted that the act of Congress did not prevent the issuance of passes under the circumstances or, that if construed as prohibiting their issuance, the statute was unconstitutional in that it deprived the Mottleys (P) of their property without due process of law. The trial court granted the relief sought, but the railroad (D) appealed directly to the United States Supreme Court.

ISSUE: May federal jurisdiction be exercised in a case if the only federal question involved will arise in connection with an anticipated defense or the response thereto?

HOLDING AND DECISION: (Moody, J.) No. A federal court may not exercise jurisdiction over a case merely because an anticipated defense or the response thereto will involve a federal question. There is no basis for diversity jurisdiction, and the federal law that the Mottleys (P) challenged need not be considered except as a defense offered by the railroad (D). Since the issue of federal law was not raised by the complaint itself, federal jurisdiction did not attach. Thus, although the railroad (D) offered no objection, the court below had no basis for exercising jurisdiction over this case, and should have dismissed the Mottleys' (P) complaint.

ANALYSIS

Federal courts may exercise jurisdiction over cases that present issues arising under the Constitution, laws, or treaties of the United States. This jurisdiction derives from the first paragraph of Article III, § 2 of the Constitution. However, the rule of *Louisville & Nashville R.R. v. Mottley*, that the federal question involved in a case must arise from the plaintiff's complaint, unaided by potential defenses, etc., has been recognized as authoritative. The *Mottley* rule seems reasonable and desirable since a plaintiff could almost always imagine a plausible defense that might reasonably be interposed by his adversary and would involve an issue of federal law.

Quicknotes

DEMURRER The assertion that the opposing party's pleadings are insufficient and that the demurring party should not be made to answer.

FEDERAL COURT JURISDICTION The authority of the federal courts to hear and determine in the first instance matters pertaining to the federal Constitution, federal law, or treaties of the United States.

SUBJECT MATTER JURISDICTION The authority of the court to hear and decide actions involving a particular type of issue or subject.

American Well Works Co. v. Layne & Bowler Co.

Manufacturer (P) v. Patent holder (D)

241 U.S. 257 (1916).

NATURE OF CASE: Suit to recover damages for injuries to a business.

FACT SUMMARY: American (P) manufactured and sold a pump. Layne & Bowler (D) alleged that the pump infringed upon its patent, and threatened to sue American (P) and all purchasers of the product.

🏛 RULE OF LAW
A suit for damages caused to one's business by a threat to sue for patent infringement is not a suit under the patent laws, and therefore may not be maintained in federal court.

FACTS: American Well Works Co. (P) produced and began selling a certain type of pump, allegedly the best on the market. Layne & Bowler (D) claimed that the pump resembled parts of the pump sold by Layne & Bowler (D), and threatened to sue both American (P) and its customers. In fact, suits were actually commenced against some of American's (P) customers. A suit was then filed in state court in which American (P) sought damages for the harm caused to its business by the litigation, threats, and accusations undertaken by Layne & Bowler (D). The action was later removed to federal district court, whereupon American (P) moved to have the case remanded to the state court. The federal tribunal ruled that, since the cause of action had arisen under the patent laws of the United States, the state court had lacked jurisdiction over the case in the first place, and that the federal court was therefore not entitled to exercise removal jurisdiction. On appeal, it was contended that the cause of action was not based on the patent laws and thus presented no federal question.

ISSUE: May a federal court exercise jurisdiction over a suit alleging damages to a business as a result of a threat to sue for patent infringement?

HOLDING AND DECISION: (Holmes, J.) No. A suit for damages caused to one's business by a threat to sue for patent infringement is not a suit under the patent laws, and therefore may not be maintained in federal court. Such an action presents no federal question because it is not the patent, but the damage caused to the business, which is the basis for the cause of action. Whether or not the type of interference that has been alleged is actionable is purely a matter of state law. Therefore, this suit is not one to which federal jurisdiction attaches. Reversed.

DISSENT: (McKenna, J.) The case clearly involves a controversy arising under the patent laws, and thus presents a federal question.

▶ ANALYSIS

The authority of the federal courts to exercise jurisdiction over patent matters is expressly conferred by 28 U.S.C. § 1338. However, federal decisional law has made it clear that the state courts have jurisdiction over many actions involving aspects of patent law. The various decisions apportioning jurisdiction over patent matters between state and federal courts are not entirely reconcilable, but they obviously demonstrate the fact that a litigant in a patent case has considerable latitude in deciding whether to proceed in a state or a federal forum.

Quicknotes

PATENT A limited monopoly conferred on the invention or discovery of any new or useful machine or process that is novel and non-obvious.

Grable & Sons Metal Products, Inc. v. Darue Engineering & Manufacturing

Former owner of seized property (P) v. New owner (D)

545 U.S. 308 (2005).

NATURE OF CASE: Review of federal appeals court decision.

FACT SUMMARY: Property owned by Grable & Sons Metal Products, Inc. (Grable) (P) that was was seized and sold because Grable (P) was delinquent in paying its federal taxes. Grable (P) sued the new owner, Darue Engineering & Manufacturing (Darue) (D), claiming that the Internal Revenue Service should have provided notice by personal service, according to federal tax law. Darue (D) removed the case to federal court.

> ## RULE OF LAW
> A case involving the interpretation of federal tax law may be removed to federal court from state court.

FACTS: In 1994, the Internal Revenue Service (IRS) seized property owned by Grable & Sons Metal Products (P) to satisfy Grable's (P) tax debt, and gave Grable (P) notice by certified mail before selling the property to Darue Engineering and Manufacturing (D). Grable (P) received the notice. Grable (P) later sued in state court, claiming Darue's (D) title was invalid because federal law required the IRS to give Grable (P) notice of the sale by personal service, not certified mail. Darue (D) removed the case to federal district court, arguing that the case presented a federal question because Grable's (P) claim depended on an interpretation of federal tax law. The district court agreed and ruled for Darue (D). The Sixth Circuit affirmed.

ISSUE: May a case involving the interpretation of federal tax law be removed to federal court from state court?

HOLDING AND DECISION: (Souter, J.) Yes. A case involving the interpretation of federal tax law may be removed to federal court from state court. The case involved a federal question and could thus be removed to federal court. The case implicated serious federal issues. The national interest in providing a federal forum for federal tax litigation warranted removing the case to federal court. Affirmed.

CONCURRENCE: (Thomas, J.) The decision authorizes federal-court jurisdiction over some cases in which state law creates the cause of action but requires determination of issues of federal law. No one in this case asked the court to overrule those precedents and adopt the rule of *American Well Works Co. v. Layne & Bowler Co.*, 241 U.S. 257 (1916), limiting jurisdiction on these facts to cases in which federal law creates the cause of action pleaded on the fact of the pleadings, but in the appropriate case, the court may go that route.

▶ ANALYSIS

The Supreme Court was unanimous in affirming the Third Circuit's decision by holding that the national interest in providing a federal forum for federal tax litigation is sufficiently substantial to support the exercise of federal question jurisdiction. The interests of the United States are affected by the case, via the federal tax law. Otherwise, the case would have been a state cause of action.

■■■

Quicknotes

CAUSE OF ACTION A fact or set of facts the occurrence of which entitles a party to seek judicial relief.

JURISDICTION The authority of a court to hear and declare judgment in respect to a particular matter.

NOTICE Communication of information to a person by one authorized or by an otherwise proper source.

TITLE The right of possession over property.

■■■

Skelly Oil Co. v. Phillips Petroleum Co.

Oil pipeline company (D) v. Subcontractor oil pipeline company (P)

339 U.S. 667 (1950).

NATURE OF CASE: Appeal from a decision of the court of appeals upholding a contract interpretation.

FACT SUMMARY: When Phillips Petroleum Co. (P), invoking the Federal Declaratory Judgment Act, sued Skelly Oil Co. (D) in federal court for breach of contract, Skelly (D) argued that the Declaratory Judgment Act did not confer jurisdiction over declaratory actions when the underlying dispute could not otherwise have been heard in a federal court.

RULE OF LAW

The Declaratory Judgment Act does not confer jurisdiction over declaratory actions when the underlying dispute could not otherwise have been heard in federal court.

FACTS: Phillips Oil Company (P) subcontracted with Skelly Oil Company (D) to provide natural gas for it. The contract provided that a certificate was required from the Federal Power Commission before oil transmission could begin. The certificate was issued with certain qualifications. Skelly (D), however, did not receive timely notice of the issuance of the certificate and gave Phillips (P) notice that it was terminating the oil distribution contract. Phillips (P), invoking the Federal Declaratory Judgment Act, thereupon brought suit in the federal district court against Skelly (D) alleging that the proper Federal Power Commission certificate had in fact been issued, hence the contract should be enforced. The district court agreed with Phillips (P), and the court of appeals affirmed. Skelly (D) appealed to the United States Supreme Court, arguing that the Declaratory Judgment Act did not confer jurisdiction over declaratory actions when, as here, the underlying dispute could not otherwise have been heard in federal court.

ISSUE: Does the Declaratory Judgment Act confer jurisdiction over declaratory actions when the underlying dispute could not otherwise have been heard in federal court?

HOLDING AND DECISION: (Frankfurter, J.) No. The Declaratory Judgment Act (Act) does not confer jurisdiction over declaratory actions when the underlying dispute could not otherwise have been heard in federal court. The operation of the Act is procedural only. By means of this legislation, Congress enlarged the range of remedies available in the federal courts but did not extend their jurisdiction. Prior to the Act, a federal court would entertain a suit on a contract only if the plaintiff asked for an immediately enforceable remedy like money damages or an injunction, but such relief could only be given if the requisites of jurisdiction, in the sense of a federal right or diversity, provided a foundation for resort to the federal courts. The Act allowed relief to be given by way of recognizing the plaintiff's right even though no immediate enforcement of it was asked. Nevertheless, the requirements of jurisdiction—the limited subject matters that alone Congress had authorized the district courts to adjudicate—were not impliedly repealed or modified. Here, for example, if Phillips (P) sought damages from Skelly Oil (D) or specific performance of their contracts, it would not bring suit in a federal district court on the theory that it was asserting a federal right. Whatever federal claim Phillips (P) may be able to urge would in any event be injected into the case only in anticipation of a defense to be asserted by Skelly Oil (D). It has long been settled that a plaintiff's claim itself must present a federal question "unaided by anything alleged in anticipation of avoidance of defenses which it is thought the defendant may interpose." To be observant of these restrictions is not to indulge in formalism or sterile technicality. To hold otherwise would turn into the federal courts a vast current of litigation indubitably arising under state law in the sense that the right to be vindicated was state-created. Reversed.

DISSENT: (Vinson, C.J.) There are "real doubts" as to whether there is a federal question here at all, even though interpretation of the contract between private parties requires an interpretation of a federal statute and the action of a federal regulatory body.

ANALYSIS

In *Skelly*, the Supreme Court explained that to permit the Declaratory Judgment Act to confer jurisdiction over declaratory actions when the underlying dispute could not otherwise have been heard in federal court, not only would unduly swell the volume of litigation in the district courts but it would also embarrass those courts and the Supreme Court on potential review since matters of local law might often be involved, and the district courts might either have to decide doubtful questions of state law or hold cases pending disposition of such state issues by state courts.

■■■

Quicknotes

DECLARATORY JUDGMENT ACT Allows prospective defendants to sue for a declaration of their rights.

■■■

United Mine Workers of America v. Gibbs

Union (D) v. Former non-union employee (P)

383 U.S. 715 (1966).

NATURE OF CASE: Action to recover damages for violation of § 303 of the Labor Management Relations Act and for interference with a business interest.

FACT SUMMARY: Gibbs (P) lost his job as superintendent of a coal mining company because of alleged unlawful influence of United Mine Workers (D).

🏛 **RULE OF LAW**
Under pendent jurisdiction, federal courts may decide state issues that are closely related to the federal issues being litigated.

FACTS: There was a dispute between United Mine Workers (D) and the Southern Labor Union over who should represent the coal miners in that area. Tennessee Consolidated Coal Company closed down a mine where more than 100 men belonging to United Mine Workers (D) were employed. Later, Grundy Company, a wholly owned subsidiary of Tennessee Consolidated Coal Company hired Gibbs (P) to open a new mine using members of the Southern Labor Union. Gibbs (P) was also given a contract to haul the mine's coal to the nearest railroad loading point. Members of Local 5881 of the United Mine Workers (D) forcibly prevented the opening of the mine. Gibbs (P) lost his job and never entered into performance of his haulage contract. He soon began to lose other trucking contracts and mine leases he held in the area. Gibbs (P) claims this was a result of a concerted union plan against him. He filed suit in the U.S. district court of the Eastern District of Tennessee for violation of § 303 of the Labor Management Relations Act and a state law claim, based on the doctrine of pendent jurisdiction, that there was an unlawful conspiracy and boycott aimed at him to interfere with his contract of employment and with his contract of haulage. The jury's verdict was that the United Mine Workers (D) had violated both § 303 and the state law. On motion, the trial court set aside the verdict for United Mine Workers (D) on the issue of violation of § 303, which was the federal claim. The award as to the state claim was sustained. The court of appeals affirmed.

ISSUE: Under pendent jurisdiction, can federal courts decide state issues that are closely related to the federal issues being litigated?

HOLDING AND DECISION: (Brennan, J.) Yes. Under pendent jurisdiction, federal courts may decide state issues that are closely related to the federal issues being litigated. When there are both state and federal claims involved in the same set of facts and the claims are such that the plaintiff would ordinarily be expected to try them all in one judicial proceeding, the federal court has the power to hear both the state and the federal claims. The federal claims must have substance sufficient to confer subject matter jurisdiction on the court. This is the doctrine of pendent jurisdiction. The court is not required to exercise this power in every case. It has consistently been recognized that pendent jurisdiction is a doctrine of discretion, not of plaintiff's right. The court should look at judicial economy, convenience, and fairness to litigants in deciding whether to exercise jurisdiction over the state claims. If the factual relationship between the state and federal claims is so close that they ought to be litigated at the same trial, the court ought to grant pendent jurisdiction in order to save an extra trial. If the issues are so complicated that they are confusing to the jury then the court probably should dismiss the state claims. The issue of whether pendent jurisdiction has been properly assumed is one that remains open throughout the litigation. If, before the trial, the federal claim is dismissed, then the state claim should also be dismissed. If it appears that a state claim constitutes the real body of a case, then it may fairly be dismissed. [The Supreme Court went on to hold that the plaintiff could not recover damages for conspiracy under the state claim. To that effect, the judgment was reversed.]

▶ *ANALYSIS*

This case helped clarify the law that had been established by the case of *Hurn v. Oursler*, 289 U.S. 238, 53 S. Ct. 586, 77 L. Ed. 1148. This case set the rule for determining if a federal court could hear the state claim. If a case had two distinct grounds in support of a single cause of action, one of which presents a federal question, then the court should hear the state claim. But if a case had two separate and distinct causes of action and only one was a federal question, then the court could not hear the state claim. Now the state and federal claims can state separate causes of action as long as they are factually closely related.

▬▬▬

Quicknotes

LABOR MANAGEMENT RELATIONS ACT Federal law prohibiting secondary boycotts.

PENDENT JURISDICTION A doctrine granting authority to a federal court to hear a claim that does not invoke diversity jurisdiction if it arises from the same transaction or occurrence as the primary action.

▬▬▬

Suits Challenging Official Action

Quick Reference Rules of Law

United States v. Lee

Federal government (D) v. Property owner (P)

106 U.S. 196 (1882).

NATURE OF CASE: Appeal from order of ejectment.

FACT SUMMARY: Lee (P), the son of General Robert E. Lee, filed an ejectment action against the government (D), alleging that the government (D) did not acquire valid title to Lee's (P) land under a tax sale proceeding.

🏛 RULE OF LAW
The doctrine of sovereign immunity is not permitted to interfere with the judicial enforcement of the established rights of plaintiffs when the United States is not a defendant or a necessary party to the suit.

FACTS: The government (D) purchased the estate of General Robert E. Lee's wife after an alleged failure to pay a $92 assessment under a tax to support the Civil War. The tax commissioners had refused a proffer of payment on behalf of the owner, under a rule (later held invalid) that only the owner in person could pay overdue taxes. The government (D) proceeded to use part of the estate for the Arlington Cemetery and a fort. Lee (P), the Lees' son, who claimed title to the property under his grandfather's will, filed an ejectment action in state court against the two federal officers who had charge of the property. The officers removed the action to the circuit court for the Eastern District of Virginia. Though the government (P) was not a party in the action, the attorney general filed a pleading in the circuit court seeking a dismissal of the suit, stating that the government (D) was in possession of the property in the exercise of its sovereign and constitutional powers, and that the court had no jurisdiction over the subject in controversy. The court ruled for Lee (P) after a jury trial and both the two federal officers and the government (D) filed a writ of error in the United States Supreme Court.

ISSUE: Is the doctrine of sovereign immunity permitted to interfere with the judicial enforcement of the established rights of plaintiffs when the United States is not a defendant or a necessary party to the suit?

HOLDING AND DECISION: (Miller, J.) No. The doctrine of sovereign immunity is not permitted to interfere with the judicial enforcement of the established rights of plaintiffs when the United States is not a defendant or a necessary party to the suit. Courts of justice are established, not only to decide upon the controverted rights of the citizens as against each other, but also upon the rights in controversy between them and the government. Shall it be said, when there is an acknowledged right of the judiciary to decide in proper cases, that statutes that

have been passed by both branches of Congress and approved by the president are unconstitutional, that the courts cannot give a remedy when the citizen has been deprived of his property by force, his estate seized and converted to the use of the government without lawful authority, without process of law, and without compensation, as has happened to Lee (P) here, because the president has ordered it and his officers are in possession? If such be the law of this country, it sanctions a tyranny that has no existence in the monarchies of Europe, nor in any government that has a just claim to well-regulated liberty and the protection of personal rights. Affirmed.

DISSENT: (Gray, J.) This case deeply affects the sovereignty of the United States, and its relations to the citizen. The sovereign is not liable to be sued in any judicial tribunal without its consent. The sovereign cannot hold property except by agents. To invade such possession of the property of the agents, by execution or other judicial process, is to invade the possession of the sovereign, and to disregard the fundamental maxim that the sovereign cannot be sued.

▶ ANALYSIS

The doctrine of sovereign immunity, as it developed in England prior to 1789, was less about whether the Crown or its agents could be sued than about how. In some instances, officers could be sued for damages, enjoined from doing wrong, or compelled to perform their duty. In other cases, relief could be obtained through resort to the petition of right, which permitted suits directly against the Crown. This remedy required consent by the sovereign, however.

Quicknotes

EJECTMENT An action to oust someone in unlawful possession of real property and to restore possession to the party lawfully entitled to it.

SOVEREIGN IMMUNITY Immunity of government from suit without its consent.

Hans v. Louisiana

Holder of state bonds (P) v. State (D)

134 U.S. 1 (1890).

NATURE OF CASE: Appeal from judgment dismissing action.

FACT SUMMARY: Hans (P), a citizen of Louisiana (D), sued the state in federal court to recover money.

🏛 RULE OF LAW
Under the Eleventh Amendment, the judicial authority of the federal court does not extend to a suit against a state by one of its citizens.

FACTS: Hans (P) purchased bonds issued by Louisiana (D) with the approval of the 1874 Louisiana legislature. The bonds Hans (P) purchased contained coupons that could be exchanged for interest payments. The Louisiana (D) legislature later amended the state constitution to include a provision that barred the state from making interest payments on the bonds. Hans (P) sued Louisiana (D) in federal court seeking interest payments on the bonds. Hans (P) alleged that the amended Louisiana Constitution violated Article I, § 10 of the Constitution, which states that no state shall pass any law impairing the obligation of contracts. The federal district court dismissed the action for failure to state a claim. Hans (P) appealed.

ISSUE: Does the Eleventh Amendment bar suits against a state by one of its citizens?

HOLDING AND DECISION: (Bradley, J.) Yes. Under the Eleventh Amendment, the judicial authority of federal courts does not extend to a suit against a state by one of its citizens. The Eleventh Amendment states, "The Judicial power of the United States shall not be construed to extend to any suit in law or equity, commenced or prosecuted against one of the United States by Citizens of another State, or by Citizens or Subjects of any Foreign State." If a citizen were allowed to sue the state government in a federal court, the language of the Constitution and the Eleventh Amendment would be constrained in a manner never imagined or contemplated by the drafters. States may only be sued with their consent. Since Louisiana (D) did not assent to Hans's (P) action, it is barred by the Eleventh Amendment. Affirmed.

CONCURRENCE: (Harlan, J.) The comments made upon the decision in *Chisholm v. Georgia* do not meet my approval. They are not necessary to the determination of the present case. Besides, the decision in that case was based upon a sound interpretation of the Constitution as that instrument then was.

▶ **ANALYSIS**

The Eleventh Amendment was adopted to prevent cases similar to the 1793 case, *Chisholm v. Georgia*, 2 U.S. 419, wherein a citizen of one state sued another state. The majority opinion attacked the validity of that decision, but Justice Harlan's concurrence defended it. The Eleventh Amendment has since been interpreted to prevent suits against a state by citizens of another state, citizens of the same state, or aliens, unless the state consents to suit.

■═■

Quicknotes

ELEVENTH AMENDMENT The Eleventh Amendment to the United States Constitution prohibits the extension of the judicial powers of the federal courts to suits brought against a state by citizens of another state, or of a foreign state, without the state's consent.

■═■

Ex parte Young

[Parties not identified.]

209 U.S. 123 (1908).

NATURE OF CASE: Derivative action challenging state railroad rates.

FACT SUMMARY: In a derivative action brought by shareholders of various railroads, alleging that state legislation regulating railroad rates was confiscatory and violated the Fourteenth Amendment, Young (D), the attorney general of Minnesota, the state in which the action was brought, defended his enforcement of the legislation under the Eleventh Amendment.

🏛 RULE OF LAW
If an act that a state attorney general seeks to enforce is a violation of the federal Constitution, the officer, in proceeding under the act, comes into conflict with the superior authority of the Constitution and is stripped of his official character and is subject, in his person, to the consequences of his individual conduct.

FACTS: Shareholders of various railroads brought a derivative action in federal court, alleging that the Minnesota state legislation regulating railroad rates was confiscatory and violated the Fourteenth Amendment. The trial court entered a temporary restraining order prohibiting Young (D), Minnesota's attorney general, from enforcing the legislation. Young (D) moved to dismiss the action under the Eleventh Amendment, and the court denied the motion, instead entering a preliminary injunction against enforcement of the legislation. Young (D) then defied the injunction by filing a state court action seeking to enforce the legislation against the railroads. The circuit court held Young (D) in contempt, again rejecting his Eleventh Amendment defense. Young (D) then filed an application in the United States Supreme Court for leave to file a petition for writs of habeas corpus and certiorari.

ISSUE: If an act that a state attorney general seeks to enforce is a violation of the federal Constitution, and the officer, in proceeding under the act, comes into conflict with the superior authority of the Constitution, is he stripped of his official character and is he subject, in his person, to the consequences of his individual conduct?

HOLDING AND DECISION: (Peckham, J.) Yes. If an act that a state attorney general seeks to enforce is a violation of the federal Constitution, the officer, in proceeding under the act, comes into conflict with the superior authority of the Constitution and is stripped of his official character and is subject, in his person, to the consequences of his individual conduct. If the act to be enforced is alleged to be unconstitutional, and if it be unconstitutional, the use of the name of the state to enforce an unconstitutional act is a proceeding without the authority of, and one that does not affect, the state in its sovereign or governmental capacity. Here, the provisions of the Minnesota legislation relating to the enforcement of rates, by imposing such enormous fines and possible imprisonment as a result of an unsuccessful effort to test the validity of the laws themselves, are unconstitutional on their face, without regard to the question of insufficiency of these rates. Here, Young (D) used the name of the state to enforce a legislative enactment that is void because unconstitutional. The state has no power to impart to him any immunity from responsibility to the supreme authority of the United States. Affirmed.

DISSENT: (Harlan, J.) It would seem clear that within the meaning of the Eleventh Amendment, this suit brought here in the federal court was one, in legal effect, against the state—as much so as if the state had been formally named on the record as a party—and, therefore, it was a suit to which, under the amendment, so far as the state or its attorney general was concerned, the judicial power of the United States did not and could not extend.

▶ ANALYSIS

The Eleventh Amendment applies by its terms only in the federal courts. The amendment does not bar suits against a state by another state or by the United States. The amendment also does not bar an individual's suit, in federal court, against a local government body on the grounds that a municipal corporation is more closely analogous to a private corporation than to a state government.

Quicknotes

ELEVENTH AMENDMENT The Eleventh Amendment to the United States Constitution prohibits the extension of the judicial powers of the federal courts to suits brought against a state by citizens of another state, or of a foreign state, without the state's consent.

IMMUNITY Exemption from a legal obligation.

STATE ACTION Actions brought pursuant to the Fourteenth Amendment claiming that the government violated the plaintiff's civil rights.

WRIT OF HABEAS CORPUS A proceeding in which a defendant brings a writ to compel a judicial determination of whether he is lawfully being held in custody.

Seminole Tribe of Florida v. Florida

Native American tribe (P) v. State (D)

517 U.S. 44 (1996).

NATURE OF CASE: Appeal from dismissal of complaint alleging failure to negotiate in good faith over the operation of gambling casinos on tribal land.

FACT SUMMARY: The Seminole Tribe (P) sued the State of Florida (D) for refusing to enter into negotiations with it as required by the Indian Gaming Regulatory Act, but Florida (D) argued that the suit was barred by the Eleventh Amendment.

🏛 RULE OF LAW
The Indian Commerce Clause does not grant Congress the power to abrogate the states' sovereign immunity.

FACTS: The Indian Gaming Regulatory Act provided that an Indian tribe may conduct certain gaming activities as long as they conformed with a valid compact between the tribe and its resident state. The Act imposed on the states a duty to negotiate in good faith with an Indian tribe in order to create the compact. It also authorized a tribe to bring suit in federal court against a state in order to compel performance of that duty. The Seminole Tribe of Indians (P) sued the State of Florida (D) and its Governor (D), alleging that they had refused to enter into any such negotiations, thereby violating the Act. Florida (D) moved to dismiss the complaint, arguing that the suit violated Florida's (D) sovereign immunity from suit in federal court. The district court rejected Florida's (D) argument and denied the motion. On interlocutory appeal, however, the Eleventh Circuit reversed, holding that the Eleventh Amendment barred the Tribe's (P) suit. It remanded to the district court with directions to dismiss the case. (But it also concluded that the rest of the Gaming Regulatory Act would remain intact, permitting a tribe immediate recourse to the Interior Department.) The Tribe (D) petitioned for certiorari, and the United States Supreme Court granted review.

ISSUE: Does the Indian Commerce Clause grant Congress the power to abrogate the states' sovereign immunity?

HOLDING AND DECISION: (Rehnquist, C.J.) No. The Indian Commerce Clause does not grant Congress the power to abrogate the states' sovereign immunity. Congress has provided an unmistakably clear statement in the Indian Gaming Regulatory Act of its intent to abrogate the immunity, but that immunity is only constitutional if the Act itself was passed pursuant to a valid exercise of power. Authority to abrogate exists under only two Constitutional provisions: the Fourteenth Amendment and the Interstate Commerce Clause, pursuant to *Pennsylvania v. Union Gas Co.*, 491 U.S. 1 (1989). However, *Union Gas* has

proven to be a solitary departure from established law, and insofar as it departs from the established understanding of Eleventh Amendment immunity and Article III jurisdiction, it is hereby overruled. Even when the Constitution vests in Congress complete law-making authority over a particular area, like the regulation of Indian commerce, the Eleventh Amendment prevents congressional authorization of suits by private parties against unconsenting states. The Indian Commerce Clause cannot be used to circumvent the constitutional limitations placed on judicial power by the Eleventh Amendment. The Eleventh Amendment prohibits Congress from making Florida (D) capable of being sued in federal court. The Tribe's (P) suit against Florida (D) and the Governor (D) must be dismissed for a lack of jurisdiction. Affirmed.

DISSENT: (Stevens, J.) The majority's misguided decision to overrule *Union Gas* does not simply preclude Congress from ensuring Indian tribes a forum in which to secure a state's good negotiations; it also prevents Congress from providing a federal forum for a broad range of actions against states, including those concerning copyright and patent law, bankruptcy, environmental, and economic regulations. In any event, since a tribe can get authorization to open a casino directly from the Executive Branch even though it cannot sue a state or its governor, this opinion may have no precedential significance.

DISSENT: (Souter, J.) Neither text, precedent, nor history supports the majority's abdication of the Court's responsibility to exercise the jurisdiction entrusted to us by Article III. First, it is not clear whether the states enjoyed sovereign immunity if sued in their own courts in the period prior to ratification of the Constitution. Second, after ratification, the states were not entitled to claim such immunity when sued in a federal court exercising jurisdiction either because the suit was between a state and a nonstate litigant who was not its citizen, or because the issue in the case raised a federal question. Passage of the Eleventh Amendment did not change this with regard to federal questions, and the Court in its decision in *Hans v. Louisiana*, 134 U.S. 1 (1890), erroneously assumed that a state could plead sovereign immunity against a noncitizen suing under federal-question jurisdiction, and for that reason held that a state must enjoy the same protection in a suit by one of its citizens. Finally, the majority's holding that no state sovereign immunity recognized in federal court may be abrogated by Congress is at odds with the Founders' view that common law, when it was received into the new American legal system, was always subject to

Continued on next page.

legislative amendment. Under the new system, sovereignty would be divided between the states and the nation, with the nation having the right to prevail against the states whenever their laws might conflict. Even during the time of the ratification, as now, there was no textual support for the proposition that Article III incorporated state sovereign immunity into the Constitution. Moreover, the Eleventh Amendment only reached suits subject to federal jurisdiction exclusively under the Citizen-State Diversity Clauses. If the Framers had meant the Eleventh Amendment to bar federal question suits, they would have more clearly done so, and could, to this end, have drawn on language already in legislation proposed at the time. Such an interpretation also comports with the Court's own repeated exercise of appellate jurisdiction in federal-question suits brought against states in their own courts by out-of-staters, since otherwise exercising appellate jurisdiction would have been patently erroneous given that the Amendment does not distinguish between trial and appellate jurisdiction. Pronouncements to the contrary, whether in *Hans*, or other subsequent cases, were either erroneous, since they were not based on the consideration of whether Congress could abrogate sovereign immunity from federal question actions, or were dicta. Instead, many subsequent decisions opined that such immunity was not of constitutional stature, and the Court ignored dicta to the contrary. Further, there is a line of cases that assumed that Congress has the power to abrogate state sovereign immunity even when § 5 of the Fourteenth Amendment has no application. The Court in *Hans* erred not only because it misread the Eleventh Amendment and misunderstood the conditions under which common-law doctrines—including state sovereign immunity—were handled by the Founders, but because it was mistaken as to the nature of such immunity in the new Republic. Thus, neither the *Hans* court nor the majority here can reasonably argue that the old common law doctrine of immunity survived the Constitution's failure to make any provision for adoption of common law as such. This view is supported by the Framers' own disagreements about the degree to which common law immunity would survive in the face of federal law questions—and their failure to directly address the question of congressional abrogation. Given "the Framers' general concern with curbing abuses by state governments, it would be amazing if the scheme of delegated powers embodied in the Constitution had left the national government powerless to render the states judicially accountable for violations of federal rights." The majority's constitutionalizing the common law at the expense of Congress flies in the face of the Framers' abhorrence of the notion that common law rules would be beyond legislative reach in the new republic. The majority's holding also raises the question of whether federal question jurisdiction exists to order prospective relief enforcing IGRA against a state officer. The answer is "yes" under *Ex Parte Young*, 209 U.S. 123 (1908); the officer is subject to suit, and the case should have been decided on that basis alone. IGRA's jurisdictional provision reads as though it had been drafted with the specific intent to apply to officer liability under *Young*, so it would not make sense that Congress would have intended to jeopardize enforcement of the statute by excluding application of *Young*'s traditional jurisdictional rule, when that rule would make the difference between success or failure in the federal court if state sovereign immunity was recognized. Barring application of *Young*, Congress's power to abrogate *Hans* immunity should be recognized, even though *Hans* may still be accepted as stare decisis, since it is not completely unworkable regarding federal common law. A plain statement requirement is sufficient to protect the states from undue federal encroachments upon their traditional immunity from suit, and this approach, which has worked well until now, should not be abandoned.

▶ *ANALYSIS*

As a practical matter, states may still be sued to enforce the right to equal protection guaranteed by the Fourteenth Amendment. The Fourteenth Amendment, Chief Justice Rehnquist conceded, was adopted well after the adoption of the Eleventh Amendment and actually altered the pre-existing balance between state and federal power. States may also be sued by the federal government and by individuals seeking to prohibit future illegal actions. Suits to enforce rights granted by Congress pursuant to the Commerce Clause, however, will most likely be strictly limited by this decision.

■■■

Quicknotes

COMMERCE CLAUSE Article 1, section 8, clause 3 of the Constitution, granting Congress the power to regulate commerce with foreign countries and among the states.

ELEVENTH AMENDMENT The Eleventh Amendment to the United States Constitution prohibits the extension of the judicial powers of the federal courts to suits brought against a state by citizens of another state, or of a foreign state, without the state's consent.

FOURTEENTH AMENDMENT Declares that no state shall make or enforce any law that shall abridge the privileges and immunities of citizens of the United States. No state shall deny to any person within its jurisdiction the equal protection of the laws.

JURISDICTION The authority of a court to hear and declare judgment in respect to a particular matter.

SOVEREIGN IMMUNITY Immunity of government from suit without its consent.

■■■

Home Telephone & Telegraph Co. v. City of Los Angeles

Utility (P) v. Municipality (D)

227 U.S. 278 (1913).

NATURE OF CASE: Suit seeking injunctive relief.

FACT SUMMARY: Los Angeles (D) passed an ordinance that established the rates that Home Telephone (P) could charge to its customers.

🏛 RULE OF LAW

The federal courts may exercise jurisdiction over suits alleging that state officials have violated the Fourteenth Amendment to the federal Constitution, even though no state court has yet considered the possibility that the conduct complained of has likewise abridged the state constitution.

FACTS: Home Telephone & Telegraph Co. (P) sued the city of Los Angeles (D) and certain of its officials (D) to enjoin the enforcement of an ordinance that established the rates that could be charged by Home (P). The rates, Home (P) alleged, were so unreasonably low that their enforcement would amount to a confiscation, without due process and therefore in violation of the Fourteenth Amendment to the federal Constitution, of Home's (P) property. The City (D) challenged the jurisdiction of the federal district court to entertain the suit, arguing that that court should not consider the matter until the state courts had had an opportunity to decide whether enforcement of the ordinance would violate a provision of the California Constitution. The district court, persuaded by the City's (D) argument, dismissed the action for want of jurisdiction. Home (P) then appealed directly to the United States Supreme Court.

ISSUE: Must a federal court await a state court consideration of possible state constitutional violations before exercising jurisdiction over a case alleging that state officials have abridged the Fourteenth Amendment to the federal Constitution?

HOLDING AND DECISION: (White, C.J.) No. The federal courts may exercise jurisdiction over suits alleging that state officials have violated the Fourteenth Amendment to the federal Constitution, even though no state court has yet considered the possibility that the conduct complained of has likewise abridged the state constitution. The trial court relied upon some ill-considered decisions that required parallel state constitutional provisions to be evaluated before a federal court could consider whether or not the conduct of a state official abrogated the Fourteenth Amendment. But this approach gravely undermines the prophylactic purposes of that amendment. Thus, the trial court's holding forecloses an effective avenue of relief from the improper conduct of state officials. This result, in view of the magnitude of the harm that may be visited upon a citizen by reason of officials' actions, is untenable. It follows that the judgment of the trial court must be reversed.

▶ ANALYSIS

At least in theory, a person has a right to redress in the federal courts if a state official acts to deprive him of a right guaranteed by the federal Constitution. This is because an action that claims that such conduct has occurred presents a federal question. Moreover, 42 U.S.C § 1983 provides: "Every person who, under color of any statute, ordinance, regulation, custom, or usage, of any state or territory, subjects, or causes to be subjected, any citizen of the United States or other person within the jurisdiction thereof to the deprivation of any rights, privileges, or immunities secured by the Constitution and laws, shall be liable to the party injured in an action at law, suit in equity, or other proper proceeding for redress."

Quicknotes

FOURTEENTH AMENDMENT Declares that no state shall make or enforce any law that shall abridge the privileges and immunities of citizens of the United States. No state shall deny to any person within its jurisdiction the equal protection of the laws.

JURISDICTION The authority of a court to hear and declare judgment in respect to a particular matter.

Monroe v. Pape

Arrestee (P) v. Municipal representative (D)

365 U.S. 167 (1961).

NATURE OF CASE: Appeal from dismissal of action brought under 42 U.S.C. § 1983.

FACT SUMMARY: Monroe (P) sued Pape (D), who represented the city of Chicago, under 42 U.S.C. § 1983 after thirteen Chicago police officers allegedly invaded Monroe's (P) home, searched without a warrant, and arrested and detained Monroe (P) without a warrant and without arraignment.

RULE OF LAW
An action under 42 U.S.C. § 1983 is supplementary to a state remedy, and the state remedy need not be first sought and refused before the federal one is invoked.

FACTS: Monroe (P) sued Pape (D), the representative for the city of Chicago, under 42 U.S.C. § 1983, after thirteen Chicago police officers allegedly invaded Monroe's (P) home, searched without a warrant, and arrested and detained Monroe (P) without a warrant and without arraignment. Monroe's (P) complaint further alleged that the officers acted under color of the statutes, ordinances, regulations, customs, and usages of the state of Illinois and the city of Chicago and that those acts deprived Monroe (P) of rights, privileges, and immunities secured by the Constitution. The city of Chicago moved to dismiss the complaint on the ground that it was not liable under the Civil Rights Acts or for acts committed in performance of its governmental functions. The city and the police officers also moved to dismiss, alleging that the complaint alleged no cause of action under the Civil Rights Acts or under the federal Constitution. The district court dismissed the complaint, the court of appeals affirmed, and Monroe (P) appealed.

ISSUE: Is an action under 42 U.S.C. § 1983 supplementary to a state remedy, and need the state remedy first be sought and refused before the federal one is invoked?

HOLDING AND DECISION: (Douglas, J.) Yes. An action under 42 U.S.C. § 1983 is supplementary to a state remedy, and the state remedy need not be first sought and refused before the federal one is invoked. It is abundantly clear that one main reason 42 U.S.C. § 1983 was passed was to afford a federal right in federal courts because, by reason of prejudice, passion, neglect, intolerance, or otherwise, state laws might not be enforced and the claims of citizens to the enjoyment of rights, privleges, and immunities guaranteed by the Fourteenth Amendment might be denied by the state agencies. Here, Pape (D) and the city argued that "under color of" enumerated state authority excludes acts of an official or policeman who can show no authority under state law. Pape (D) also argued that the police, in breaking into Monroe's (P) apartment, violated the laws of Illinois,

that under Illinois law a simple remedy is offered for that violation, and that, thus, Illinois courts are available to give Monroe (P) full redress. However, it is no answer that a state has a law that, if enforced, would give relief. The fact that Illinois by its constitution outlaws unreasonable searches and seizures is no barrier to the present suit in federal court. Reversed and remanded.

CONCURRENCE: (Harlan, J.) One should hesitate to assume that the proponents of the present statute, who regarded it as necessary even though they knew that the provisions of the Fourteenth Amendment were self-executing, would have thought the remedies unnecessary whenever there were self-executing provisions of state constitutions also forbidding what the Fourteenth Amendment forbids.

DISSENT: (Frankfurter, J.) The jurisdiction that Article III of the Constitution conferred on the national judiciary reflected the assumption that the state courts, not the federal courts, would remain the primary guardians of that fundamental security of person and property that the long evaluation of the common law had secured to one individual as against other individuals. The Fourteenth Amendment did not alter this basic aspect of our federalism.

ANALYSIS

To recover under 42 U.S.C. § 1983 for a constitutional tort in violation of the Fourteenth Amendment, a plaintiff must establish that the violation resulted from "state action." In a suit against a governmental official, the state action requirement is identical to § 1983's requirement of conduct under color of state law; satisfying the former necessarily safisfies the latter. Section 1983 does not extend to conduct of federal officers.

■■■

Quicknotes

FOURTEENTH AMENDMENT Declares that no state shall make or enforce any law that shall abridge the privileges and immunities of citizens of the United States. No state shall deny to any person within its jurisdiction the equal protection of the laws.

SEARCH AND SEIZURE An inspection conducted in order to obtain evidence to be utilized for the prosecution of a crime and the subsequent taking of such evidence.

STATE ACTION Actions brought pursuant to the Fourteenth Amendment claiming that the government violated the plaintiff's civil rights.

■■■

Parratt v. Taylor

Prison inmate (P) v. Nebraska prison warden (D)

451 U.S. 527 (1981).

NATURE OF CASE: Appeal from a federal court decision holding a prison inmate entitled to being suit against a state under federal civil rights legislation.

FACT SUMMARY: When Parratt (P), a prison inmate ordered by mail hobby materials valued at $23.50 that were negligently lost by prison officials, he sued the state (D) under the federal Civil Rights Act to recover their value, arguing the denial of his Fourteenth Amendment due process rights.

🏛 RULE OF LAW
Even though an individual has been deprived of property under color of state law, a Fourteenth Amendment Due Process violation arises only if the deprivation is a result of some established state procedure.

FACTS: Parratt (P), an inmate of the Nebraska prison system, ordered by mail certain hobby materials valued at $23.50 that were negligently lost by prison officials. Parratt (P) brought suit in federal district court under Section 1983 of the federal Civil Rights Act to recover their value. His claim was that the negligent loss violated his due process rights under the Fourteenth Amendment. The federal district court entered summary judgment for Parratt (P), and the court of appeals affirmed. The state (D) appealed to the United States Supreme Court.

ISSUE: Even though an individual has been deprived of property under color of state law, does a Fourteenth Amendment Due Process violation arise only if the deprivation is a result of some established state procedure?

HOLDING AND DECISION: (Rehnquist, J.) Yes. Even though an individual has been deprived of property under color of state law, a Fourteenth Amendment Due Process violation arises only if the deprivation is a result of some established state procedure. Nothing in the Fourteenth Amendment protects against *all* deprivations of life, liberty, or property by the state. The protection is only against deprivations without due process of law. Here, post-deprivation remedies made available by the state satisfied the due process clause. Justifications sufficient to uphold takings of property without any pre-deprivation process are applicable to a situation such as the present one involving a tortious loss of a prisoner's property as a result of a random and unauthorized act by a state employee. Hence, the loss is not the result of some established state procedure and the state cannot predict precisely when the loss will occur. It is, therefore, difficult to conceive how the state could provide a meaningful hearing before the

deprivation takes place. Indeed, here the deprivation occurred as a result of the unauthorized failure of agents of the state to follow established procedure. There was no contention that the procedures themselves were inadequate nor was there any contention that it was practicable for the state to provide a pre-deprivation hearing. Reversed.

CONCURRENCE: (Stewart, J.) Even if Nebraska has deprived the inmate of his property in the constitutional sense, it has not deprived him of it without due process of law. By making available to the inmate a reparations remedy, Nebraska has done all that the Fourteenth Amendment requires in this context.

CONCURRENCE: (Blackmun, J.) The mere availability of a subsequent tort remedy before tribunals of the same authority that, through its employees, deliberately inflicted the harm complained of, might well not provide the due process of which the Fourteenth Amendment speaks.

CONCURRENCE: (Powell, J.) In the due process area, the question is whether intent is required before there can be a "deprivation" of life, liberty, or property. A "deprivation" connotes an intentional act denying something to someone, or at the very least, a deliberate decision not to act to prevent a loss.

CONCURRENCE IN PART AND DISSENT IN PART: (Marshall, J.) Here, there was no adequate state law remedy available to the inmate. Furthermore, the prison officials never informed this inmate as to his rights under state law.

▶ ANALYSIS

In *Parratt*, the Supreme Court made clear that although the statutory state remedies may not have provided the inmate with all the relief which may have been available if he could have proceeded under Section 1983 of the federal Civil Rights Act, that did not mean that the state remedies were inadequate to satisfy the requirements of due process.

■=■

Quicknotes

FOURTEENTH AMENDMENT DUE PROCESS CLAUSE Provides that protections mandated by the U.S. Constitution and observed by the federal government are equally applicable, and therefore must be observed by the states.

■=■

Harlow v. Fitzgerald

President's aide (D) v. Whistleblower (P)

457 U.S. 800 (1982).

NATURE OF CASE: Appeal from denial of defense motion for summary judgment in action for damages for violations of constitutional rights.

FACT SUMMARY: Harlow (D) and Butterfield (D), aides to President Nixon, claimed that they were entitled to absolute immunity for their official acts.

RULE OF LAW
(1) Presidential aides are entitled to only qualified immunity for their acts as officials.
(2) In order to defeat qualified immunity, government officials must have violated clearly established statutory or constitutional rights.

FACTS: Fitzgerald (P) was terminated from his federal job and claimed it was due to his whistle-blowing. He filed suit against Harlow (D) and Butterfield (D), aides to President Nixon, for participating in an alleged conspiracy to violate his rights. Harlow (D) and Butterfield (D) moved for summary judgment, contending that they were entitled to official immunity for any alleged wrongful acts as presidential aides. The district court denied the motion, and the defendants brought an interlocutory appeal, which was dismissed by the court of appeals.

ISSUE:
(1) Are presidential aides entitled to absolute immunity for their acts as officials?
(2) Must government officials have violated clearly established statutory or constitutional rights in order to lose their qualified immunity?

HOLDING AND DECISION: (Powell, J.)
(1) No. Presidential aides are entitled to only qualified immunity for their acts as officials. Government officials are entitled to some form of immunity from suits for damages. Previous decisions have recognized immunity defenses of two kinds: absolute immunity and qualified immunity. Legislators conducting their legislative functions, prosecutors, and executive officers engaged in adjudicative functions are all entitled to absolute immunity. However, qualified immunity is more the norm and reflects an attempt to balance the competing values at issue. Officials must be able to exercise their discretion, while the rights of citizens must also be protected. Of course, courts may still quickly terminate insubstantial lawsuits against officials with only qualified immunity. In the present case, this Court has previously ruled that Cabinet members are given only qualified immunity. Thus, presidential aides are not allowed any greater protection. Harlow (D) and Butterfield (D) have not yet demonstrated that the responsibilities of their offices embrace a function so sensitive as to require a total shield from liability.
(2) Yes. In order to defeat qualified immunity, government officials must have violated clearly established statutory or constitutional rights. Good faith immunity is an affirmative defense for government officials. It contains both a subjective and objective element. Qualified immunity is not available if the official knew or should have known that his actions were illegal. This reliance on an objective element should avoid excessive disruption of government and permit the resolution of many claims on summary judgment. In the present case, the record is not developed enough to reach this issue. Therefore, the judgment of the court of appeals is vacated and the case remanded.

CONCURRENCE: (Brennan, J.) Some measure of discovery may sometimes be required to determine the extent of an official's knowledge.

DISSENT: (Burger, C.J.) Since this Court has decided that aides to legislators are entitled to absolute immunity, the same protection should be available to presidential aides. This decision might undermine the functioning of the Office of the President.

▶ ANALYSIS

Until 1896, officials sued in tort action were treated like regular defendants. Immunity evolved over a number of cases until *Spalding v. Vilas*, 161 U.S. 483 (1896), brought immunity to the forefront. In 1988, the Federal Employees Liability Reform and Tort Compensation Act became the sole remedy for alleged torts committed by federal officials.

■■■

Quicknotes

INTERLOCUTORY APPEAL The appeal of an issue that does not resolve the disposition of the case, but is essential to a determination of the parties' legal rights.

QUALIFIED IMMUNITY An affirmative defense relieving officials from civil liability for the performance of activities within their discretion so long as such conduct is not in violation of an individual's rights pursuant to law as determined by a reasonable person standard.

■■■

Judicial Federalism: Limitations on District Court Jurisdiction or its Exercise

Quick Reference Rules of Law

Kline v. Burke Construction Company

Contracting party (D) v. Contracting party (P)

260 U.S. 226 (1922).

NATURE OF CASE: Review of order enjoining prosecution of breach of contract suit in state court.

FACT SUMMARY: Burke Construction (Burke) (P) sought to enjoin Kline (D) from suing the company in state court over a contract on which Burke (P) had based its federal diversity suit.

RULE OF LAW
The state or federal court that first acquires jurisdiction in an in rem case has exclusive authority to decide the dispute.

FACTS: Burke (P) brought a breach of contract action against Kline (D) in federal district court based on diversity of citizenship. After this suit was under way, Kline (D) brought its own suit in equity in state court alleging that Burke (P) had abandoned the contract. The second case was based on the same facts and alleged the same cause of action, but it included additional parties. The federal suit was declared a mistrial. Burke (P) filed a dependent complaint asking the district court to enjoin the state court proceedings. The district court refused to grant the injunction. However, the court of appeals reversed and remanded to the district court with an order to issue the injunction. Kline (D) appealed.

ISSUE: Does the state or federal court that first acquires jurisdiction in an in rem case have exclusive authority to decide the dispute?

HOLDING AND DECISION: (Sutherland, J.) Yes. The state or federal court that first acquires jurisdiction in an in rem case has exclusive authority to decide the dispute. However, if an action is in personam, then a similar second action in a different jurisdiction is not precluded. A federal court is permitted to enjoin a similar state proceeding in an in rem action when the federal court has taken possession of the res first in order to avoid friction between the two court systems. But the same justification does not apply when the action, like the instant case, is in personam and only claims monetary damages. Burke (P) argues that this procedure potentially deprives it of its right to maintain an action in federal court under the Constitution. But the right to bring a suit in diversity is not a constitutional right. Therefore, any res judicata effect from the state court cannot deprive Burke (P) of its constitutional right to invoke the jurisdiction of the federal court. Reversed.

ANALYSIS

In *Atlantic Cost Line R.R. v. Brotherhood of Locomotive Engineers*, 398 U.S. 281 (1970), the Court interpreted the "in aid of jurisdiction" exception to the Anti-Injunction Act as preventing the severe disruption of the federal court exercising jurisdiction. In that case, a federal court had granted an injunction against a state court injunction preventing union members from picketing. The Court, however, concluded that the state and federal courts had concurrent jurisdiction and neither court could prevent management or the union from pursuing claims in both courts. The "in aid of jurisdiction" exception, it ruled, may only be invoked when state court interference seriously impairs the federal court's flexibility and authority to decide a case.

Quicknotes

ENJOIN The ordering of a party to cease the conduct of a specific activity.

INJUNCTION A court order requiring a person to do, or prohibiting that person from doing, a specific act.

IN PERSONAM An action against a person seeking a judgment to impose personal liability.

IN REM An action against property.

RES Thing; subject matter of a dispute to establish rights therein.

RES JUDICATA The rule of law that a final judgment by a court precludes subsequent litigation between the parties regarding the same cause of action.

Atlantic Coast Line R.R. v. Brotherhood of Locomotive Engineers

Railroad (P) v. Union (D)

398 U.S. 281 (1970).

NATURE OF CASE: Appeal from an action seeking an injunction.

FACT SUMMARY: After a state court of Florida granted an injunction sought by Atlantic Coast Line R.R. (Atlantic) (P) against the picketing of the Brotherhood of Locomotive Engineers (D) (Brotherhood), the Brotherhood (D) in federal district court sought and was granted an injunction against the enforcement of the state court injunction.

> 🏛 **RULE OF LAW**
> Under § 2283 of the Anti-Injunction Statute, a federal court may not enjoin a state court proceeding unless the injunction is expressly authorized by an Act of Congress, necessary in aid of the court's jurisdiction, or to protect or effectuate the court's judgment.

FACTS: In 1967, the Brotherhood (D) began picketing a railroad yard in Florida, wholly owned and operated by Atlantic (P). Atlantic (P) went immediately into federal court seeking an injunction against the picketing. When the federal judge denied the request, Atlantic (P) went into state court and there succeeded in obtaining an injunction. No further legal action was taken until 1969, when the Supreme Court in the Jacksonville Terminal Case held that the unions had a federally protected right to picket that could not be interfered with by state court injunctions. The Brotherhood (D) filed a motion in state court to dissolve the injunction. The state court denied the motion. Electing not to appeal that decision directly, the Brotherhood (D) went back into federal court and requested an injunction against enforcement of the state court injunction. The federal court granted that injunction and the court of appeals affirmed.

ISSUE: May a federal court enjoin a state court proceeding if the injunction is not necessary in aid of its jurisdiction or to protect or effectuate the court's judgment?

HOLDING AND DECISION: (Black, J.) No. On its face the present Anti-Injunction Statute is an absolute prohibition against enjoining state court proceedings unless the injunction falls within one of the three statutory exceptions to § 2283. Thus, if the injunction against the Florida court proceedings is to be upheld, it must be "expressly authorized by an Act of Congress," "necessary in aid of the district court's jurisdiction," or "to protect or effectuate the court's judgments." Neither party argues that there is any congressional authorization. The Court agrees. However, the Brotherhood (D) contends that the injunction was proper, either as a means to protect or effectuate the district court's 1967 order, or in aid of that court's jurisdiction. This Court does not think either contention can be supported. The

Brotherhood (D) in effect tried to get the federal district court to decide that the state court judge was wrong in distinguishing the Jacksonville case. Such an attempt to seek appellate review of a state decision in a federal district court cannot be justified as necessary to protect or effectuate the 1967 order. As to the Brotherhood's (D) contention that the injunction was necessary to aid the lower court's jurisdiction, this Court concludes that the state and federal courts had concurrent jurisdiction, neither being free to prevent the parties from simultaneously pursuing claims in both courts. Therefore, the state court's assumption of jurisdiction over the state law claims and the federal preclusion issue did not hinder the federal court's jurisdiction so as to make an injunction necessary to aid jurisdiction. The injunction issued by the district court is vacated.

DISSENT: (Brennan, J.) Section 2283 evinces a congressional intent to resort to state proceedings not be permitted to undermine a prior judgment of a federal court. But that is exactly what has occurred in the present case. The federal determination that the Brotherhood (D) may picket has been rendered wholly ineffective by the state court injunction.

▶ *ANALYSIS*

The Supreme Court has twice been called on to interpret the 1948 revised draft of the Anti-Injunction Statute involved in the case at bar. In one case, the state court lacked jurisdiction to issue an injunction against peaceful picketing because Congress had preempted the field, leaving such problems to be solved by the National Labor Relations Board (NLRB). The Supreme Court held that the federal court could not restrain the state court proceedings. However, if the injunction was sought by the NLRB, it was proper. The second case involved the issue of whether a federal court could restrain state court proceedings when the United States sought the injunction. The Court held that a federal court could not so enjoin a state court proceeding.

■==■

Quicknotes

ENJOIN The ordering of a party to cease the conduct of a specific activity.

INJUNCTION A court order requiring a person to do, or prohibiting that person from doing, a specific act.

JURISDICTION The authority of a court to hear and declare judgment in respect to a particular matter.

■==■

Mitchum v. Foster

Bookstore owner (P) v. State official (D)

407 U.S. 225 (1972).

NATURE OF CASE: Direct appeal from an order of the court of appeals denying an injunction against state court proceedings.

FACT SUMMARY: Mitchum (P) sought an injunction against state proceedings he alleged had unconstitutionally ordered his bookstore closed. The court of appeals refused to enjoin, and Mitchum (P) appealed directly to the Supreme Court.

RULE OF LAW
42 U.S.C. § 1983 is an "Act of Congress" that comes within the "expressly authorized" exception of the Anti-Injunction Statute (28 U.S.C. § 2283) so as to permit a federal court to grant an injunction to stay proceedings pending in a state court.

FACTS: The Florida prosecutor brought a proceeding in state court to close down Mitchum's (P) bookstore as a public nuisance under Florida law. The state court preliminarily enjoined operation of the bookstore, and Mitchum (P) brought an action in U.S. district court alleging the state officials were depriving him of rights protected by the First and Fourteenth Amendments. Relying on 42 U.S.C. § 1983, he sought an injunction against the state court proceedings. The district court ordered a temporary injunction, the court of appeals dissolved the injunction, and Mitchum (P) appealed directly to the United States Supreme Court.

ISSUE: Is 42 U.S.C. § 1983 an "Act of Congress" that comes within the "expressly authorized" exception of the federal Anti-Injunction Statute so as to permit a federal court to grant an injunction to stay proceedings pending in a state court?

HOLDING AND DECISION: (Stewart, J.) Yes. 42 U.S.C. § 1983 is an "Act of Congress" that comes within the "expressly authorized" exception of the Anti-Injunction Statute so as to permit a federal court to grant an injunction to stay proceedings pending in a state court. The test is whether an act of Congress, clearly creating a federal right or remedy enforceable in a federal court of equity, could be given its intended scope only by the stay of a state court proceedings. The very purpose of § 1983 was to interpose the federal courts between the states and the people, as guardians of the people's federal rights—to protect the people from unconstitutional action under color of state law, "whether that action be executive, legislative, or judicial." In carrying out that purpose, Congress plainly authorized the federal courts to issue injunctions in § 1983 actions, by expressly authorizing a "suit in equity"

as one of the means of redress. For these reasons we conclude that § 1983 is an act of Congress that falls within the "expressly authorized" exception of the Anti-Injunction Statute. Reversed and remanded.

CONCURRENCE: (Burger, C.J.) Since the Court had not yet decided whether the principles of equity, comity, and federalism set forth in *Younger v. Harris*, 401 U.S 37 (1971), restricted federal injunctive relief against pending state civil proceedings, the federal district court on remand should consider that question before proceeding to the merits.

ANALYSIS

This fairly recent case is the third in the trilogy of the Court's interpretation of § 2283. The opinion here decidedly favors the "flexible" interpretation of 2283. Compare *Baines v. City of Danville*, 337 F.2d 579 (4th Circuit, 1964), where at 593, Judge Haynsworth noted that since § 2283 had been "fathered by the principles of comity," it "should be read in the light of those principles and, though absolute in its terms, is inapplicable in extraordinary cases in which an injunction against state court proceedings is the only means of avoiding grave and irreparable injury."

Quicknotes

ENJOIN The ordering of a party to cease the conduct of a specific activity.

FIRST AMENDMENT RIGHTS Rights conferred by the First Amendment to the United States Constitution prohibiting Congress from enacting any law respecting an establishment of religion, prohibiting the free exercise of religion, abridging freedom of speech or the press, the right of peaceful assembly and the right to petition for a redress of grievances.

FOURTEENTH AMENDMENT Declares that no state shall make or enforce any law that shall abridge the privileges and immunities of citizens of the United States. No state shall deny to any person within its jurisdiction the equal protection of the laws.

INJUNCTION A court order requiring a person to do, or prohibiting that person from doing, a specific act.

Railroad Commission of Texas v. Pullman Co.

State railroad commission (D) v. Sleeping car manufacturer (P)

312 U.S. 496 (1941).

NATURE OF CASE: Suit seeking injunctive relief.

FACT SUMMARY: An order of the Railroad Commission of Texas (D) required that a conductor, rather than a porter, be in charge of all Pullman Co. (P) cars.

RULE OF LAW
Federal courts should abstain from deciding cases involving issues of state law that can easily be resolved by a state court.

FACTS: When passenger traffic was light, certain trains operating in Texas were served by only one sleeping car. On these occasions, the cars were supervised by the porters (P), most of whom were black, instead of by conductors, who were white. In response to this situation, the Railroad Commission of Texas (Commission) (D) promulgated an order that forbade the operation of sleeping cars unless they were continuously in the charge of a conductor. The Pullman Co. (P), which manufactured sleeping cars, together with the railroads (P) affected, brought suit in federal district court to enjoin the Commission's (D) order, and the porters (P) were permitted to intervene in the action. The railroads (P) and the Pullman Co. (P) contended that the order contravened Texas law as well as the federal Constitution. The porters (P) argued that the discriminatory effects of the order violated the Fourteenth Amendment. A three-judge panel enjoined enforcement of the order, denying that the applicable Texas statutes sustained the Commission's injunction.

ISSUE: Should federal courts resolve issues of state law that could be decided by state courts?

HOLDING AND DECISION: (Frankfurter, J.) No. Federal courts should abstain from deciding cases involving issues of state law that can easily be resolved by a state court. The porters (P) have raised a significant constitutional issue, but they have also touched upon a sensitive social question of considerable moment. It is preferable that the case be resolved by resorting to state law, rather than by determining the merits of the constitutional issue. The outcome can turn on whether or not the contested order is consistent with the Commission's (D) authority to prevent discrimination and other abuses. A state court may determine whether the order is within the ambit of the Commission's (D) authority, thus precluding the necessity for a federal court to decide the case in a manner that might ultimately create friction between state and federal law. Since Texas law facilitates a state court resolution of this dispute, the federal action should not be given effect until the appropriate Texas court has had a chance to consider the merits of this controversy. Reversed and remanded.

ANALYSIS

The abstention doctrine compels federal courts to refrain, at least temporarily, from deciding cases that may be resolved by reference to state law or that require a preliminary consideration of state law issues. The doctrine had been recognized and applied in cases that predated the *Pullman Co.* case, and has been utilized by subsequent cases as well. The purpose of the doctrine is to ensure that federal courts will not interfere with their state counterparts by rendering decisions that are inconsistent with ultimate state court resolutions of identical issues.

Quicknotes

ABSTENTION A doctrine pursuant to which a federal court may decline to assert its authority to hear a case involving a federal question pending resolution of an issue in the matter in state court involving a question of state law, or if the matter seems more appropriately determined by a state court.

ENJOIN The ordering of a party to cease the conduct of a specific activity.

FOURTEENTH AMENDMENT Declares that no state shall make or enforce any law that shall abridge the privileges and immunities of citizens of the United States. No state shall deny to any person within its jurisdiction the equal protection of the laws.

INJUNCTION A court order requiring a person to do, or prohibiting that person from doing, a specific act.

Younger v. Harris

State attorney (D) v. Convicted criminal (P)

401 U.S. 37 (1971).

NATURE OF CASE: Appeal from an injunction against a pending state prosecution.

FACT SUMMARY: After being indicted in a California state court for violation of the California Criminal Syndicalism Act, Harris (P) filed suit in the federal district court seeking an injunction against Younger (D), the district attorney, restraining him from further prosecution on the ground that the Act was overbroad and violated Harris's (P) First and Fourteenth Amendment rights.

🏛 RULE OF LAW
Federal courts should not interfere with pending state court proceedings except where it can be shown that the defendant will suffer irreparable injury.

FACTS: Harris (P) was indicted in a state court for violation of the California Criminal Syndicalism Act. Harris (P) then filed a complaint in the federal district court seeking an injunction against Younger (D), the district attorney in charge of the state prosecution, restraining him from prosecuting Harris (P) further. Harris (P) alleged that the prosecution and even the presence of the Act violated his First and Fourteenth Amendment rights. A three-judge district court held that the Act was void for vagueness and overbreadth in violation of the First and Fourteenth Amendments and granted the injunction. Younger (D) appealed on the ground that national policy forbids federal courts from enjoining pending state proceedings.

ISSUE: Can federal courts stay or enjoin pending state court proceedings absent special circumstances showing irreparable injury?

HOLDING AND DECISION: (Black, J.) No. There is a national policy forbidding federal courts from staying or enjoining pending state court proceedings except under special circumstances where a person about to be prosecuted in a state court can show that he will suffer irreparable injury. In the instant case a proceeding was already pending in the state court, affording Harris (P) an opportunity to raise his constitutional claims. Furthermore, there is no suggestion that this single prosecution against Harris is brought in bad faith or is meant to be one of a series of repeated prosecutions designed to harass him. The existence of a chilling effect, even in the area of First Amendment rights, has never been considered a sufficient basis, in and of itself, for prohibiting state action. In the first place, the chilling effect cannot be satisfactorily eliminated by federal injunctive relief. Secondly, where a statute does not directly abridge free speech, but tends to have an incidental effect, it is well established that the statute can be upheld if the effect is minor in relation to the need for control of the conduct. Therefore, this Court holds that the possible unconstitutionality of a statute on its face does not itself justify an injunction against good-faith attempts to enforce it. Harris (P) has failed to make any showing of bad faith, harassment, or any other unusual circumstance that would result in irreparable injury and call for equitable relief.

CONCURRENCE: (Brennan, J.) Harris was indicted in state court before he sued in federal court and his constitutional contentions may be adequately adjudicated in the state criminal proceeding.

CONCURRENCE: (Stewart, J.) Since this case and the others considered in the decision all involve state criminal prosecutions, the Court does not deal with the factors that should govern a federal court when it is asked to intervene in state civil proceedings. The balance in such cases might be struck differently.

DISSENT: (Douglas, J.) The *Dombrowski* decision, 380 U.S. 479 (1965), which should govern this case, represents an exception to the general rule that federal courts should not interfere with state criminal prosecutions. The exception governs statutes that have an overbroad sweep. In *Younger,* criminal syndicalism is defined so broadly as to jeopardize teaching that socialism is preferable to free enterprise. Harris (P) tried unsuccessfully in the state courts to have the indictment dismissed, but to no avail. He went to the federal court as a manner of last resort in an effort to keep this unconstitutional trial from continuing.

▶ ANALYSIS

In state criminal prosecutions unrelated to freedom of expression, defendants have been unable to attain *Dombrowski*-type relief. However, in cases where state action has been found to have a chilling effect on First Amendment rights, lower courts have granted *Dombrowski*-sanctioned relief in a wide range of cases. These cases have usually involved prosecutions against civil rights workers or protest demonstrators under statutes unconstitutional on their face or under statutes applied in an unconstitutional manner.

Quicknotes

CHILLING EFFECT Any practice that results in discouraging the exercise of a right.

ENJOIN The ordering of a party to cease the conduct of a specific activity.

Continued on next page.

FIRST AMENDMENT RIGHTS Rights conferred by the First Amendment to the United States Constitution prohibiting Congress from enacting any law respecting an establishment of religion, prohibiting the free exercise of religion, abridging freedom of speech or the press, the right of peaceful assembly and the right to petition for a redress of grievances.

FOURTEENTH AMENDMENT Declares that no state shall make or enforce any law that shall abridge the privileges and immunities of citizens of the United States. No state shall deny to any person within its jurisdiction the equal protection of the laws.

INJUNCTION A court order requiring a person to do, or prohibiting that person from doing, a specific act.

SYNDICALISM The advocating of unlawful conduct to effect a change in ownership or control.

Steffel v. Thompson

Handbill distributor (P) v. State official (D)

415 U.S. 452 (1974).

NATURE OF CASE: Appeal in a federal action seeking injunctive and declaratory relief from enforcement of a state statute.

FACT SUMMARY: Steffel (P) had been told he would be arrested if he persisted in distributing handbills protesting the Vietnam War, so he sought a federal declaratory judgment that the state statute involved was unconstitutional and an injunction against its enforcement.

> ## RULE OF LAW
> A federal district court can entertain an action to declare a state statute unconstitutional when criminal prosecution thereunder is only threatened but not pending.

FACTS: On two occasions, Steffel (P) was threatened with arrest and prosecution if he continued to distribute handbills against the Vietnam War on the sidewalk of a shopping center. He stopped distribution, but brought an action in federal court for a declaratory judgment that application of the Georgia criminal trespass statute would violate his First and Fourteenth Amendment rights. He also sought an injunction to keep Thompson (D) and others from enforcing the statute under the circumstances. The district court dismissed the action on the ground that bad-faith harassment was a prerequisite for declaratory relief just as it was for injunctive relief. The court of appeals affirmed.

ISSUE: Can a federal district court entertain an action to declare a state statute unconstitutional when criminal prosecution thereunder is only threatened but not pending?

HOLDING AND DECISION: (Brennan, J.) Yes. A federal district court can entertain an action to declare a state statute unconstitutional when criminal prosecution thereunder is only threatened but not pending. While principles of equity, comity, and federalism lead to the conclusion that federal courts should ordinarily refrain from enjoining ongoing state criminal prosecutions, they do not preclude a federal court from entertaining an action to declare a state criminal statute unconstitutional (either facially or as applied) when a federal plaintiff demonstrates a genuine threat of prosecution thereunder although prosecution is not then actually pending. The fact that irreparable injury is a prerequisite to injunctive relief in this type of case does not mean it is also a prerequisite for declaratory relief. Declaratory relief is a less harsh and abrasive remedy and does not interfere with state proceedings by barring future state prosecutions. A state prosecutor can go on to bring a state prosecution under the statute even if a federal court issues a declaratory judgment that the statute is unconstitutional. Reversed and remanded.

CONCURRENCE: (Stewart, J.) This type of declaratory relief is possible only when a plaintiff demonstrates "a genuine threat" of prosecution under the subject state statute, and those cases will be exceedingly rare.

CONCURRENCE: (White, J.) A final federal declaratory judgment holding particular conduct of the plaintiff to be immune from prosecution under state law on federal constitutional grounds should be accorded res judicata effect in any later prosecution of that very conduct. Furthermore, the federal court that rendered such a declaratory judgment in favor of the plaintiff may subsequently enjoin a later state prosecution for the very conduct it has declared immune. Finally, a federal suit challenging a state criminal statute on federal constitutional grounds could be sufficiently far along so that ordinary considerations of economy would warrant refusal to dismiss the federal case solely because a state prosecution has subsequently been filed and the federal question may be litigated there.

CONCURRENCE: (Rehnquist, J.) In providing for declaratory actions, Congress did not intend to provide persons wishing to violate state laws with a federal shield behind which they could carry on their contemplated conduct. Therefore, the mere filing of such an action should not prevent a state from prosecuting the plaintiff under the subject state statute. Any arrest prior to resolution of the federal action would constitute a pending prosecution and bar declaratory relief. Thus, the plaintiff who continues to violate a state statute after filing his federal complaint for declaratory relief does so both at the risk of state prosecution and at the risk of dismissal of his federal lawsuit.

ANALYSIS

Declaratory relief can also be had when a state prosecution is under way, but only if injunctive relief would be appropriate under the circumstances. *Samuels v. Mackell*, 401 U.S. 66 (1971). Injunctive relief is appropriate only if the plaintiff can show bad faith, harassment, or any other unusual circumstances that would result in irreparable injury. If he can make such a showing, a pending state prosecution can be enjoined or declaratory relief granted. Recent cases have extended this rationale to state-initiated civil proceedings that are closely related to a criminal statute. *Huffman v. Pursue, Ltd.*, 420 U.S. 592 (1975) (civil

Continued on next page.

action under obscenity statutes to "abate" the showing of obscene films).

◼══◼

Quicknotes

ENJOIN The ordering of a party to cease the conduct of a specific activity.

FIRST AMENDMENT RIGHTS Rights conferred by the First Amendment to the United States Constitution prohibiting Congress from enacting any law respecting an establishment of religion, prohibiting the free exercise of religion, abridging freedom of speech or the press, the right of peaceful assembly and the right to petition for a redress of grievances.

FOURTEENTH AMENDMENT Declares that no state shall make or enforce any law that shall abridge the privileges and immunities of citizens of the United States. No state shall deny to any person within its jurisdiction the equal protection of the laws.

INJUNCTION A court order requiring a person to do, or prohibiting that person from doing, a specific act.

RES JUDICATA The rule of law that a final judgment by a court precludes subsequent litigation between the parties regarding the same cause of action.

◼══◼

Hicks v. Miranda

District attorney (D) v. Theater owner (P)

422 U.S. 332 (1975).

NATURE OF CASE: Direct appeal from a judgment of a three-judge district court in an action for an injunction.

FACT SUMMARY: Hicks (D), the district attorney, claimed that the three-judge federal court by its enjoining his seizure of an obscene film and subsequent prosecution of Miranda (P) therefor, violated the rule of *Younger v. Harris.*

🏛 **RULE OF LAW**
Where state criminal proceedings are begun against federal plaintiffs after the federal complaint is filed, but before any proceeding of substance on the merits has taken place, the principles of *Younger v. Harris* should apply in full force.

FACTS: Miranda (P) was one of the owners (P) of four copies of the film "Deep Throat" seized by police from an Orange County, California, theater. On November 26, 1973, criminal charges, stemming from the seizure, were filed in the municipal court against two of Miranda's (P) theater employees. Also on November 26, the Superior Court ordered Miranda (P) to show cause why the film should not be ruled obscene. Miranda (P), objecting to the court's jurisdiction—and purporting to reserve all federal questions, refused to participate. Thereupon, on November 27, the Superior Court ruled the film obscene and seized the copies. Miranda (P) then filed this suit in the district court seeking: (1) an injunction against the enforcement of the California obscenity statute; (2) a declaration that the statute was unconstitutional; and (3) an injunction ordering the return of the film. A three-judge court was convened on January 8, 1974, to consider the constitutionality of the statute. However, in the meantime, on January 15 the pending municipal court action was amended to add Miranda (P) and his associates (P) as parties defendant. On June 4, the three-judge court declared the California obscenity statute unconstitutional and ordered Hicks (D) to return the film. Hicks (D) argued that *Younger v. Harris,* 401 U.S. 37 (1971), required dismissal of the federal case due to the pending state criminal charges. The three-judge court rejected this argument since no criminal charges had been filed against Miranda (P) when he first brought the case in federal court. After the three-judge court denied Hicks's (D) further motions, Hicks (D) appealed.

ISSUE: Should the principles of *Younger v. Harris* apply when state criminal proceedings are begun against federal plaintiffs after the federal complaint is filed, but before any proceeding of substance on the merits has taken place?

HOLDING AND DECISION: (White, J.) Yes. Where state criminal proceedings are begun against a federal plaintiff after the federal complaint is filed, but before any proceedings of substance on the merits have taken place, the principles of *Younger v. Harris* should apply in full force. The rule in *Younger v. Harris* is designed to permit state courts to try state cases free from interference by federal courts, particularly where the party to the federal action may fully litigate his claim before the state court. While it is true, as Miranda (P) claims, that when he filed his federal complaint no state criminal proceedings were pending against him, nevertheless his employees had been already charged and the film belonging to Miranda (P) had been declared obscene. Therefore, Miranda (P) had a substantial stake in those state proceedings to the degree that he sought to interfere with them by seeking federal relief. Therefore, absent a clear showing by Miranda (P) that he could not have achieved relief in the state court, the requirements of *Younger v. Harris* cannot be avoided by Miranda's (P) claim. Reversed.

DISSENT: (Stewart, J.) The federal court is primarily involved as the guarantor of constitutional rights. Yet the majority holding allows the state, by the process of filing subsequent criminal charges after the federal case has begun, to oust the federal court. This is no less offensive to federalism than is the federal injunction restraining pending state actions condemned in *Younger v. Harris.*

▶ *ANALYSIS*

Shortly after the above decision, the Court decided *Doran v. Salem Inn, Inc.,* 422 U.S. 922 (1975), wherein three local bars, facing an ordinance prohibiting topless dancing, complied with the ordinance but, at the same time, sued in federal court to have the ordinance declared unconstitutional and its enforcement enjoined. The day after the federal filing, one bar resumed topless dancing and criminal procedures were immediately commenced against it. The Court held that *Younger* barred that federal plaintiff (M&L) from securing its federal injunction since the federal litigation was in its "embryonic stage" when the criminal summons was issued against M&L.

■▬■

Quicknotes

ENJOIN The ordering of a party to cease the conduct of a specific activity.

Continued on next page.

INJUNCTION A court order requiring a person to do, or prohibiting that person from doing, a specific act.

JURISDICTION The authority of a court to hear and declare judgment in respect to a particular matter.

Colorado River Water Conservation District v. United States

State district (D) v. Federal government (P)

424 U.S. 800 (1976).

NATURE OF CASE: Appeal from reversal of dismissal of action to determine water rights.

FACT SUMMARY: The government (P) filed suit in federal court to obtain a declaration of its water rights in part of Colorado, and the District et al. (D) moved that the action be dismissed.

RULE OF LAW
A federal court may, under limited circumstances, refuse to exercise jurisdiction over a proceeding due to the presence of a concurrent state proceeding for reasons of wise judicial administration.

FACTS: The government (P) was brought into a suit by a water user (D) who was seeking declaration of its right to waters in certain rivers and their tributaries located in Division 7, one of seven divisions into which Colorado is divided for the purpose of allocating water. This suit, brought in federal district court, was based on state and federal claims and also asserted rights on behalf of certain Indian tribes. Previously, the government (P) had pursued adjudication of non-Indian reserved rights and other water claims based on state law in state court for Water Divisions 4, 5, and 6, and the government (P) continued to participate fully in those divisions. Federal jurisdiction was invoked under 28 U.S.C. § 1345, which provides that district courts shall have original jurisdiction over all civil actions brought by the federal government "except as otherwise provided by an act of Congress." Several defendants claimed that under the McCarran Amendment, the court was without jurisdiction to determine federal water rights. That amendment gives the consent of the United States to be joined in certain suits involving water rights. The Colorado River Water Conservation District (D) appealed the reversal by the court of appeals of the dismissal of the government's (P) suit by the district court.

ISSUE: May a federal court, under limited circumstances, refuse to exercise jurisdiction over a matter due to the presence of a concurrent state proceeding for reasons of wise judicial administration?

HOLDING AND DECISION: (Brennan, J.) Yes. For reasons of wise judicial administration, a federal court may, under limited circumstances, refuse to exercise jurisdiction over a matter due to the presence of a concurrent state proceeding. The McCarran Amendment in no way diminished federal district court jurisdiction under § 1345, and the district court had jurisdiction to hear this case. The dismissal cannot be supported under the doctrine of abstention in any of its forms. Abstention from the exercise of federal jurisdiction is the exception, not the rule, and this case falls into none of the categories of circumstances appropriate for abstention. However, a number of factors clearly counsel against the federal proceedings. The McCarran Amendment indicates a policy that recognizes the availability of state systems for adjudication of water rights as a means of avoiding piecemeal adjudication of such rights. That alone might not justify dismissal, but added to other factors in this case, dismissal was justified. Reversed.

DISSENT: (Stewart, J.) The Court's principal reason for deciding to close the doors of the federal courthouse to the government (P) in this case seems to stem from the view that its decision will avoid piecemeal adjudication of water rights. To the extent that the Court's view is based on the realistic practicalities of this case, it is simply wrong because the relegation of the government to the state courts will not avoid piecemeal litigation. Furthermore, the issues involved are issues of federal law. A federal court is more likely than a state court to be familiar with federal water law and to have had experience in interpreting the relevant federal statutes, regulations, and Indian treaties.

DISSENT: (Stevens, J.) The holding that the government (P) may not litigate a federal claim in a federal court having jurisdiction thereof is particularly anomalous; the Court's holding would restrict private water users' access to federal courts, and the Court should defer to the judgment of the court of appeals, rather than evaluate itself the balance of factors for and against the exercise of jurisdiction.

ANALYSIS

Colorado River can be taken as both broadening and, at the same time, narrowing the category of cases over which federal courts can refuse jurisdiction. The case emphasized that federal courts can refuse jurisdiction over matters being heard in state courts, aside from the narrow doctrines of abstention and forum non conveniens. However, most circuits had already been upholding stays of federal jurisdiction in deference to state proceedings; and *Colorado River* limited the power of federal courts to dismiss to the "virtually unflagging obligation" of the federal courts to exercise the jurisdiction given them.

Quicknotes

ABSTENTION A doctrine pursuant to which a federal court may decline to assert its authority to hear a case involving a federal question pending resolution of an issue in the matter in state court involving a question of

Continued on next page.

state law, or if the matter seems more appropriately determined by a state court.

FORUM NON CONVENIENS An equitable doctrine permitting a court to refrain from hearing and determining a case when the matter may be more properly and fairly heard in another forum.

INJUNCTION A court order requiring a person to do, or prohibiting that person from doing, a specific act.

Ankenbrandt v. Richards

Former wife (P) v. Former husband (D)

504 U.S. 689 (1992).

NATURE OF CASE: Appeal from dismissal of tort action seeking monetary damages for sexual and physical abuse.

FACT SUMMARY: The district court dismissed Ankenbrandt's (P) lawsuit against Richards (D), her former husband, for alleged sexual and physical abuse of their children, concluding that it fell within the domestic relations exception to diversity jurisdiction.

🏛 RULE OF LAW
The domestic relations exception to diversity jurisdiction encompasses only cases involving the issuance of a divorce, alimony, or child custody decree.

FACTS: Ankenbrandt (P) brought a tort suit against her former husband, Richards (D), alleging that Richards (D) sexually and physically abused their children. The lawsuit was brought in federal court pursuant to diversity jurisdiction. The district court dismissed the complaint on the ground that it lacked jurisdiction over the case because it fell within the "domestic relations" exception to diversity jurisdiction. Ankenbrandt (P) appealed, and the Supreme Court granted certiorari.

ISSUE: Does the domestic relations exception to diversity jurisdiction encompass only cases involving the issuance of a divorce, alimony, or child custody decree?

HOLDING AND DECISION: (White, J.) Yes. The domestic relations exception to diversity jurisdiction encompasses only cases involving the issuance of a divorce, alimony, or child custody decree. This rule, although based on dicta from the 1859 case of *Barber v. Barber*, 21 How. 582, has been recognized for nearly 150 years. However, the *Barber* case did not intend to strip the federal courts of authority to hear cases arising from the domestic relations of persons unless they seek the granting or modification of a divorce or alimony decree. Subsequent cases expanded the exception to include decrees in child custody cases. The lawsuit in this case does not seek any of these three decrees; it alleges that Richards (D) committed torts against his children. Federal subject-matter jurisdiction is proper. Reversed.

CONCURRENCE: (Blackmun, J.) The diversity statute does not contain an exception for domestic relations matters. The majority's decision regarding the intentions of Congress is incorrect. Furthermore, standard principles of statutory construction reveal that a domestic relations exception does not exist. The proper reason for declining jurisdiction is for abstention purposes, since states generally have a greater interest in domestic relations issues.

CONCURRENCE: (Stevens, J.) This case falls outside the scope of any plausible "domestic relations exception," and whether such an exception in fact exists need not be decided at present.

▶ *ANALYSIS*

The rationale behind the domestic relations exception is that family relations are unique because they involve matters of state policy and concern. Furthermore, they may involve retention of jurisdiction by the court and compliance monitoring. In addition, state courts are closely associated with the types of local government organization dedicated to handling conflicts arising from divorce and child custody decrees.

■■■

Quicknotes

CERTIORARI A discretionary writ issued by a superior court to an inferior court in order to review the lower court's decisions; the Supreme Court's writ ordering such review.

JURISDICTION The authority of a court to hear and declare judgment in respect to a particular matter.

TORT A legal wrong resulting in a breach of duty by the wrongdoer, causing damages as a result of the breach.

■■■

Federal Habeas Corpus

Quick Reference Rules of Law

Boumediene v. Bush

Alien detainees (P) v. President (D)

__ U.S. __, 128 S. Ct. 2229, 171 L. Ed. 2d 41 (2008).

NATURE OF CASE: Appeal from decisions holding that alien detainees designated as enemy combatants at the U.S. Naval Station at Guantanamo Bay, Cuba, did not have the privilege of habeas corpus.

FACT SUMMARY: Aliens (P) designated as enemy combatants detained at Guantanamo Bay, Cuba, contended they had the constitutional privilege of habeas corpus, despite the procedures provided by the Detainee Treatment Act of 2005 (DTA) for review of the detainees' status, and that the Military Commissions Act of 2006 (MCA) operated as an unconstitutional suspension of the writ.

RULE OF LAW
Alien detainees have the constitutional privilege of habeas corpus even though they are designated as enemy combatants and are located outside the country in an area over which the United States has de facto jurisdiction.

FACTS: The United States government (D) captured aliens (P) abroad on the battlefields of Afghanistan or elsewhere. These aliens (P) were sent to the U.S. Naval Station at Guantanamo Bay, Cuba, over which Cuba has sovereignty. However, the government (D), which leases the naval station from Cuba, exercises complete jurisdiction and control over the site. The aliens (P) denied membership in the al Qaeda terrorist network that carried out the September 11 attacks and the Taliban regime that supported al Qaeda. At the time, none of the aliens (P) was a citizen of a nation at war with the United States. Each alien (P) appeared before a Combatant Status Review Tribunal (CSRT), was determined to be an "enemy combatant," and each alien (P) sought a writ of habeas corpus in the district court. While the cases were on remand from the United States Supreme Court, Congress passed the Detainee Treatment Act of 2005 (DTA), which amended 28 U.S.C. § 2241 to provide that "no court, justice, or judge shall have jurisdiction to hear or consider . . . an application for a writ of habeas corpus filed by or on behalf of an alien detained by the Department of Defense at Guantanamo," and gave the court of appeals "exclusive" jurisdiction to review CSRT decisions. After the Court's decision in *Hamdan v. Rumsfeld*, 548 U.S. 557 (2006), Congress enacted the Military Commissions Act of 2006 (MCA), § 7(a), which again amended § 2241 in an attempt to deprive federal courts of jurisdiction to hear the aliens' (P) habeas corpus petitions or other claims. The court of appeals ruled that the MCA deprived it of jurisdiction to hear the habeas petitions, and the United States Supreme Court granted certiorari.

ISSUE: Do alien detainees have the constitutional privilege of habeas corpus even though they are designated as enemy combatants and are located outside the country in an area over which the United States has de facto jurisdiction?

HOLDING AND DECISION: (Kennedy, J.) Yes. Alien detainees have the constitutional privilege of habeas corpus even though they are designated as enemy combatants and are located outside the country in an area over which the United States has de facto jurisdiction. The issue is made up of two subsidiary issues: whether the aliens (P) are barred from seeking the habeas writ or invoking the Suspension Clause's protections because of their status as designated enemy combatants or because of their geographic presence at Guantanamo. A brief account of the writ's history and origins shows that protection for the habeas privilege is one of the few safeguards of liberty specified in the Constitution and that in the system the Framers conceived, the writ has a centrality that must inform proper interpretation of the Suspension Clause. That the Framers considered the writ a vital instrument for the protection of individual liberty is evident from the care taken in the Suspension Clause to specify the limited grounds for its suspension: The writ may be suspended only when public safety requires it in times of rebellion or invasion. It protects detainee rights by a means consistent with the Constitution's essential design, ensuring that, except during periods of formal suspension, the Judiciary will have a time-tested device, the writ, to maintain the "delicate balance of governance." Separation-of-powers principles, and the history that influenced their design, inform the Clause's reach and purpose. A diligent search of founding-era precedents and legal commentaries reveals no certain conclusions. None of the cases the parties cite reveal whether a common-law court would have granted, or refused to hear for lack of jurisdiction, a habeas petition by a prisoner deemed an enemy combatant, under a standard like the Defense Department's in these cases, and when held in a territory, like Guantanamo, over which the government (D) has total military and civil control. The evidence as to the writ's geographic scope at common law is informative, but, again, not dispositive. The aliens (P) argue that the site of their detention is analogous to two territories outside England to which the common-law writ ran, the exempt jurisdictions and India, but critical differences between these places and Guantanamo render these claims unpersuasive. The government (D) argues that

Continued on next page.

Guantanamo is more closely analogous to Scotland and Hanover, where the writ did not run, but it is unclear whether the common-law courts lacked the power to issue the writ there, or whether they refrained from doing so for prudential reasons. The parties' arguments that the very lack of a precedent on point supports their respective positions are premised upon the doubtful assumptions that the historical record is complete and that the common law, if properly understood, yields a definite answer to the questions before the Court. Given the unique status of Guantanamo and the particular dangers of terrorism in the modern age, the common-law courts simply may not have confronted cases with close parallels to this one. Therefore, too much cannot be inferred, one way or the other, from the lack of historical evidence on point. The government's (D) argument that the Suspension Clause affords the aliens (P) no rights because the United States does not claim sovereignty over the naval station is rejected. While Guantanamo is subject to Cuba's de jure sovereignty, it is clear that the government (D) exercises de facto sovereignty over this territory. Common-law habeas history provides scant support for the proposition that de jure sovereignty is the touchstone of habeas jurisdiction, and such a proposition is inconsistent with the Court's precedents and contrary to fundamental separation-of-powers principles. Fundamental questions regarding the Constitution's geographic scope first arose when the Nation acquired Hawaii and the noncontiguous Territories ceded by Spain after the Spanish-American War, and Congress discontinued its prior practice of extending constitutional rights to territories by statute. In the so-called Insular Cases, the Court held that the Constitution had independent force in the territories that was not contingent upon acts of legislative grace. Yet because of the difficulties and disruption inherent in transforming the former Spanish colonies' civil-law system into an Anglo-American system, the Court adopted the doctrine of territorial incorporation, under which the Constitution applies in full in incorporated Territories surely destined for statehood but only in part in unincorporated Territories. Practical considerations likewise influenced the Court's analysis in a case where American civilians were being tried by the U.S. military abroad, and in a case where enemy aliens, convicted of violating the laws of war, were detained in a German prison during the Allied Powers' post-World War II occupation (*Johnson v. Eisentrager,* 339 U.S. 763 (1950)). The government's (D) reading of *Eisentrager* as adopting a formalistic test for determining the Suspension Clause's reach is rejected because: (1) the discussion of practical considerations in that case was integral to a part of the Court's opinion that came before it announced its holding; (2) it mentioned the concept of territorial sovereignty only twice in its opinion, in contrast to its significant discussion of practical barriers to the running of the writ; and (3) if the Government's reading were correct, the opinion would have marked not only a change in, but a complete repudiation of, the Insular Cases' (and later cases') functional approach. A constricted reading of *Eisentrager* overlooks what the Court sees as a common

thread uniting all these cases: the idea that extraterritoriality questions turn on objective factors and practical concerns, not formalism. Under the government's (D) approach, it could lease territory from a third-party sovereign, exercise complete control over the territory, and govern the territory without legal constraints. The Constitution, however, cannot be contracted away in such a manner. Based on *Eisentrager* and other precedential cases, there are at least three factors that are relevant in determining the reach of the Suspension Clause: (1) the detainees' citizenship and status and the adequacy of the process through which that status was determined; (2) the nature of the sites where apprehension and then detention took place; and (3) the practical obstacles inherent in resolving the prisoner's entitlement to the writ. Application of this framework reveals, first, that the aliens' (P) status is in dispute: They are not American citizens, but deny they are enemy combatants; and although they have been afforded some process in CSRT proceedings, there has been no trial by military commission for violations of the laws of war. Second, while the sites of the aliens' (P) apprehension and detention weigh against finding they have Suspension Clause rights, the government (D) has absolute and indefinite control over the naval station. Third, although the Court is sensitive to the financial and administrative costs of holding the Suspension Clause applicable in a case of military detention abroad, these factors are not dispositive because the government (D) presents no credible arguments that the military mission at Guantanamo would be compromised if habeas courts had jurisdiction. For these reasons, the Suspension Clause applies with full effect at Guantanamo Bay. The aliens (P) thus are entitled to the privilege of habeas corpus to challenge the legality of their detention. Reversed and remanded to the court of appeals with instructions to remand to the district court.

DISSENT: (Scalia, J.) "The writ of habeas corpus does not, and never has, run in favor of aliens abroad; the Suspension Clause thus has no application, and the Court's intervention in this military matter is entirely ultra vires." The country is at war with radical terrorists, and the majority's decision will make it more difficult for the government (D) to fight terrorism and will "almost certainly cause more Americans to be killed." Such consequences are intolerable because they do not even protect a time-honored constitutional principle. It is already difficult enough for the military to determine in the theater of battle who is an enemy combatant and who is not; the majority's decision makes it even more difficult by requiring military officials to appear before civilian courts to defend their decisions. With higher standards of proof, more enemies will be returned to battle. Providing classified information to detainees' defense counsel will only lead to its getting into enemy hands. Congress and the President (D) have already determined that limiting the role of civilian courts in these matters is important to the

Continued on next page.

war's success. Given that the Court must be especially deferential to Congress in military matters, and given that the majority concedes that common law is not dispositive of the issue, the majority has no basis on which to strike down the MCA, and should have left undisturbed the considered judgment of the coequal branches. The majority's reliance on separation-of-powers principles is also misplaced, as those must be considered individually, so that if the scope of the writ is understood to restrain the Executive's actions, the limits of that scope are likewise intended to restrain the judiciary's incursions. In the past, alien combatants who have not been on U.S. soil have not been accorded the habeas privilege. The majority's finding that *Eisentrager* was grounded in practical considerations is a "rewriting" of that case. The practical considerations in that case were merely being used to support the Court's holding that the writ is unavailable to aliens abroad under any circumstance. Such a reading is also not supported by the Insular Cases. The aliens here are akin to prisoners of war, and such prisoners have never been accorded the writ—even when they were present on U.S. soil. Moreover, the original understanding of the Suspension Clause was that habeas was not available to aliens abroad, and such an understanding is supported by historical evidence. Finally, the Constitution provides for suspension of the writ during times of rebellion or invasion—it would make little sense for suspension to be limited to domestic crises, as there is an even greater justification for suspension in foreign lands where the United States might hold prisoners of war during an ongoing conflict. Correspondingly, there is less threat to liberty when the government (D) suspends the writ's application in foreign lands, where even in the most extreme view prisoners are entitled to fewer constitutional rights. And the writ's availability to citizens held abroad does not disprove such a limited reach of the writ, since the Constitution provides citizens with defined protections against the government (D).

▶ *ANALYSIS*

This decision held that the aliens (P) were entitled to seek the writ of habeas corpus, not that the writ would have to issue; that the DTA review procedures were an inadequate substitute for habeas corpus; that the aliens (P) did not need to exhaust the review procedures in the court of appeal before proceeding with their habeas actions in the district court; and that MCA § 7 was unconstitutional. Accordingly, both the DTA and the CSRT process remain intact. The case did not address whether the government (D) had the authority in the first place to detain the aliens (P), and left that issue for decision in the district court. The court expressly declined to decide whether the CSRT procedures satisfied due process.

■═■

Quicknotes

CERTIORARI A discretionary writ issued by a superior court to an inferior court in order to review the lower court's decisions; the Supreme Court's writ ordering such review.

DE FACTO GOVERNMENT A government that sustains its power against the lawful government by force.

DE JURE GOVERNMENT Government legally vested with the authority to govern.

DUE PROCESS The constitutional mandate requiring the courts to protect and enforce individuals' rights and liberties consistent with prevailing principles of fairness and justice and prohibiting the federal and state governments from such activities that deprive its citizens of life, liberty, or property interest.

HABEAS CORPUS A proceeding in which a defendant brings a writ to compel a judicial determination of whether he is lawfully being held in custody.

ULTRA VIRES An act undertaken by a corporation that is beyond the scope of its authority pursuant to law or its articles of incorporation.

■═■

Boumediene v. Bush

Alien detainees (P) v. President (D)

___ U.S. ___, 128 S. Ct. 2229, ___ L. Ed. 2d ___ (2008).

NATURE OF CASE: Appeal from decisions holding that alien detainees designated as enemy combatants at the U.S. Naval Station at Guantanamo Bay, Cuba, did not have the privilege of habeas corpus.

FACT SUMMARY: Aliens (P) designated as enemy combatants detained at Guantanamo Bay, Cuba, contended they had the constitutional privilege of habeas corpus, despite the procedures provided by the Detainee Treatment Act of 2005 (DTA) for review of the detainees' status, and that the Military Commissions Act of 2006 (MCA) operated as an unconstitutional suspension of the writ.

🏛 **RULE OF LAW**
Procedures provided in the Detainee Treatment Act of 2005 (DTA) for reviewing the status of alien detainees designated as enemy combatants are not an adequate and effective substitute for habeas corpus review.

FACTS: The United States government (D) captured aliens (P) abroad on the battlefields of Afghanistan or elsewhere. These aliens (P) were sent to the U.S. Naval Station at Guantanamo Bay, Cuba, over which Cuba has sovereignty. However, the government (D), which leases the naval station from Cuba, exercises complete jurisdiction and control over the site. The aliens (P) denied membership in the al Qaeda terrorist network that carried out the September 11 attacks and the Taliban regime that supported al Qaeda. At the time, none of the aliens (P) was a citizen of a nation at war with the United States. Each alien (P) appeared before a Combatant Status Review Tribunal (CSRT), was determined to be an "enemy combatant," and each alien (P) sought a writ of habeas corpus in the district court. While the cases were on remand from the United States Supreme Court, Congress passed the Detainee Treatment Act of 2005 (DTA), which amended 28 U.S.C. § 2241 to provide that "no court, justice, or judge shall have jurisdiction to hear or consider . . . an application for a writ of habeas corpus filed by or on behalf of an alien detained by the Department of Defense at Guantanamo," and gave the court of appeals "exclusive" jurisdiction to review CSRT decisions. After the Court's decision in *Hamdan v. Rumsfeld*, 548 U.S. 557 (2006), Congress enacted the Military Commissions Act of 2006 (MCA), § 7(a), which again amended § 2241 in an attempt to deprive federal courts of jurisdiction to hear the aliens' (P) habeas corpus petitions or other claims. The court of appeals ruled that the MCA deprived it of jurisdiction to hear the habeas petitions, and the United States Supreme Court granted certiorari.

ISSUE: Are procedures provided in the Detainee Treatment Act of 2005 (DTA) for reviewing the status of alien detainees designated as enemy combatants an adequate and effective substitute for habeas corpus review?

HOLDING AND DECISION: (Kennedy, J.) No. Procedures provided in the Detainee Treatment Act of 2005 (DTA) for reviewing the status of alien detainees designated as enemy combatants are not an adequate and effective substitute for habeas corpus review. Alien detainees designated as enemy combatants have the constitutional privilege of habeas corpus where procedures provided for review of their status are not an adequate and effective substitute for habeas corpus. The issue is whether the Suspension Clause has been complied with because the DTA review process provides an adequate substitute for the right to habeas review, to which the aliens (P) are entitled. Given its holding that the writ does not run to the aliens (P), the court of appeals found it unnecessary to consider whether there was an adequate substitute for habeas. This Court usually remands for consideration of questions not decided below, but departure from this rule is appropriate in "exceptional circumstances," where, as here, the costs of further delay substantially outweigh any benefits of remanding, and given the grave separation-of-powers issues raised by these cases and the fact that the aliens (P) have been denied meaningful access to a judicial forum for years. The Court's leading precedents on addressing habeas substitutes provide little guidance here because the statutes in question in those cases gave the courts broad remedial powers to secure the historic office of the writ, and included saving clauses to preserve habeas review as an avenue of last resort. In contrast, Congress intended the DTA and the MCA to circumscribe habeas review. The DTA's text limits the court of appeals' jurisdiction to assessing whether the CSRT complied with the "standards and procedures specified by the Secretary of Defense," and whether those were lawful. Thus, it was not intended by Congress to be coextensive with habeas corpus, and instead of preserving habeas review as a last resort, the MCA eliminates it for the aliens (P). That Congress intended to create a more limited procedure is also confirmed by its limiting factfinding. Ordinarily any justice or circuit judge is authorized to issue the writ, thereby accommodating the necessity for factfinding that will arise in some cases by allowing the appellate judge or Justice to transfer the case to a district court. However, by granting the court of appeals exclusive jurisdiction over the cases at bar, Congress has foreclosed that option in these cases. It is uncontroversial

Continued on next page.

that the habeas privilege entitles the prisoner to a meaningful opportunity to demonstrate that he is being held pursuant to "the erroneous application or interpretation" of relevant law, and the habeas court must have the power to order the conditional release of an individual unlawfully detained. However, more may be required depending on the circumstances, and, indeed, common-law habeas was an adaptable remedy. Also, the idea that the necessary scope of habeas review in part depends upon the rigor of any earlier proceedings accords with the test for procedural adequacy in the due process context. Where a person is detained by executive order, rather than, say, after being tried and convicted in a court, the need for collateral review is most pressing. Thus, here, to determine the necessary scope of habeas corpus review, the CSRT process must be assessed. The aliens (P) identify what they see as myriad deficiencies in the CSRTs, the most relevant being the constraints upon the detainee's (P) ability to rebut the factual basis for the government's (D) assertion that he is an enemy combatant. At the CSRT stage, the detainee (P) has limited means to find or present evidence to challenge the government's (D) case, does not have the assistance of counsel, and may not be aware of the most critical allegations that the government (D) relied upon to order his detention. His opportunity to confront witnesses is likely to be more theoretical than real, given that there are no limits on the admission of hearsay. Even if the CSRTs satisfied due process, however, that would not end the inquiry, because, for the habeas writ, or its substitute, to function as an effective and meaningful remedy in this context, the court conducting the collateral proceeding must have some ability to correct any errors, to assess the sufficiency of the government's (D) evidence, and to admit and consider relevant exculpatory evidence that was not introduced during the earlier proceeding. There also must be authority for directing the prisoner's release. The DTA does not meet these standards. Among the constitutional infirmities from which the DTA potentially suffers are the absence of provisions allowing the aliens (P) to challenge the President's (D) authority under the AUMF to detain them indefinitely, to contest the CSRT's findings of fact, to supplement the record on review with exculpatory evidence discovered after the CSRT proceedings, and to request release. Because the statute cannot be read to contain each of these constitutionally required procedures, the aliens (P) have met their burden of establishing that the DTA review process is, on its face, an inadequate substitute for habeas corpus and that there is no bar to the district court's entertaining their claims. MCA § 7 thus effects an unconstitutional suspension of the writ. A remaining question, nevertheless, is whether there are prudential barriers to habeas review under these circumstances. The government (D) argues that the aliens (P) must seek review of their CSRT determinations in the court of appeals before they can proceed with their habeas corpus actions in the district court. In other contexts and for prudential reasons, this Court has required exhaustion of alternative remedies before a prisoner can seek federal habeas relief. The cases here involve detainees (P) who have been held for years without judicial oversight,

and there has been no showing that it would be excessively burdensome to respond to the habeas corpus actions. To require these detainees (P) to pursue the limited structure of DTA review before proceeding with habeas actions would be to require additional months, if not years, of delay. This does not mean that a habeas court should intervene the moment an enemy combatant steps foot in a territory where the writ runs. Except in cases of undue delay, such as the present, federal courts should refrain from entertaining an enemy combatant's habeas petition at least until after the CSRT has had a chance to review his status. To reduce the burden habeas proceedings will place on the military, without impermissibly diluting the writ's protections, due consideration must be given to channeling future cases to a single district court and requiring that court to use its discretion to accommodate to the greatest extent possible the government's (D) legitimate interest in protecting sources and intelligence gathering methods. Also, proper deference must be accorded to the political branches. Reversed and remanded to the court of appeals with instructions to remand to the district court.

DISSENT: (Roberts, C.J.) The majority has struck down as inadequate "the most generous set of procedural protections ever afforded aliens detained by this country," and replaced them with "a set of shapeless procedures to be defined by the federal court at some future date." The procedures under the DTA are a sufficient substitute for habeas review and adequately protect whatever constitutional rights aliens (P) captured abroad and detained as enemy combatants may enjoy. The undefined habeas process will most likely be like the DTA system it replaces, since the district courts will have to balance the need to review a prisoner's detention with the need to protect Americans from terrorism. The DTA system the political branches constructed adequately protects any constitutional rights aliens captured abroad and detained as enemy combatants may enjoy, and the cases should be dismissed on that ground. In addition, the Court should never have granted certiorari to hear the cases until the court of appeals had made its rulings on the nature and validity of the congressionally mandated proceedings in a given alien's (P) case and until the alien detainees (P) had exhausted their remedies under the DTA. It is premature to decide that the aliens (P) have a right to habeas without first assessing whether the remedies under the DTA system vindicate their rights. If the CSRT procedures meet minimal due process requirements, and if an Article III court is available to ensure that these procedures are followed in future cases, there is no need to reach the Suspension Clause question. While the majority believes that requiring the aliens (P) to pursue DTA review before proceeding with their habeas actions will inject additional delay, there is no reason to believe that habeas review by the federal courts will proceed any faster. On the contrary, it will take

Continued on next page.

longer because it will precede review at the court of appeals—where review starts under the DTA system. The CSRTs mirror the procedural model of habeas for enemy combatants, and they operate much as habeas courts would upon hearing a defendant's collateral challenge for the first time. Based on the posture it has assumed, the majority must evaluate whether the DTA system is an adequate substitute for habeas review without knowing what rights either habeas or the DTA is supposed to protect. In part this is because habeas review may be more limited in some circumstances than in others, depending on the detainee's status and the rights he is asserting. Also, because there is no disagreement that the Suspension Clause protects the writ as it existed at the time of ratification, when common-law courts abstained altogether from matters involving prisoners of war, the process provided the aliens (P) under the DTA must be more than constitutionally sufficient. At the CSRT stage, the detainees (P) are accorded significant access to classified materials, may call any witness who is "reasonably available," and have a Personal Representative. Then, at the court of appeals, they have full access to appellate counsel and the right to challenge the factual and legal bases of their detention. This statutory scheme provides the enemy combatants held at Guantanamo greater procedural protections than have ever been afforded alleged enemy detainees—whether citizens or aliens—in our national history. The only weak argument to all these procedural protections that the majority has is that detainees are unable to introduce at the appeal stage exculpatory evidence discovered after the conclusion of their CSRT proceedings. While this is true, a detainee who finds such evidence can have the court of appeals remand the case for a new CSRT determination, and the court of appeals can later review any new or reinstated decision in light of the supplemented record. In addition, the DTA provides for periodic review of any new evidence that may become available relating to the enemy combatant status of a detainee. Additionally, the DTA can and should be read to authorize the court of appeals to order release to avoid serious constitutional difficulties. In sum, the majority finds that any interpretation that would make the statute an adequate substitute for habeas must be rejected. This disserves the detainees, who will be subjected to further litigation; Congress, whose attempts to balance the needs of national security and detainees' liberty interests have been brushed aside; and the American people, who lose some control over foreign policy to unelected judges.

▶ ANALYSIS

In determining the adequacy of the DTA as a substitute for habeas review, the majority observes that it is not holding that an adequate substitute must duplicate practice under 28 U.S.C. § 2241 (which codified the common law writ of habeas corpus) in all respects. It also notes that to hold that the detainees at Guantanamo may, under the DTA, challenge the President's legal authority to detain them,

contest the CSRT's findings of fact, supplement the record on review with exculpatory evidence, and request an order of release would come close to reinstating the § 2241 habeas corpus process Congress sought to deny them. These observations seem to acknowledge that Congress has the power to statutorily expand habeas jurisdiction more than is required by the Suspension Clause, but also that limiting such jurisdiction can go only so far as permitted by the Constitution. The Court thus leaves open the question of which habeas "practice" must be looked to in ascertaining such a constitutional limitation—the practice at common law, the practice at the time of ratification, or current practice.

Quicknotes

ARTICLE III, U.S. CONSTITUTION Limits federal judicial power to cases and controversies.

CERTIORARI A discretionary writ issued by a superior court to an inferior court in order to review the lower court's decisions; the Supreme Court's writ ordering such review.

DUE PROCESS The constitutional mandate requiring the courts to protect and enforce individuals' rights and liberties consistent with prevailing principles of fairness and justice and prohibiting the federal and state governments from such activities that deprive its citizens of life, liberty, or property interest.

EXCULPATORY EVIDENCE A statement or other evidence that tends to excuse, justify, or absolve the defendant from alleged fault or guilt.

HABEAS CORPUS COLLATERAL REVIEW An independent review of whether a prisoner is being lawfully imprisoned.

Brown v. Allen

Death row inmate (D) v. State official (P)

344 U.S. 443 (1953).

NATURE OF CASE: Consolidated appeals from convictions for rape and murder.

FACT SUMMARY: Brown (D) filed a habeas petition in federal court after the North Carolina Supreme Court rejected his appeal.

RULE OF LAW
Federal courts have habeas jurisdiction to review convictions after state remedies have been exhausted.

FACTS: Brown (D), Daniels (D), and Speller (D) were convicted and sentenced to death in North Carolina. All three were black men who claimed that jury selection in the original trial had involved racial discrimination. After the North Carolina Supreme Court had rejected their appeals, they filed habeas petitions in federal court. Their cases were then consolidated. In Speller's (D) case, the district court ruled that a habeas corpus proceeding could not raise the same question already rejected in state court. The Fourth Circuit affirmed, and the United States Supreme Court granted certiorari.

ISSUE: Do federal courts have habeas jurisdiction to review convictions after state remedies have been exhausted?

HOLDING AND DECISION: (Frankfurter, J.) [Justice Reed provided the opinion of the Court. However, the casebook indicates that Frankfurter's opinion was clearer and has since been used as the law on this issue.] Yes. Federal courts have habeas jurisdiction to review convictions after state remedies have been exhausted. Most habeas claims are frivolous; the meritorious claims are few. However, the Act of 1867 gave federal courts the right to hear habeas cases for state convictions. Therefore, habeas corpus jurisdiction was provided to federal courts by Congress and must be given effect even if most habeas claims are insubstantial. Still, the reality of frivolous claims does bear upon the procedure that district courts should use to judge these claims. The correct procedure includes: (1) a prima facie case must be made by the habeas petitioner; (2) state remedies must be exhausted; (3) a record of the state proceedings is favored; (4) judges should accept the state court's finding of basic facts. Federal district courts must retain their own judgment on matters of federal law and mixed questions of law and fact. Only by following these rules can habeas corpus, deemed the principal bulwark of liberty, be an effective means of justice. [The disposition of the three cases is unclear from the footnotes explaining the various opinions filed.]

CONCURRENCE: (Jackson, J.) Substantive due process law must remain somewhat vague but it is important to adhere to procedures that enable courts to quickly distinguish frivolous claims. Federal courts should review only habeas petitions that raise jurisdictional questions involving federal law or that show the defendant was improperly obstructed from making a record and presenting a constitutional issue.

ANALYSIS

The scope of habeas reviews has never included basic facts from the underlying case. Statutory amendments in 1966 narrowed this discretion by making state court findings of fact presumptively binding. Thus, there are very few evidentiary proceedings in federal courts for habeas proceedings.

■=■

Quicknotes

CERTIORARI A discretionary writ issued by a superior court to an inferior court in order to review the lower court's decisions; the Supreme Court's writ ordering such review.

HABEAS CORPUS A proceeding in which a defendant brings a writ to compel a judicial determination of whether he is lawfully being held in custody.

JURISDICTION The authority of a court to hear and declare judgment in respect to a particular matter.

PRIMA FACIE CASE An action where the plaintiff introduces sufficient evidence to submit the issue to the judge or jury for determination.

■=■

Terry Williams v. Taylor

Death sentence defendant (P) v. State official (D)

529 U.S. 362 (2000).

NATURE OF CASE: Appeal from a federal court of appeals decision denying habeas corpus relief to a death sentence convict.

FACT SUMMARY: When Terry Williams (P), who had been sentenced to death, sought federal habeas corpus relief on grounds of ineffective assistance of counsel at his penalty hearing, the federal court of appeals denied habeas relief, construing the federal habeas corpus statute (Section 2254(d)(1)) as barring relief under the circumstances of the case.

🏛 RULE OF LAW
(1) The constitutional right to effective assistance of counsel is violated when defense counsel fails to introduce mitigating evidence at the penalty phase of a death sentence case.
(2) The Antiterrorism and Effective Death Penalty Act of 1996 (AEDPA) does not alter the underlying grant of jurisdiction to federal courts to exercise federal habeas corpus relief.

FACTS: Having been sentenced to death, Terry Williams (P) alleged, in a state post-conviction proceeding, ineffective assistance of counsel at the penalty phase since his defense counsel failed to produce mitigating evidence. The state trial court agreed under the federal *Strickland v. Washington*, 466 U.S. 668 (1984), standard, and reversed the conviction. The Virginia Supreme Court disagreed and reversed the trial court. Williams (P) sought federal habeas corpus relief in the federal district court, which upheld the claim of ineffective assistance of counsel. The federal court of appeal, however, reversed the district court, construing the federal habeas corpus statute (Section 2254(d)(1)) as barring relief unless the state court decided the question by interpreting or applying the relevant precedent in a manner that reasonable jurists would all agree was unreasonable. Williams (P) appealed to the United States Supreme Court.

ISSUE:
(1) Is the constitutional right to effective assistance of counsel violated when defense counsel fails to introduce mitigating evidence at the penalty phase of a death sentence case?
(2) Does the Antiterrorism and Effective Death Penalty Act of 1996 (AEDPA) alter the underlying grant of jurisdiction to federal courts to exercise federal habeas corpus relief?

HOLDING AND DECISION: (Stevens, J.)
(1) Yes. The constitutional right to effective assistance of counsel is violated when defense counsel fails to introduce mitigating evidence at the penalty phase of a death sentence case. Here, the sole argument in mitigation

that trial counsel advanced was that Williams (P) turned himself in, expressed remorse, and cooperated with the police. While this, coupled with the prison records and guard testimony, may not have overcome a finding of future dangerousness, the graphic description of Williams's (P) childhood, filled with abuse and privation, or the reality that he was "borderline mentally retarded," might well have influenced the jury's appraisal of his moral culpability. Mitigating evidence unrelated to dangerousness may alter the jury's selection of penalty, even if it does not undermine or rebut the prosecution's death-eligibility case. In neglecting to present evidence of the latter, defense counsel in this case failed to provide Williams (P) with effective assistance of counsel as mandated in *Strickland v. Washington* since defense counsel's performance at sentencing fell below the range of competent assistance of counsel, and such deficiency was prejudicial as there was a reasonable probability that the sentencing outcome would have differed had counsel been effective.
(2) No. The Antiterrorism and Effective Death Penalty Act of 1996 (AEDPA) does not alter the underlying grant of jurisdiction to federal courts to exercise federal habeas corpus relief. The inquiry mandated by the AEDPA amendment to the federal habeas corpus legislation relates only to the way in which a federal habeas court exercises its duty to decide constitutional questions. When federal judges exercise their federal-question jurisdiction under the "judicial power" of Article III of the Constitution, it is "emphatically the province and duty" of those judges to say what the law is. While the AEDPA amendment directs federal courts to attend to every state-court judgment with utmost care, it does not require them to defer to the opinion of every reasonable state-court judge on the content of federal law. Otherwise, federal law might be applied by the federal courts one way in Virginia and another way in California. Reversed.

CONCURRENCE: (O'Connor, J.) Federal courts, even on habeas corpus review, have an independent obligation to say what the law is.

DISSENT IN PART: (Rehnquist, C.J.) The Virginia court's prejudice standard was not contrary to clearly established precedent. Nor was its decision an unreasonable application of federal law since, given the strong evidence of Williams's (P) dangerousness, the state court could reasonably have determined that evidence of Williams's (P) terrible childhood and low IQ would not have swayed the jury.

Continued on next page.

ANALYSIS

In the *Williams* decision, the Supreme Court noted that certain basic premises govern its interpretation of the federal habeas corpus statute: first, the requirement that the determinations of state courts be tested only against clearly established federal law, as determined by the Supreme Court, and, second, the prohibition on the issuance of the writ unless the state court's decision is contrary to, or involves an unreasonable application of, that clearly established law.

■═■

Quicknotes

ARTICLE III, U.S. CONSTITUTION Limits federal judicial power to cases and controversies.

HABEAS CORPUS A proceeding in which a defendant brings a writ to compel a judicial determination of whether he is lawfully being held in custody.

■═■

Wainwright v. Sykes

State official (D) v. Convicted murderer (P)

433 U.S. 72 (1977).

NATURE OF CASE: Federal habeas corpus petition.

FACT SUMMARY: Sykes (P) confessed to a murder after being given his Miranda rights, but he was drunk at the time and the voluntariness of the confession and the validity of the Miranda waiver were not raised during the trial.

🏛 RULE OF LAW
Federal habeas corpus petitions may not challenge convictions based on the failure to raise objections under the state's contemporary objection rule.

FACTS: Sykes (P) murdered a man. Sykes (P) confessed after being given his Miranda warnings. At the time, Sykes (P) was allegedly in a highly inebriated state. Neither the voluntariness of the confession nor the validity of the waiver of Miranda rights was ever raised before or during the trial. When it was subsequently raised on appeal, the state courts refused to review the matter or hold a hearing on it since the objections were deemed waived under the state contemporary objection rule. The failure to properly object waived the alleged defect. Sykes (P) then filed a federal habeas corpus petition. The court granted the petition ordering as to whether there had been a knowing and intelligible waiver of rights since it found no prejudice to the state. Wainwright (D), the warden, appealed alleging that the contemporary objection rule was a matter of substantive law and the federal courts should not interfere with such matters.

ISSUE: May federal habeas corpus petitions challenge convictions based on the failure to raise objections under the state's contemporary objection rule?

HOLDING AND DECISION: (Rehnquist, J.) No. Federal habeas corpus petitions may not challenge convictions based on the failure to raise objections under the state's contemporary objection rule. One of the questions that must be considered in deciding whether to entertain a habeas corpus petition is whether there is an independent state ground that bars such considerations even though they may involve federally cognizable issues/rights. Until recently, federal courts would not interfere with state procedural rules that barred the consideration of such issue by state courts, e.g., failure to object, or failure to file a timely appeal. The failure of the defendant to comply with state substantive law barred consideration by the federal judiciary on the ground that it could not simply ignore such rules/ laws. In *Fay v. Noia*, 372 U.S. 391 (1963), the Court stated that, absent a knowing and intelligent waiver of such rights and if no prejudice resulted to the state, an independent hearing could be held to determine whether such rights had been adequately waived even though they could not be

raised in state proceedings because of its substantive law. *Noia* was too broadly worded. At least with respect to state contemporary objection rules, we reject its rationale. Failure to promptly and properly object to defects as herein bars federal habeas corpus review of such defects if barred under state law. Our holding applies only to situations where the state court never decides the issue since it was not properly raised. In proper situations where there is adequate "cause" or "prejudice," neither of which we attempt to define herein, justice may require a different finding. Reversed.

CONCURRENCE: (Burger, C.J.) The touchstone of *Noia* was that the choice therein was solely Noia's. It was his waiver of constitutional rights that was at issue. Here, Sykes's (P) attorney made the decision/error not to challenge the admissibility of the confession. The two cases are dissimilar.

CONCURRENCE: (Stevens, J.) A client does not consent to decisions concerning trial tactics, and *Noia* applies only to issues involving consent. Further, since the police fully complied with Miranda, the alleged rule violation is inapplicable.

DISSENT: (Brennan, J.) No guidelines are presented herein as to what situations qualify as either "cause" or "prejudice." Further, the state suffers a very minor injury by allowing federal habeas corpus inquiry into such matters as compared to the much greater harm suffered by the defendant were habeas corpus inquiry to be denied. The fear of the majority that attorneys might not raise constitutional questions to have a second shot at an acquittal/ new trial is irrational. If these claims prevail their clients may obtain an immediate dismissal. Deference to local rules at the expense of constitutional claims is a mistake. *Noia* applies to the intentional bypass of constitutional rights rather than unintentional errors.

▶ ANALYSIS

Denial of counsel has been said to go to the very power and authority of the trial court and is an independent ground for granting habeas corpus regardless of state substantive law. *Johnson v. Zerbst*, 304 U.S. 458 (1938). However, in *Davis v. United States*, 411 U.S. 233 (1973), the makeup of a federal grand jury was challenged for the first time on appeal. The appeal was dismissed since it failed to comply with Fed. R. Crim. P. 12(b)(2) requiring such objections to be raised before trial.

■■■

Continued on next page.

Quicknotes

HABEAS CORPUS A proceeding in which a defendant brings a writ to compel a judicial determination of whether he is lawfully being held in custody.

MIRANDA RULE A required warning given before any questioning by law enforcement authorities can take place. Individuals in custody receive warnings regarding their privilege against self-incrimination, right to remain silent, and right to be represented by an attorney.

■══■

Advanced Problems in Judicial Federalism

Quick Reference Rules of Law

United States v. Mendoza

Federal government (D) v. Filipino national (P)

464 U.S. 154 (1984).

NATURE OF CASE: Appeal from finding of due process denial under the Nationality Act.

FACT SUMMARY: Mendoza (P) brought an action against the government (D) in which Mendoza (P) alleged that the government's (D) administration of the Nationality Act denied Mendoza (P) due process of law.

🏛 RULE OF LAW
Nonmutual offensive collateral estoppel does not apply against the government in such a way as to preclude relitigation of constitutional issues.

FACTS: Mendoza (P), a Filipino national, filed a petition for naturalization under a statute that by its terms had expired thirty-two years earlier. Mendoza's (P) claim for naturalization was based on the assertion that the government's (D) administration of the Nationality Act denied him due process of law. Neither the district court nor the court of appeals ever reached the merits of Mendoza's (P) claim because they held that the government (D) was collaterally estopped from litigating the constitutional issue of due process because of an earlier decision against the government (D) in a case brought by other Filipino nationals in U.S. district court. The government (D) appealed, and the United States Supreme Court reviewed the lower decisions.

ISSUE: Does nonmutual offensive collateral estoppel apply against the government in such a way as to preclude relitigation of constitutional issues?

HOLDING AND DECISION: (Rehnquist, J.) No. Nonmutual offensive collateral estoppel does not apply against the government in such a way as to preclude relitigation of constitutional issues. The conduct of government (D) litigation in the federal courts is sufficiently different from the conduct of private civil litigation in these courts so that what might otherwise be economy interests underlying a broad application of collateral estoppel are outweighed by the constraints that peculiarly affect the government (D). Here, the court of appeals found no "record evidence" indicating there was a "crucial need" in the administration of immigration laws for a redetermination of the due process question decided in earlier litigation, *In re Naturalization of 68 Filipino War Veterans*, 406 F. Supp. 931 (N.D. Cal. 1975). The standard announced by the court of appeals—that is, "crucial need"—is so wholly subjective that it affords no guidance to the courts or the government. This Court believes its present disposition of this case will better allow thorough development of legal doctrine and avoid the problem of freezing the development of the law. Reversed.

▶ ANALYSIS

Difficult questions about the fair administration of justice arise when the government is faced with lower court rulings it believes to be wrong. *Mendoza* established that res judicata does not bar the government from relitigating the issue against a new party. The policy arguments relied upon by the Supreme Court in *Mendoza* show that it is not improper for the government to relitigate issues in order to persuade other courts that the first decision was erroneous.

Quicknotes

COLLATERAL ESTOPPEL A doctrine whereby issues litigated and determined in a prior proceeding are binding upon all subsequent litigation between the parties regarding that issue.

DUE PROCESS The constitutional mandate requiring the courts to protect and enforce individuals' rights and liberties consistent with prevailing principles of fairness and justice and prohibiting the federal and state governments from such activities that deprive its citizens of life, liberty, or property interest.

RES JUDICATA The rule of law that a final judgment by a court precludes subsequent litigation between the parties regarding the same cause of action.

Allen v. McCurry

Police officer (D) v. Convicted criminal (P)

449 U.S. 90 (1980).

NATURE OF CASE: Action for damages under 42 U.S.C. § 1983.

FACT SUMMARY: In McCurry's (P) action against Allen (D) (one of several police officers who entered McCurry's (P) home and seized evidence used in McCurry's (P) trial), McCurry (P) contended that Allen et al. (D) conspired to violate McCurry's (P) Fourth Amendment rights by conducting an unconstitutional search and seizure in McCurry's (P) home.

🏛 RULE OF LAW
42 U.S.C. § 1983 is not a substitute for a federal writ of habeas corpus, the purpose of which is not to redress civil injury, but to release the applicant from unlawful physical confinement.

FACTS: At a hearing before his criminal trial in state court, McCurry (P) invoked the Fourth and Fourteenth Amendments to suppress evidence that had been seized by the police. The trial court denied the suppression motion and McCurry (P) was convicted after a jury trial. On appeal, the conviction was affirmed. McCurry (P) also was barred from seeking a writ of habeas corpus in a federal district court because he did not assert that the state courts had denied him a full and fair opportunity to litigate his search and seizure claim. McCurry (P) then sought federal court redress for the alleged constitutional violations by bringing a damages suit under 42 U.S.C. § 1983 against Allen (D) and other police officers who had entered his home and seized the evidence. The United States Supreme Court granted certiorari.

ISSUE: Is 42 U.S.C § 1983 a substitute for a federal writ of habeas corpus, the purpose of which is not to redress civil injury, but to release the applicant from unlawful physical confinement?

HOLDING AND DECISION: (Stewart, J.) No. 42 U.S.C. § 1983 is not a substitute for a federal writ of habeas corpus, the purpose of which is not to redress civil injury, but to release the applicant from unlawful physical confinement. Here, the court of appeals concluded that McCurry's (P) suit was his only route to a federal forum for his constitutional claim and directed the trial court to allow him to proceed to trial unencumbered by collateral estoppel. However, nothing in the language or legislative history of § 1983 proves any congressional intent to deny binding effect to a state court judgment or decision when the state court, acting within its proper jurisdiction, has given the parties a full and fair opportunity to litigate federal claims, and thereby has shown itself willing and able to protect federal rights. There is, in short, no reason to believe that Congress intended to provide a person claiming a federal right an unrestricted opportunity to relitigate an issue already decided in state court simply because the issue arose in a state proceeding in which he would rather not have been engaged at all. Thus, the court of appeals erred in holding that McCurry's (P) inability to obtain federal habeas corpus relief upon his Fourth Amendment claim rendered the doctrine of collateral estoppal inapplicable to his § 1983 suit. Reversed and remanded.

DISSENT: (Blackmun, J.) To hold that a criminal defendant who raises a Fourth Amendment claim at his criminal trial "freely and without reservation submits his federal claims for decision by the state courts" is to deny reality. The criminal defendant is an involuntary litigant in the state tribunal, and against him all the forces of the state are arrayed. To force him to choose between forgoing either a potential defense or a federal forum for hearing his constitutional civil claim is fundamentally unfair.

▶ ANALYSIS

Allen v. McCurry affirmed that § 1983 does not just negate the application of res judicata and that "normal" res judicata principles apply. There are, however, many ambiguities in the opinion. For instance, the Court reserved the question whether preclusion could apply to claims that could have been but were not raised in the state courts. Nor did the Court specify the source or content of the rule that res judicata does not apply when there was no "full and fair opportunity" to litigate.

■═■

Quicknotes

CERTIORARI A discretionary writ issued by a superior court to an inferior court in order to review the lower court's decisions; the Supreme Court's writ ordering such review.

COLLATERAL ESTOPPEL A doctrine whereby issues litigated and determined in a prior proceeding are binding upon all subsequent litigation between the parties regarding that issue.

RES JUDICATA The rule of law that a final judgment by a court precludes subsequent litigation between the parties regarding the same cause of action.

WRIT OF HABEAS CORPUS A proceeding in which a defendant brings a writ to compel a judicial determination of whether he is lawfully being held in custody.

■═■

Heck v. Humphrey

Prison inmate (P) v. Prosecutor (D)

512 U.S. 477 (1994).

NATURE OF CASE: Appeal from dismissal of a § 1983 claim for damages.

FACT SUMMARY: Heck (P), a prison inmate, filed a § 1983 action for damages alleging that his manslaughter conviction was due to violations of law by Humphrey (D), the prosecutor.

🏛 **RULE OF LAW**
In order to recover damages for an unconstitutional conviction, a § 1983 plaintiff must prove that the conviction has been reversed on direct appeal or otherwise invalidated.

FACTS: Heck (P) was convicted in Indiana of voluntary manslaughter. While his appeal of this conviction was pending, Heck (P) filed a § 1983 civil rights lawsuit against the prosecutors, including Humphrey (D), for destroying exculpatory evidence in violation of the law. The complaint sought monetary damages. The district court dismissed the action, holding that the issues it raised would directly implicate Heck's (P) confinement. While this decision was being appealed, Heck's (P) criminal appeals failed at both the state and federal level. The Seventh Circuit affirmed dismissal of the § 1983 action, ruling that it was essentially challenging the legality of his conviction. The United States Supreme Court granted certiorari.

ISSUE: Must a § 1983 plaintiff prove that the conviction has been reversed on direct appeal or otherwise invalidated in order to recover damages for an unconstitutional conviction?

HOLDING AND DECISION: (Scalia, J.) Yes. In order to recover damages for an unconstitutional conviction, a § 1983 plaintiff must prove that the conviction has been reversed on direct appeal or otherwise invalidated. The two most fertile sources of federal court prisoner litigation are the Civil Rights Act, § 1983, and the federal Habeas Corpus Statute. Both provide federal forums for claims of unconstitutional treatment by state officials. Generally, exhaustion of state remedies is not a prerequisite for § 1983 actions but is required for federal habeas cases. Previously, this Court has ruled that habeas proceedings are the exclusive remedy for prisoners challenging their imprisonment. However, Heck (P) brought his § 1983 action for damages and could not have obtained this remedy through habeas corpus. The proper way to handle this potential conflict is not to add an exhaustion requirement to § 1983. Rather, it is evident that certain claims are not cognizable under § 1983 at all. In the analogous situation of a malicious prosecution action, termination of the criminal proceedings in favor of the defendant is a necessary element. Therefore, a state prisoner who seeks damages in a § 1983 suit must be required to show that the conviction has been invalidated for some reason. Even prisoners who have fully exhausted their available state remedies have no cause of action under § 1983 unless their convictions are reversed. Accordingly, Heck's (P) damages action is barred because he is not able to show that his manslaughter conviction was reversed or invalidated. Affirmed.

CONCURRENCE: (Thomas, J.) The Court's expansion of the two jurisdiction statutes has caused the conflict. Thus, it must attempt to limit the scope of the statutes in order to fix the problem.

CONCURRENCE: (Souter, J.) Justice Scalia's opinion should not have simply grafted malicious prosecution requirements onto § 1983. The analogy is not necessarily adequate. The reason that § 1983 attacks on convictions are improper is that they frustrate the intentions of Congress. The majority decision should be read narrowly. Individuals who are not in custody do not have a conflict with habeas jurisdiction and should not be bound by the requirements set forth by the majority for favorable termination.

▶ **ANALYSIS**

This decision leaves many questions unanswered. It is unclear what the effect of res judicata will be on a case in which a state prisoner is allowed to pursue a § 1983 action. The Supreme Court has yet to deal with this and similar issues in the wake of the *Heck* case.

■=■

Quicknotes

CERTIORARI A discretionary writ issued by a superior court to an inferior court in order to review the lower court's decisions; the Supreme Court's writ ordering such review.

HABEAS CORPUS A proceeding in which a defendant brings a writ to compel a judicial determination of whether he is lawfully being held in custody.

RES JUDICATA The rule of law that a final judgment by a court precludes subsequent litigation between the parties regarding the same cause of action.

■=■

Exxon Mobil Corporation v. Saudi Basic Industries Corporation

Joint venturer (P) v. Joint venturer (D)

544 U.S. 280 (2005).

NATURE OF CASE: Appeal from dismissal for lack of subject-matter jurisdiction, on interlocutory appeal, of declaratory action to determine whether royalties were overcharged to joint ventures.

FACT SUMMARY: Exxon Mobil Corporation (Exxon Mobil) (P) contended that its action in federal court against Saudi Basic Industries Corporation (SABIC) (D) to determine whether SABIC (D) had properly charged royalties to joint ventures between the parties should not be dismissed under the *Rooker-Feldman* doctrine merely because a judgment had been entered in a previously filed state-court action that had litigated the same claims as made in the federal action.

🏛 RULE OF LAW
The *Rooker-Feldman* doctrine applies only to cases brought by state-court losers complaining of injuries caused by state-court judgments rendered before federal district court proceedings have been commenced and inviting district court review and rejection of those judgments.

FACTS: Two subsidiaries of Exxon Mobil (P) formed joint ventures with SABIC (D) to produce polyethylene in Saudi Arabia. When a dispute arose over royalties that SABIC (D) had charged the joint ventures, SABIC (D) preemptively sued the two subsidiaries in state court, seeking a declaratory judgment that the royalties were proper. Exxon Mobil (P) then countersued in federal district court two weeks later, alleging that SABIC (D) overcharged them. Before the state-court trial, which ultimately yielded a jury verdict of over $400 million for Exxon Mobil (P), the district court denied SABIC's (D) motion to dismiss the federal suit. On interlocutory appeal, over eight months after the state-court jury verdict, the court of appeals, on its own motion, raised the question of whether subject-matter jurisdiction over the federal suit failed under the *Rooker-Feldman* doctrine because Exxon Mobil's (P) claims had already been litigated in state court. The court did not question the district court's subject-matter jurisdiction at the suit's outset, but held that federal jurisdiction terminated when the state court entered judgment on the jury verdict. The United States Supreme Court granted certiorari to resolve conflict among the circuits over the scope of the *Rooker-Feldman* doctrine.

ISSUE: Does the *Rooker-Feldman* doctrine apply only to cases brought by state-court losers complaining of injuries caused by state-court judgments rendered before federal district court proceedings have been commenced

and inviting district court review and rejection of those judgments?

HOLDING AND DECISION: (Ginsburg, J.) Yes. The *Rooker-Feldman* doctrine applies only to cases brought by state-court losers complaining of injuries caused by state-court judgments rendered before federal district court proceedings have been commenced and inviting district court review and rejection of those judgments. Here, the court of appeals erred in holding that *Rooker-Feldman* applied merely because the state-court judgment preceded a federal judgment on the same claim. The *Rooker-Feldman* doctrine has been applied by the Court only twice, in *Rooker v. Fidelity Trust Co.*, 263 U.S. 413 (1923), and in *District of Columbia Court of Appeals v. Feldman*, 460 U.S. 462 (1983). In *Rooker*, the plaintiffs previously defeated in state court filed suit in federal district court alleging that the adverse state-court judgment was unconstitutional and asking that it be declared "null and void." Noting preliminarily that the state court had acted within its jurisdiction, the Court explained that if the state-court decision was wrong, "that did not make the judgment void, but merely left it open to reversal or modification in an appropriate and timely appellate proceeding." Federal district courts, *Rooker* recognized, are empowered to exercise only original, not appellate, jurisdiction. Because Congress has empowered the Supreme Court alone to exercise appellate authority "to reverse or modify" a state-court judgment, the Court affirmed a decree dismissing the federal suit for lack of jurisdiction. In *Feldman*, two plaintiffs, Hickey and Feldman, neither of whom had graduated from an accredited law school, brought federal-court actions after the District of Columbia's highest court denied their petitions to waive a court rule requiring D. C. bar applicants to have graduated from an accredited law school. Citing *Rooker*, the Court observed that the district court lacked authority to review a final judicial determination of the D. C. high court because such review "can be obtained only in this Court." Concluding that the D.C. court's proceedings applying the accreditation rule to the plaintiffs were "judicial in nature," the Court ruled that the federal district court lacked subject-matter jurisdiction. However, concluding also that, in promulgating the bar admission rule, the D.C. court had acted legislatively, the Court held that the district court was not barred from addressing the validity of the rule itself, so long as the plaintiffs did not seek review of the rule's application in a particular case. Since *Feldman*, the Court has never applied *Rooker-Feldman* to dismiss an action for want of jurisdiction. However, the lower federal courts

Continued on next page.

have variously interpreted the *Rooker-Feldman* doctrine to extend far beyond the contours of the *Rooker* and *Feldman* cases, overriding Congress's conferral of federal-court jurisdiction concurrent with jurisdiction exercised by state courts, and superseding the ordinary application of preclusion law under 28 U.S.C. § 1738. *Rooker* and *Feldman* exhibit the limited circumstances in which this Court's appellate jurisdiction over state-court judgments, 28 U.S.C. § 1257, precludes a federal district court from exercising subject-matter jurisdiction in an action it would otherwise be empowered to adjudicate under a congressional grant of authority. In both cases, the plaintiffs, alleging federal-question jurisdiction, called upon the district court to overturn an injurious state-court judgment. Because § 1257, as long interpreted, vests authority to review a state-court judgment solely in the United States Supreme Court, the district courts lacked subject-matter jurisdiction. Contrary to the court of appeals' ruling, when there is parallel state and federal litigation, *Rooker-Feldman* is not triggered simply by the entry of judgment in state court, because the pendency of an action in state court is not a bar to proceedings concerning the same matter in federal court having jurisdiction over those claims. Instead, the disposition of the federal action, once the state-court adjudication is complete, is governed by preclusion law. Under such law, while a federal court may be required to give preclusive effect to the state-court judgment, federal jurisdiction over the action does not terminate automatically on mere entry of judgment in the state action. Section 1257 does not stop a district court from exercising subject-matter jurisdiction simply because a party attempts to litigate in federal court a matter previously litigated in state court. If a federal plaintiff presents an independent claim, even one that denies a state court's legal conclusion in a case to which the plaintiff was a party, there is jurisdiction, and state law determines whether the defendant prevails under preclusion principles. *Rooker-Feldman* does not otherwise override or supplant preclusion doctrine or augment the circumscribed doctrines allowing federal courts to stay or dismiss proceedings in deference to state-court actions. Accordingly, this is not a case to which *Rooker-Feldman* applies, since it is clear that Exxon Mobil (P) did not enter federal court to undo the state judgment in its favor, but filed its federal-court suit to protect itself in the event it lost in state court on grounds (such as the state statute of limitations) that might not preclude relief in the federal venue. *Rooker-Feldman* did not prevent the district court from exercising jurisdiction when Exxon Mobil (P) filed the federal action, and it did not emerge to vanquish jurisdiction after Exxon Mobil (P) prevailed in the state courts. Reversed and remanded.

▎ *ANALYSIS*

One of the purposes of the Court's decision was to rein in the lower courts, which the Court noted had construed the *Rooker-Feldman* doctrine to "extend far beyond the con-

tours of the *Rooker* and *Feldman* cases. The decision should have the desired effect of discouraging the lower federal courts from applying the doctrine except in a very narrow set of circumstances. In fact, in *Lance v. Dennis,* 546 U.S. 459 (2006), Justice Stevens indicated that in *Exxon Mobil,* "the Court finally interred the so-called 'Rooker-Feldman* doctrine.' And today, the Court quite properly disapproves of the district court's resuscitation of a doctrine that has produced nothing but mischief for 23 years."

■═■

Quicknotes

CERTIORARI A discretionary writ issued by a superior court to an inferior court in order to review the lower court's decisions; the Supreme Court's writ ordering such review.

INTERLOCUTORY APPEAL The appeal of an issue that does not resolve the disposition of the case, but is essential to a determination of the parties' legal rights.

JURISDICTION The authority of a court to hear and declare judgment in respect to a particular matter.

■═■

CHAPTER 13

The Diversity Jurisdiction of the Federal District Courts

Quick Reference Rules of Law

Strawbridge v. Curtiss

[Parties not identified.]

7 U.S. (3 Cranch) 267 (1806).

NATURE OF CASE: Suit seeking relief against parties residing in different jurisdictions.

FACT SUMMARY: [Facts not stated in casebook excerpt.]

🏛 RULE OF LAW
If several parties to a lawsuit represent several distinct interests, federal jurisdiction may not be predicated upon diversity of citizenship unless there is diversity between the parties representing each interest and their adversary.

FACTS: [Facts not stated in casebook excerpt.]

ISSUE: In order for federal jurisdiction to attach by reason of diversity of citizenship, must there be diversity between the plaintiff and the representatives of each of the separate interests involved in the litigation?

HOLDING AND DECISION: (Marshall, C.J.) Yes. If several parties to a lawsuit represent several distinct interests, federal jurisdiction may not be predicated upon diversity of citizenship unless there is diversity between the parties representing each interest and their adversary. Where a joint interest is involved, each person involved must enjoy citizenship different from that of the opposing party. Congress has provided that diversity of citizenship may be established "where an alien is a party; or the suit is between a citizen of a state where the suit is brought, and a citizen of another state." This standard is not met unless there is diversity between the representatives of each interest involved in a lawsuit and the adverse litigant. Thus, the lower court properly concluded that Strawbridge had failed to establish federal jurisdiction on the basis of diversity of citizenship. Affirmed.

▶ ANALYSIS

Although the case may be susceptible to a narrower reading, *Strawbridge v. Curtiss* has traditionally been interpreted as requiring diversity of citizenship between each plaintiff and each defendant. Thus, in cases where numerous parties were involved on each side of a lawsuit, the *Strawbridge* rule precluded federal jurisdiction on the basis of diversity of citizenship if a single defendant resided in the same state as any one of the plaintiffs. However, in the 1967 case of *State Farm Fire & Cas. Co. v. Tashire,* 386 U.S. 523, the Supreme Court responded to pressure from many learned commentators and ruled that "minimal diversity," i.e., diversity between any plaintiff and any defendant, was sufficient to establish federal jurisdiction.

Quicknotes

DIVERSITY JURISDICTION The authority of a federal court to hear and determine cases involving a statutory sum and in which the parties are citizens of different states, or in which one party is an alien.

State Farm Fire & Casualty Co. v. Tashire

Insurer (P) v. Injured passenger (D)

386 U.S. 523 (1967).

NATURE OF CASE: Appeal from reversal of grant of preliminary injunction in an interpleader action brought by an insurer under the Interpleader Act of 1935, 28 U.S.C. § 1335.

FACT SUMMARY: State Farm Fire & Casualty Co. (State Farm) (P), which had insured a truck driver against bodily injury liability to the extent of $10,000 per person, and $20,000 per accident, contended in a federal interpleader action against injured passengers (D) who had brought pending state-court suits for over $1,000,000 and all other potential claimants that because the damages requested in the pending actions already far exceeded State Farm's (P) liability under the policy, all claims against it and the truck driver be established only in a single interpleader proceeding and that it be discharged from all further obligations under its policy.

🏛 RULE OF LAW
A minimal diversity requirement under the Interpleader Act of 1935 is constitutional under Article III of the Constitution.

FACTS: A bus and a truck collided. Four victims brought suits in courts in the state where the collision occurred for damages exceeding $1,000,000 against the bus and truck drivers and the owners of the truck and bus. State Farm (P) had insured the truck driver against bodily injury liability to the extent of $10,000 per person, and $20,000 per accident, and accordingly it filed a federal interpleader action against the plaintiff-victims (D) and all other potential claimants on the grounds that the damages requested in the pending actions already far exceeded State Farm's (P) liability under the policy. State Farm (P) asked that all claims against it and the truck driver be established only in this single proceeding and that it be discharged from all further obligations under its policy. State Farms (P) based jurisdiction on general diversity of citizenship and the Interpleader Act of 1935, 28 U.S.C. § 1335, which provides, inter alia, that a district has jurisdiction in an interpleader action where a corporation has issued an insurance policy in the amount of $500 or more if two or more "adverse claimants, of diverse citizenship" claim or may claim to be entitled to money or the benefits arising under that policy. The district court issued a preliminary injunction providing that all suits against State Farm (P) and its insured relating to the accident had to be prosecuted in the interpleader proceeding. The court of appeals reversed, and the United States Supreme Court granted certiorari.

ISSUE: Is a minimal diversity requirement under the Interpleader Act of 1935 constitutional under Article III of the Constitution?

HOLDING AND DECISION: (Fortas, J.) Yes. A minimal diversity requirement under the Interpleader Act of 1935 is constitutional under Article III of the Constitution. The interpleader statute has been construed to require only "minimal diversity," meaning diversity of citizenship between two or more claimants, without regard to the circumstance that other rival claimants may be co-citizens. The statute's language and purpose confirm that no more is required. Nevertheless, the issue remains whether such a statutory construction is consistent with Article III of the Constitution, which extends the federal judicial power to "Controversies . . . between Citizens of different States . . . and between a State, or the Citizens thereof, and foreign States, Citizens or Subjects." Some prior decisions have held that diversity required "complete" diversity, so that if co-citizens appeared on both sides of a dispute, diversity was lost. However, in those cases, the Court was only construing a statute, not the Constitution itself. However, the Court and the lower courts have concluded that Article III itself poses no obstacle to the legislative extension of federal jurisdiction founded on diversity provided any two adverse parties are not co-citizens. Therefore, the interpleader action is properly before the federal courts. Although State Farm (P) properly invoked federal interpleader jurisdiction, it is not, under the circumstances, entitled to the injunctive relief it sought. Reversed and remanded.

DISSENT: (Douglas, J.) The majority's conclusion as to "minimal diversity" is correct. Nonetheless, the majority erred in finding that federal interpleader was available under the particular circumstances of this case.

▶ ANALYSIS

While this case settled the constitutionality of diversity jurisdiction based on less than complete diversity between adversaries in interpleader actions, it is unclear whether such diversity will always satisfy Article III's requirements. Some commentators have argued that the expansion of federal jurisdiction through "minimal diversity" in such enactments as the Class Action Fairness Act of 2005 may not be sufficient or proper to achieve Article III's goals.

■■■

Quicknotes

ARTICLE III, U.S. CONSTITUTION Limits federal judicial power to cases and controversies.

Continued on next page.

DIVERSITY OF CITIZENSHIP Parties are citizens of different states, or one party is an alien.

INTER ALIA Among other things.

INTERPLEADER An equitable proceeding whereby a person holding property which is subject to the claims of multiple parties may require such parties to resolve the matter through litigation.

■━■

Burns v. Anderson

Car accident victim (P) v. Alleged tortfeasor (D)

502 F.2d 970 (1974).

NATURE OF CASE: Appeal from an action for damages for personal injuries.

FACT SUMMARY: The district court dismissed a suit for personal injuries brought by Burns (P) as the result of an automobile accident with Anderson (D) in which Burns (P) sustained a broken thumb but prayed for $1,026 in lost wages and medical expenses and another $60,000 for pain and suffering.

🏛 RULE OF LAW
A district court may dismiss a diversity suit where it appears to a legal certainty that the claim was really for less than the jurisdictional amount.

FACTS: This suit grew out of an auto accident in which Burns's (P) automobile was struck by that of Anderson (D). Burns's (P) principal injury was a broken thumb. Burns (P) brought the action in the District Court of Louisiana, claiming $1,026 in lost wages and medical expenses and another $60,000 for pain and suffering. After a pretrial conference and considerable discovery, the district court dismissed for want of jurisdiction. Burns (P) appealed.

ISSUE: May a district court dismiss a diversity suit where it appears to a legal certainty that the claim was really for less than the jurisdictional amount?

HOLDING AND DECISION: (Brown, C.J.) Yes. A district court may dismiss a diversity suit where it appears to a legal certainty that the claim was really for less than the jurisdictional amount. The test for jurisdictional amount is a plaintiff's good faith claim. To justify dismissal, it must appear to a legal certainty that the claim is really for less than the jurisdictional amount. The test is an objective one and, once it is clear that as a matter of law the claim is for less than $10,000, the trial judge is required to dismiss. In the instant case, the district judge dismissed only after examination of an extensive record. The record shows that Burns (P) was back working only a month after the accident doing heavy manual labor. Burns (P) admitted that after three months there was no pain whatsoever. Burns's (P) total medical bills were less than $250. It really does appear to a legal certainty that the amount in controversy is less than $10,000. Therefore, the court holds the case was properly dismissed. Affirmed.

▶ ANALYSIS

That it may appear highly unlikely that a plaintiff can recover the amount prayed for is not controlling, unless it can be shown to a legal certainty that the plaintiff will be unable to recover the requisite jurisdictional amount of $10,000. For example, if a plaintiff prays for actual damages of $5,000 and punitive damages of $15,000, and the applicable law disallows recovery of punitive damages, then there is a legal certainty that the plaintiff will not recover the jurisdictional amount of $10,000 and the case must be dismissed.

Quicknotes

DIVERSITY ACTION An action commenced by a citizen of one state against a citizen of another state or against an alien, involving an amount in controversy set by statute, over which the federal court has jurisdiction.

JURISDICTION The authority of a court to hear and declare judgment in respect to a particular matter.

TORTFEASOR Party that commits a tort or wrongful act.

Exxon Mobil Corporation v. Allapattah Services, Inc.

Corporation (D) v. Class member (P)

545 U.S. 546 (2005).

NATURE OF CASE: Appeal of judgment regarding supplemental jurisdiction.

FACT SUMMARY: Only some members of a class met the amount-in-controversy to establish diversity jurisdiction, and the circuit courts were split as to whether each member's claim must meet the requirement in order for their claims to go forward, if the claims of other members of the class meet the requirement.

🏛 RULE OF LAW
Where one plaintiff's claim satisfies the minimum amount-in-controversy requirement for federal diversity jurisdiction, and another plaintiff's related claim does not, 28 U.S.C. § 1367 allows federal courts to exercise supplemental jurisdiction over the claim that is less than the required amount.

FACTS: Two cases were consolidated and the Supreme Court granted certiorari to resolve a circuit split over the federal supplemental jurisdiction statute, 28 U.S.C. § 1367. The plaintiffs in the *Exxon* case are a class of approximately 10,000 gas dealers (P) who claimed that Exxon (D) overcharged them for fuel purchases. The court of appeals affirmed the district court's verdict for the dealers (P), and held that the federal supplemental jurisdiction statute allows a district court in a class action lawsuit to exercise supplemental jurisdiction over class members whose claims do not meet the jurisdictional minimum amount. In the *Ortega* case, a nine-year-old girl injured her finger on a can of Star-Kist tuna. The girl (P) and her family (P) sued in federal court, on the basis of diversity jurisdiction. The district court dismissed the claims for lack of jurisdiction, holding that the girl's (P) and family members' (P) claims did not meet the minimum amount for jurisdiction. The First Circuit Court of Appeals reversed as to the girl (P), but upheld the district court's conclusion that none of the family members (P) satisfied the amount-in-controversy requirement.

ISSUE: Where one plaintiff's claim satisfies the minimum amount-in-controversy requirement for federal diversity jurisdiction, and another plaintiff's related claim does not, does 28 U.S.C. § 1367 allow federal courts to exercise supplemental jurisdiction over the claim that is less than the required amount?

HOLDING AND DECISION: (Kennedy, J.) Yes. Where one plaintiff's claim satisfies the minimum amount-in-controversy requirement for federal diversity jurisdiction, and another plaintiff's related claim does not, 28 U.S.C. § 1367 allows federal courts to exercise supplemental jurisdiction over the claim that is less than the required amount. Courts only need to determine whether they have original

jurisdiction over one of the claims in a case. If they do, courts can then decide to extend supplemental jurisdiction to the other related claims. The indivisibility and contamination theories are easily dismissed. The indivisibility theory is inconsistent with the whole notion of supplemental jurisdiction, and the contamination theory is inconsistent with the amount-in-controversy requirement. The unambiguous text of the statute indicates that jurisdiction should extend to the other plaintiffs, regardless of legislative history or other extrinsic material.

DISSENT: (Stevens, J.) The majority should have consulted the legislative history of the statute. It is unwise to treat the ambiguity of a statute as determinative of whether legislative history is consulted. The legislative history of the statute suggests that Congress intended to codify and preserve authorization for and limits on other forms of supplemental jurisdiction, not to support the expansive view of jurisdiction held by the majority.

DISSENT: (Ginsburg, J.) The majority's reading of the statute is plausible, but broad. It should be read as instructing that the district court have original jurisdiction over the action first, before supplemental jurisdiction can attach. This would be a less disruptive reading of the statute.

▶ ANALYSIS

The Court's holding greatly expands the limits of diversity jurisdiction. This case overrules *Zahn v. International Paper*, which held that in order for a federal court to exercise diversity jurisdiction, all plaintiffs in the case had to satisfy 28 U.S.C. 1332's amount-in-controversy requirement. The courts of appeal had divided on the question and the Supreme Court had previously failed to resolve the issue in the 2000 case *Free v. Abbott Laboratories*.

■—■

Quicknotes

CERTIORARI A discretionary writ issued by a superior court to an inferior court in order to review the lower court's decisions; the Supreme Court's writ ordering such review.

DIVERSITY JURISDICTION The authority of a federal court to hear and determine cases involving a statutory sum and in which the parties are citizens of different states, or in which one party is an alien.

SUPPLEMENTAL JURISDICTION A doctrine granting authority to a federal court to hear a claim that does not invoke diversity jurisdiction if it arises from the same transaction or occurrence as the primary action.

■—■

Kramer v. Caribbean Mills, Inc.

Assignee of claim (P) v. Foreign corporation (D)

394 U.S. 823 (1969).

NATURE OF CASE: Certiorari to resolve whether a district court had proper diversity jurisdiction under the Judicial Code.

FACT SUMMARY: After receiving an assignment of a contract cause of action for nominal consideration from a Panamanian corporation, Kramer (P) sued Caribbean Mills, Inc. (D), a Haitian corporation, in a district court in diversity jurisdiction. The district court judge denied a motion to dismiss for improper jurisdiction by Caribbean Mills, Inc. (D), and found for Kramer (P).

RULE OF LAW
Under the Judicial Code, where an assignment of a cause of action is improper or collusively made to invoke federal diversity jurisdiction, a district court may not have cognizance of the suit.

FACTS: Kramer (P) received an assignment of a contract cause of action from a Panamanian corporation against Caribbean Mills, Inc. (D), a Haitian corporation. Kramer (P) paid one dollar for the assignment and promised to pay back 95 percent of any net recovery. Kramer (P) sued Caribbean Mills, Inc. (D), in district court involving diversity jurisdiction, and Caribbean Mills, Inc. (D), moved to dismiss for improper and collusively created jurisdiction under the Judicial Code. Motion denied. Judgment for Kramer (P). Reversed on appeal.

ISSUE: Does the Judicial Code permit the creation of diversity jurisdiction through the collusive assignment of a cause of action?

HOLDING AND DECISION: (Harlan, J.) No. Under the Judicial Code, where an assignment of a cause of action is collusively or otherwise improperly made merely to invoke federal diversity jurisdiction, a district court may not take cognizance of the suit. One purpose of the revised Judicial Code is to prevent the manufacture of federal jurisdiction in diversity jurisdiction. The mere fact the assignment was valid under state law and involves a foreign national corporation is irrelevant. Judgment of the court of appeals affirmed.

ANALYSIS

Federal courts jealously guard their limited jurisdiction. Because of this, devices used to create federal diversity jurisdiction are frowned upon. It is elementary of course that Fed. R. Civ. P. 8a requires that federal diversity jurisdiction be pleaded in any complaint seeking it. This case points out an extension of the policy of carefulness in determining the existence of true diversity—the policy that diversity cannot be created by collusion. Most commonly, this rule is applied where an administrator, guardian, or trustee is appointed solely for the purpose of creating diversity. Note, however, that while such is true, most writers agree that there is no reason why diversity could not be defeated by a collusive joinder—since the statute that prevents the former, 28 U.S.C. 1359, does not apply to the latter situation.

Quicknotes

CERTIORARI A discretionary writ issued by a superior court to an inferior court in order to review the lower court's decisions; the Supreme Court's writ ordering such review.

COLLUSION An agreement between two or more parties to engage in unlawful conduct or in other activities with an unlawful goal, typically involving fraud.

DIVERSITY JURISDICTION The authority of a federal court to hear and determine cases involving a statutory sum and in which the parties are citizens of different states, or in which one party is an alien.

JOINDER The joining of claims or parties in one lawsuit.

Additional Problems of District Court Authority to Adjudicate

Quick Reference Rules of Law

Ruhrgas AG v. Marathon Oil Company

Foreign company (D) v. U.S. company (P)

526 U.S. 574 (1999).

NATURE OF CASE: Appeal from en banc decision overturning panel's decision to vacate a judgment dismissing for lack of personal jurisdiction a federal action based on various state law business torts.

FACT SUMMARY: Ruhrgas AG (D) contended that a federal district court does not have to consider subject-matter jurisdiction before dismissing a removed case for lack of personal jurisdiction.

🏛 RULE OF LAW
A federal district court is not absolutely barred in all circumstances from dismissing a removed case for lack of personal jurisdiction without first deciding subject-matter jurisdiction.

FACTS: Marathon Oil Co. (Marathon) (P) and some of its subsidiaries sued Ruhrgas (D), a German company, in state court for various state-law business torts allegedly arising from the parties' agreement for Marathon (P) to sell to Ruhrgas (D) and others a significant portion of gas production from a field in the Norwegian North Sea. Marathon (P) premised personal jurisdiction on three meetings held in the state, and on correspondence directed to Marathon (P) in the state. Ruhrgas (D) removed the case to federal district court, asserting three bases for federal jurisdiction: (1) diversity of citizenship, on the theory that Marathon Petroleum Norge (Norge), a Marathon (P) subsidiary and the only nondiverse plaintiff, had been fraudulently joined; (2) federal question, because Marathon's (P) claims raised questions of international relations; and (3) 9 U.S.C. § 205, which authorizes removal of cases relating to international arbitration agreements. Ruhrgas (D) moved to dismiss the complaint for lack of personal jurisdiction, whereas Marathon (P) moved to remand the case to the state court for lack of federal subject-matter jurisdiction. The district court granted Ruhrgas's (D) motion. A panel of the court of appeals, believing it had to consider the issue of subject-matter jurisdiction first, considered and rejected each of Ruhrgas's (D) asserted bases of federal jurisdiction, vacated the district court's judgment, and remanded the case to state court. The court of appeals granted a rehearing en banc, and vacated the panel's decision. The en banc court held that in removed cases, district courts must decide issues of subject-matter jurisdiction first, reaching issues of personal jurisdiction only if subject-matter jurisdiction is found to exist. The United States Supreme Court granted certiorari.

ISSUE: Is a federal district court absolutely barred in all circumstances from dismissing a removed case for lack of personal jurisdiction without first deciding subject-matter jurisdiction?

HOLDING AND DECISION: (Ginsburg, J.) No. A federal district court is not absolutely barred in all circumstances from dismissing a removed case for lack of personal jurisdiction without first deciding subject-matter jurisdiction. The court of appeals erred in according absolute priority to the subject-matter jurisdiction requirement on the ground that it is nonwaivable and delimits federal-court power, while restrictions on a court's jurisdiction over the person are waivable and protect individual rights. Although the character of the two jurisdictional bedrocks unquestionably differs, the distinctions do not mean that subject-matter jurisdiction is ever and always the more "fundamental." Personal jurisdiction, too, is an essential element of district court jurisdiction, without which the court is powerless to proceed to an adjudication. Here, the impediment to subject-matter jurisdiction on which Marathon (P) relies—lack of complete diversity—rests on statutory interpretation, not constitutional command. In contrast, Ruhrgas (D) relies on the constitutional due process safeguard to stop the court from proceeding to the merits of the case. While subject-matter jurisdiction necessarily precedes a ruling on the merits, this does not mean that it must be considered before personal jurisdiction. A court that dismisses for want of personal jurisdiction, without first ruling on subject-matter jurisdiction, makes no assumption of law-declaring power that violates the separation of powers principles. The Court rejects Marathon's (P) argument that it is particularly offensive in removed cases to rule on personal jurisdiction without first deciding subject-matter jurisdiction, because the federal court's personal jurisdiction determination may preclude the parties from relitigating the very same issue in state court. Issue preclusion in subsequent state-court litigation may also attend a federal court's subject-matter determination. This is in keeping with the federal design, which emphasizes cooperation, not conflict, between the state and federal courts. A state's dignitary interest bears consideration when a district court exercises discretion in a case of this order. If personal jurisdiction raises difficult questions of state law, and subject-matter jurisdiction is resolved as easily as personal jurisdiction, a district court will ordinarily conclude that federalism concerns tip the scales in favor of initially ruling on the motion to remand. In other cases, as here, however, the district court may find that overriding concerns of judicial economy and restraint warrant immediate dismissal for lack of personal jurisdiction. The federal design allows leeway for sensitive, discretionary judgments of this sort. Marathon's (P) and the court of appeals' fear that such a discretionary rule will

Continued on next page.

lead to abuse, with the creation of convoluted subject-matter jurisdiction theories, is unfounded since the district courts will be able to discern when removal is unwarranted. Reversed and remanded.

▶ ANALYSIS

The approach taken by the Court in this case is a pragmatic one that should enhance the efficient operation of the judicial system, notwithstanding that some problematic areas will persist, such as where a federal court without personal or subject-matter jurisdiction dismisses a case not on the merits and the dismissal entails rulings or consequences that are themselves problematic. In any event, the Court has indicated that questions of jurisdiction do not need to be resolved prior to a non-merits dismissal, such as a dismissal on forum non conveniens grounds, since jurisdiction is necessary only when the court proposes to issue a judgment on the merits.

■══■

Quicknotes

CERTIORARI A discretionary writ issued by a superior court to an inferior court in order to review the lower court's decisions; the Supreme Court's writ ordering such review.

EN BANC The hearing of a matter by all the judges of the court, rather than only the necessary quorum.

FORUM NON CONVENIENS An equitable doctrine permitting a court to refrain from hearing and determining a case when the matter may be more properly and fairly heard in another forum.

JURISDICTION The authority of a court to hear and declare judgment in respect to a particular matter.

■══■

Kingsepp v. Wesleyan University

Student (P) v. University (D)

763 F. Supp. 22 (S.D.N.Y. 1991).

NATURE OF CASE: Motion to dismiss class action antitrust case.

FACT SUMMARY: Kingsepp (P), a student, brought an antitrust action against Wesleyan University (D), Williams College (D), and Dartmouth College (D) in a New York federal court.

🏛 RULE OF LAW
Corporate defendants are subject to nationwide federal jurisdiction under the antitrust provisions of the Clayton Act.

FACTS: Kingsepp (P), a student, brought an antitrust action under the Clayton Act against Wesleyan University (D), Williams College (D), and Dartmouth College (D). The action was filed in a New York district court. The schools (D) responded that they were not subject to jurisdiction under the nationwide service of process provisions or under the New York long-arm statute and moved to dismiss the case.

ISSUE: Are corporate defendants subject to nationwide federal jurisdiction under the antitrust provisions of the Clayton Act?

HOLDING AND DECISION: (Edelstein, J.) Yes. Corporate defendants are subject to nationwide federal jurisdiction under the antitrust provisions of the Clayton Act. Personal jurisdiction in an antitrust action is governed by § 12 of the Clayton Act, which provides for out-of-state service of process. The section does not expressly mention personal jurisdiction. However, in cases where Congress authorizes nationwide service, the court's jurisdiction is usually co-extensive with the boundaries of the United States. It is not necessary that the resident defendant have minimum contacts within the state exercising jurisdiction. Since Wesleyan (D) and Williams (D) are non-profit corporations that reside in the United States, they are subject to nationwide service of process under the Clayton Act and are subject to personal jurisdiction in this case. However, Dartmouth (D) is not a corporation and not subject to nationwide process because it is a charitable trust organized under a charter issue in the name of King George III. Thus, Dartmouth (D) is subject to personal jurisdiction only if it is engaged in "doing business" in New York according to the state's long-arm statute. Since Dartmouth (D) solicits for students in the state and has numerous other financial activities in New York, it has enough presence in the state to be subject to personal jurisdiction. Motion to dismiss denied.

▶ ANALYSIS

The decision also rejected the schools' (D) contention that venue was improper. Section 1391(c), the general federal venue provision, provides that corporations are deemed to reside in any district where they are subject to personal jurisdiction. Thus, venue was deemed proper in the New York district court.

■=■

Quicknotes

ANTITRUST Body of federal law prohibiting business conduct that constitutes a restraint on trade.

CLASS ACTION A suit commenced by a representative on behalf of an ascertainable group that is too large to appear in court, who share a commonality of interests and who will benefit from a successful result.

JURISDICTION The authority of a court to hear and declare judgment in respect to a particular matter.

■=■

Granny Goose Foods, Inc. v. Brotherhood of Teamsters

Employer (P) v. Union (D)

415 U.S. 423 (1974).

NATURE OF CASE: Appeal from judgment of willful violation of restraining order.

FACT SUMMARY: Granny Goose Foods, Inc. (Granny Goose) (P), filed a complaint against the Brotherhood of Teamsters (Teamsters) (D) in state court, alleging that the Teamsters (D) were engaging in strike activity in breach of collective bargaining agreements between Granny Goose (P) and the Teamsters (D), and a temporary restraining order was issued by the court to prohibit the Teamster's (D) strike activities.

🏛 RULE OF LAW
An ex parte temporary restraining order issued by a state court prior to removal remains in force after removal no longer than it would have remained in effect under state law, and in no event, longer than the time limitations imposed by Fed. R. Civ. P. 65(b).

FACTS: Granny Goose (P) filed a complaint in state court against the Brotherhood of Teamsters (D), alleging that the Teamsters (D) were engaging in strike activity in breach of collective bargaining agreements between Granny Goose (P) and the Teamsters (D). The court issued a temporary restraining order enjoining all strike activity. The Teamsters (D) then removed the action to federal court and filed a motion to dissolve the temporary restraining order. The federal court denied the motion to dissolve. When strike activity began a few months later, Granny Goose (P) moved to hold the Teamsters (D) in contempt. The Teamsters (D) argued that the temporary restraining order had long since expired. The federal court rejected the Teamsters' (D) argument, stating that the order continued in force and effect because of that court's earlier denial of the motion to dissolve, and also that 28 U.S.C. § 1450 continued the order in effect until affirmatively dissolved or modified by the court. The Teamsters (D) appealed.

ISSUE: Does an ex parte temporary restraining order issued by a state court prior to removal remain in force after removal any longer than it would have remained in effect under state law, and in any event, longer than the time limitations imposed by Fed. R. Civ. P. 65(b)?

HOLDING AND DECISION: (Marshall, J.) No. An ex parte temporary restraining order issued by a state court prior to removal remains in force after removal no longer than it would have remained in effect under state law, and in no event, longer than the time limitations imposed by Fed. R. Civ. P. 65(b). Here, the temporary restraining order issued by the state court expired long before the date of the alleged contempt. This fact is clear,

whether California law or whether Rule 65(b) is controlling. Section 527 of the California Code of Civil Procedure, under which the order was issued, provides that temporary restraining orders must be returnable no later than fifteen days from the date of the order, twenty days if good cause is shown, and unless the party obtaining the order then proceeds to submit its case for a preliminary injunction, the temporary restraining order must be dissolved. Similarly, under Rule 65(b), temporary restraining orders must expire by their own terms within ten days after entry, twenty days if good cause is shown. Accordingly, no order was in effect, and the Teamsters (D) violated no order when they resumed their strike. Affirmed.

CONCURRENCE: (Rehnquist, J.) There was no injunctive order in effect at the time the Teamsters' (D) allegedly contemptuous conduct occurred. However, the determination that mere removal of a case to a federal district court does not extend the duration of a previously issued state court order past its original termination date makes it quite unnecessary, in this case, to further discuss the time limitations contained in Rule 65(b).

▶ ANALYSIS

Before 1948, removal procedure differed according to the ground of removal. A 1948 revision eliminated these discrepancies and promulgated a more uniform procedure. The key difference between the old and the new rules is that now the petition for removal and the bond required by federal law are filed in federal court instead of state court.

■━■

Quicknotes

CONTEMPT OF COURT Conduct that is intended to obstruct the court's effective administration of justice or to otherwise disrespect its authority.

EX PARTE A proceeding commenced by one party.

TEMPORARY RESTRAINING ORDER A court order preserving the status quo pending a hearing regarding injunctive relief.

■━■

CHAPTER 15

Obligatory and Discretionary Supreme Court Review

Quick Reference Rules of Law

Davis v. Jacobs

State prisoner (P) v. State official (D)

454 U.S. 911 (1981).

NATURE OF CASE: Appeal from dismissal of habeas corpus action.

FACT SUMMARY: Davis (P), a state prisoner, brought a habeas corpus action in federal court that was denied in the lower court and dismissed by the court of appeals because Davis (P) did not have a certificate of probable cause.

🏛 RULE OF LAW
Under 28 U.S.C. § 1651, the United States Supreme Court may grant a writ of certiorari to review the action of the court of appeals in declining to allow an appeal and review questions on the merits sought to be raised by the appeal.

FACTS: Davis (P) and other state prisoners brought habeas corpus actions in federal court. The actions were denied and dismissed by the lower court, and Davis (P) appealed. The court of appeals would not grant review of the case because Davis (P) had not obtained a certificate of probable cause, and, therefore, that court could not have jurisdiction over the matter. Davis (P) then sought review by way of a writ of certiorari from the United States Supreme Court.

ISSUE: Under 28 U.S.C. § 1651, may the United States Supreme Court grant a writ of certiorari to review the action of the court of appeals in declining to allow an appeal to it and review questions on the merits sought to be raised by the appeal?

HOLDING AND DECISION: (Stevens, J.) Yes. Under 28 U.S.C. § 1651, the United States Supreme Court may grant a writ of certiorari to review the action of the court of appeals in declining to allow an appeal to it and review questions on the merits sought to be raised by the appeal. Also, this Court itself may issue a certificate of probable cause if it determines that a petition has arguable merit notwithstanding the failure of a district or circuit judge to authorize an appeal to the court of appeals. Here, Davis (P) does not have a meritorious claim and neither the circuit justice nor this Court has decided to issue a certificate of probable cause. Our work is facilitated by the practice of simply denying certiorari once a determination is made that there is no merit to a claim. Affirmed.

DISSENT: (Rehnquist, J.) The effect of 28 U.S.C. § 2253 is clear: a certificate of probable cause is an indispensable prerequisite to an appeal from the district court to the appropriate court of appeals. Where the statutory scheme permits appellate review only upon the issuance of such a certificate, review by extraordinary writ in the absence of a certificate collides with Congress's express purpose to foreclose review.

▶ ANALYSIS

A statutory writ runs to the court of appeals in any case before or after rendition of judgment or decree. A final judgment in the court of appeals is not required. But grant of certiorari before any court of appeals judgment is rare, generally being reserved for cases of imperative public importance where there is prompt need for settlement of the issues.

Quicknotes

CERTIORARI A discretionary writ issued by a superior court to an inferior court in order to review the lower court's decisions; the Supreme Court's writ ordering such review.

HABEAS CORPUS A proceeding in which a defendant brings a writ to compel a judicial determination of whether he is lawfully being held in custody.

PROBABLE CAUSE A reasonable basis for believing that a crime has been committed.

Singleton v. Commissioner of Internal Revenue

Taxpayer-shareholder (P) v. Federal official (D)

439 U.S. 940 (1978).

NATURE OF CASE: Appeal from judgment that cash distribution from stock shares was a taxable dividend.

FACT SUMMARY: Singleton (P) brought suit against the Commissioner of Internal Revenue (D), alleging that a cash distribution respecting shares in a corporation was a return of capital, not a dividend, and, therefore, not taxable.

🏛 RULE OF LAW
Denial of certiorari carries with it no implication regarding the Court's views on the merits of a case that it has declined to review.

FACTS: Singleton (P) brought an action against the Commissioner of Internal Revenue (D), alleging that a cash distribution that Singleton (P) received from Capital Southwest Corporation was return of capital and, therefore, not taxable. The Commissioner (D) contended that the distribution was a dividend and was taxable to Singleton (P). The district court and the Court of Appeals for the Fifth Circuit agreed with the Commissioner (D) that the distribution was a taxable dividend and ruled against Singleton (P). Singleton (P) then petitioned the United States Supreme Court for a writ of certiorari.

ISSUE: Does the denial of certiorari carry with it any implication regarding the Court's views on the merits of a case that it has declined to review?

HOLDING AND DECISION: (Stevens, J.) No. Denial of certiorari carries with it no implication regarding the Court's views on the merits of a case that it has declined to review. The sole significance of such a denial is that fewer than four members of the Court deemed it desirable to review a decision of the lower court as a matter of sound judicial discretion. There is no need to explain the Court's action in denying a writ and there is even less reason for individual expressions of opinion about why certiorari should have been granted in particular cases. In this case, for example, the dissent suggests that the Court may have refused to grant certiorari because the case is "devoid of glamour and emotion." This suggestion is puzzling because there has never been any indication that any of the Court's justices have ever considered "glamour and emotion" as a relevant consideration in the exercise of his discretion or in his analysis of the law. With respect to the Court's action in this case, the absence of any conflict in the circuits is plainly a sufficient reason for denying certiorari. Affirmed.

DISSENT: (Blackmun, J.) It is hoped that the Court's decision to pass this case by is not due to a natural reluctance to take on another complicated tax case that is devoid of glamour and emotion and that would be remindful of the recent struggles, upon argument and reargument, in *United States v. Foster Lumber Co.*, 429 U.S. 32 (1976), and *Laing v. United States*, 423 U.S. 161 (1976).

▶ ANALYSIS

The practice of noting dissents from denials of certiorari, and of writing opinions in support of such dissents, has become increasingly common. Justice Douglas alone dissented from denial of certiorari 477 times in the 1973 term. Had certiorari been granted in all of these cases, the Court's plenary docket at that time would have more than doubled.

■═■

Quicknotes

CAPITAL In tax, is often used synonymously with basis; in accounting, refers to an account that represents the equity (ownership) interests of the owners, i.e., the amounts they would obtain if the business were liquidated.

CERTIORARI A discretionary writ issued by a superior court to an inferior court in order to review the lower court's decisions; the Supreme Court's writ ordering such review.

DIVIDEND The payment of earnings to a corporation's shareholders in proportion to the amount of shares held.

■═■

Glossary

Common Latin Words and Phrases Encountered in the Law

A FORTIORI: Because one fact exists or has been proven, therefore a second fact that is related to the first fact must also exist.

A PRIORI: From the cause to the effect. A term of logic used to denote that when one generally accepted truth is shown to be a cause, another particular effect must necessarily follow.

AB INITIO: From the beginning; a condition which has existed throughout, as in a marriage which was void ab initio.

ACTUS REUS: The wrongful act; in criminal law, such action sufficient to trigger criminal liability.

AD VALOREM: According to value; an ad valorem tax is imposed upon an item located within the taxing jurisdiction calculated by the value of such item.

AMICUS CURIAE: Friend of the court. Its most common usage takes the form of an amicus curiae brief, filed by a person who is not a party to an action but is nonetheless allowed to offer an argument supporting his legal interests.

ARGUENDO: In arguing. A statement, possibly hypothetical, made for the purpose of argument, is one made arguendo.

BILL QUIA TIMET: A bill to quiet title (establish ownership) to real property.

BONA FIDE: True, honest, or genuine. May refer to a person's legal position based on good faith or lacking notice of fraud (such as a bona fide purchaser for value) or to the authenticity of a particular document (such as a bona fide last will and testament).

CAUSA MORTIS: With approaching death in mind. A gift causa mortis is a gift given by a party who feels certain that death is imminent.

CAVEAT EMPTOR: Let the buyer beware. This maxim is reflected in the rule of law that a buyer purchases at his own risk because it is his responsibility to examine, judge, test, and otherwise inspect what he is buying.

CERTIORARI: A writ of review. Petitions for review of a case by the United States Supreme Court are most often done by means of a writ of certiorari.

CONTRA: On the other hand. Opposite. Contrary to.

CORAM NOBIS: Before us; writs of error directed to the court that originally rendered the judgment.

CORAM VOBIS: Before you; writs of error directed by an appellate court to a lower court to correct a factual error.

CORPUS DELICTI: The body of the crime; the requisite elements of a crime amounting to objective proof that a crime has been committed.

CUM TESTAMENTO ANNEXO, ADMINISTRATOR (ADMINISTRATOR C.T.A.): With will annexed; an administrator c.t.a. settles an estate pursuant to a will in which he is not appointed.

DE BONIS NON, ADMINISTRATOR (ADMINISTRATOR D.B.N.): Of goods not administered; an administrator d.b.n. settles a partially settled estate.

DE FACTO: In fact; in reality; actually. Existing in fact but not officially approved or engendered.

DE JURE: By right; lawful. Describes a condition that is legitimate "as a matter of law," in contrast to the term "de facto," which connotes something existing in fact but not legally sanctioned or authorized. For example, de facto segregation refers to segregation brought about by housing patterns, etc., whereas de jure segregation refers to segregation created by law.

DE MINIMIS: Of minimal importance; insignificant; a trifle; not worth bothering about.

DE NOVO: Anew; a second time; afresh. A trial de novo is a new trial held at the appellate level as if the case originated there and the trial at a lower level had not taken place.

DICTA: Generally used as an abbreviated form of obiter dicta, a term describing those portions of a judicial opinion incidental or not necessary to resolution of the specific question before the court. Such nonessential statements and remarks are not considered to be binding precedent.

DUCES TECUM: Refers to a particular type of writ or subpoena requesting a party or organization to produce certain documents in their possession.

EN BANC: Full bench. Where a court sits with all justices present rather than the usual quorum.

EX PARTE: For one side or one party only. An ex parte proceeding is one undertaken for the benefit of only one party, without notice to, or an appearance by, an adverse party.

EX POST FACTO: After the fact. An ex post facto law is a law that retroactively changes the consequences of a prior act.

EX REL.: Abbreviated form of the term "ex relatione," meaning upon relation or information. When the state brings an action in which it has no interest against an individual at the instigation of one who has a private interest in the matter.

FORUM NON CONVENIENS: Inconvenient forum. Although a court may have jurisdiction over the case, the action should be tried in a more conveniently located court, one to which parties and witnesses may more easily travel, for example.

GUARDIAN AD LITEM: A guardian of an infant as to litigation, appointed to represent the infant and pursue his/her rights.

HABEAS CORPUS: You have the body. The modern writ of habeas corpus is a writ directing that a person (body) being detained (such as a prisoner) be brought before the court so that the legality of his detention can be judicially ascertained.

IN CAMERA: In private, in chambers. When a hearing is held before a judge in his chambers or when all spectators are excluded from the courtroom.

IN FORMA PAUPERIS: In the manner of a pauper. A party who proceeds in forma pauperis because of his poverty is one who is allowed to bring suit without liability for costs.

INFRA: Below, under. A word referring the reader to a later part of a book. (The opposite of supra.)

IN LOCO PARENTIS: In the place of a parent.

IN PARI DELICTO: Equally wrong; a court of equity will not grant requested relief to an applicant who is in pari delicto, or as much at fault in the transactions giving rise to the controversy as is the opponent of the applicant.

IN PARI MATERIA: On like subject matter or upon the same matter. Statutes relating to the same person or things are said to be in pari materia. It is a general rule of statutory construction that such statutes should be construed together, i.e., looked at as if they together constituted one law.

IN PERSONAM: Against the person. Jurisdiction over the person of an individual.

IN RE: In the matter of. Used to designate a proceeding involving an estate or other property.

IN REM: A term that signifies an action against the res, or thing. An action in rem is basically one that is taken directly against property, as distinguished from an action in personam, i.e., against the person.

INTER ALIA: Among other things. Used to show that the whole of a statement, pleading, list, statute, etc., has not been set forth in its entirety.

INTER PARTES: Between the parties. May refer to contracts, conveyances or other transactions having legal significance.

INTER VIVOS: Between the living. An inter vivos gift is a gift made by a living grantor, as distinguished from bequests contained in a will, which pass upon the death of the testator.

IPSO FACTO: By the mere fact itself.

JUS: Law or the entire body of law.

LEX LOCI: The law of the place; the notion that the rights of parties to a legal proceeding are governed by the law of the place where those rights arose.

MALUM IN SE: Evil or wrong in and of itself; inherently wrong. This term describes an act that is wrong by its very nature, as opposed to one which would not be wrong but for the fact that there is a specific legal prohibition against it (malum prohibitum).

MALUM PROHIBITUM: Wrong because prohibited, but not inherently evil. Used to describe something that is wrong because it is expressly forbidden by law but that is not in and of itself evil, e.g., speeding.

MANDAMUS: We command. A writ directing an official to take a certain action.

MENS REA: A guilty mind; a criminal intent. A term used to signify the mental state that accompanies a crime or other prohibited act. Some crimes require only a general mens rea (general intent to do the prohibited act), but others, like assault with intent to murder, require the existence of a specific mens rea.

MODUS OPERANDI: Method of operating; generally refers to the manner or style of a criminal in committing crimes, admissible in appropriate cases as evidence of the identity of a defendant.

NEXUS: A connection to.

NISI PRIUS: A court of first impression. A nisi prius court is one where issues of fact are tried before a judge or jury.

N.O.V. (NON OBSTANTE VEREDICTO): Notwithstanding the verdict. A judgment n.o.v. is a judgment given in favor of one party despite the fact that a verdict was returned in favor of the other party, the justification being that the verdict either had no reasonable support in fact or was contrary to law.

NUNC PRO TUNC: Now for then. This phrase refers to actions that may be taken and will then have full retroactive effect.

PENDENTE LITE: Pending the suit; pending litigation underway.

PER CAPITA: By head; beneficiaries of an estate, if they take in equal shares, take per capita.

PER CURIAM: By the court; signifies an opinion ostensibly written "by the whole court" and with no identified author.

PER SE: By itself, in itself; inherently.

PER STIRPES: By representation. Used primarily in the law of wills to describe the method of distribution where a person, generally because of death, is unable to take that which is left to him by the will of another, and therefore his heirs divide such property between them rather than take under the will individually.

PRIMA FACIE: On its face, at first sight. A prima facie case is one that is sufficient on its face, meaning that the evidence supporting it is adequate to establish the case until contradicted or overcome by other evidence.

PRO TANTO: For so much; as far as it goes. Often used in eminent domain cases when a property owner receives partial payment for his land without prejudice to his right to bring suit for the full amount he claims his land to be worth.

QUANTUM MERUIT: As much as he deserves. Refers to recovery based on the doctrine of unjust enrichment in those cases in which a party has rendered valuable services or furnished materials that were accepted and enjoyed by another under circumstances that would reasonably notify the recipient that the rendering party expected to be paid. In essence, the law implies a contract to pay the reasonable value of the services or materials furnished.

QUASI: Almost like; as if; nearly. This term is essentially used to signify that one subject or thing is almost analogous to another but that material differences between them do exist. For example, a quasi-criminal proceeding is one that is not strictly criminal but shares enough of the same characteristics to require some of the same safeguards (e.g., procedural due process must be followed in a parole hearing).

QUID PRO QUO: Something for something. In contract law, the consideration, something of value, passed between the parties to render the contract binding.

RES GESTAE: Things done; in evidence law, this principle justifies the admission of a statement that would otherwise be hearsay when it is made so closely to the event in question as to be said to be a part of it, or with such spontaneity as not to have the possibility of falsehood.

RES IPSA LOQUITUR: The thing speaks for itself. This doctrine gives rise to a rebuttable presumption of negligence when the instrumentality causing the injury was within the exclusive control of the defendant, and the injury was one that does not normally occur unless a person has been negligent.

RES JUDICATA: A matter adjudged. Doctrine which provides that once a court of competent jurisdiction has rendered a final judgment or decree on the merits, that judgment or decree is conclusive upon the parties to the case and prevents them from engaging in any other litigation on the points and issues determined therein.

RESPONDEAT SUPERIOR: Let the master reply. This doctrine holds the master liable for the wrongful acts of his servant (or the principal for his agent) in those cases in which the servant (or agent) was acting within the scope of his authority at the time of the injury.

STARE DECISIS: To stand by or adhere to that which has been decided. The common law doctrine of stare decisis attempts to give security and certainty to the law by following the policy that once a principle of law as applicable to a certain set of facts has been set forth in a decision, it forms a precedent which will subsequently be followed, even though a different decision might be made were it the first time the question had arisen. Of course, stare decisis is not an inviolable principle and is departed from in instances where there is good cause (e.g., considerations of public policy led the Supreme Court to disregard prior decisions sanctioning segregation).

SUPRA: Above. A word referring a reader to an earlier part of a book.

ULTRA VIRES: Beyond the power. This phrase is most commonly used to refer to actions taken by a corporation that are beyond the power or legal authority of the corporation.

Addendum of French Derivatives

IN PAIS: Not pursuant to legal proceedings.

CHATTEL: Tangible personal property.

CY PRES: Doctrine permitting courts to apply trust funds to purposes not expressed in the trust but necessary to carry out the settlor's intent.

PER AUTRE VIE: For another's life; during another's life. In property law, an estate may be granted that will terminate upon the death of someone other than the grantee.

PROFIT A PRENDRE: A license to remove minerals or other produce from land.

VOIR DIRE: Process of questioning jurors as to their predispositions about the case or parties to a proceeding in order to identify those jurors displaying bias or prejudice.

Casenote Legal Briefs

CPSIA information can be obtained at www.ICGtesting.com
Printed in the USA
BVOW06s1437210415

397069BV00005B/142/P

9 780735 589476